IN THE IMAGE OF MAN

The Indian perception of the Universe through 2000 years of painting and sculpture

Hayward Gallery, London   25 March–13 June 1982

Catalogue published in association with Weidenfeld and Nicolson · London

Arts Council of Great Britain

EXHIBITION STAFF

Exhibition Officer: Catherine Lampert
Exhibition Assistant: Rosalie Cass
Foreign Transport: Jeffery Watson
United Kingdom Transport: Stanley Leppard
Installation: Norman McManus, Sidney Pottier
Gallery Superintendent: Lesley Kendall
Publicity: Joan Asquith
Publications: Tania Butler
Hayward Bookstall: Anna Sixsmith

Exhibition organized by Catherine Lampert
assisted by Rosalie Cass, Hilary Westlake and Muriel Walker

Exhibition designed by Ross Owen Feller

Catalogue edited by George Michell,
Catherine Lampert and Tristram Holland

Copyright © The Arts Council
of Great Britain 1982

Catalogue designed by Sara Komar
assisted by Joy FitzSimmons
for George Weidenfeld and Nicolson Limited
91 Clapham High Street, London sw4

ISBN 0 7287 0311 4

Set in Monophoto Ehrhardt and printed by
BAS Printers Limited, Over Wallop, Hampshire
Colour separations by Newsele Litho Ltd

IN THE IMAGE OF MAN

CONTENTS

IN THE IMAGE OF MAN

British Advisory Committee
Dr Raymond Allchin
Dr James Harle
Mrs Dalu Jones
Dr Linda Leach
Dr T. S. Maxwell
Dr George Michell
Mr Robert Skelton

Indian Advisory Committee
Dr N. Banerjee
Sri C. Sivaramamurti
Dr B. K. Thapar
Dr Kapila Vatsyayan

Exhibition organized by Catherine Lampert, Arts Council
Exhibition designed by Ross Owen Feller

PREFACE

The fascination for British travellers of the monumental sculptures adorning temples, shrines and *stūpas* in India is enduring, and miniatures of the Hindu and Mughal schools have been appreciated and collected in this country for three hundred years. However, the assembly of material from a cultural history extending over several millennia across a vast country has discouraged the formation of comprehensive exhibitions. The post-Independence exhibition at Burlington House in 1947/8 was the last great landmark. Fully aware of the potential obstacles, His Excellency Sir John Thomson, British High Commissioner in India, in 1977 bravely suggested attempting a celebration of India in Britain. He had discussed the idea with friends in both countries, and they agreed the time had come for British and Indian scholars to collaborate on an ambitious exhibition. Sir John asked Mr Bryan Swingler, then British Council representative in India, Mr T. F. Scott, former Director of the Visiting Arts Unit in London and Mr J. A. L. Morgan, at that time head of the Cultural Relations Department of the Foreign and Commonwealth Office, to explore the feasibility of the idea. Mr Scott turned for advice to Mr Robert Skelton, Keeper of the Indian Section of the Victoria and Albert Museum, who had been independently considering an Indian exhibition. They pooled ideas on the content, timing and location of such an event with Mr Wladimir Zwalf, Assistant Keeper in the Oriental Antiquities Department of the British Museum, Mr Malcolm McLeod, Keeper of the Museum of Mankind, Dr James Harle, Keeper of the Department of Eastern Art at the Ashmolean Museum, Mr Jerry Losty, Assistant Keeper in the Department of Oriental Manuscripts and Printed Books of the British Library and the Arts Council. The 'event' quickly took the form of a series of exhibitions jointly focusing on the Indian-ness of Indian art and the creative attitudes behind the historic objects themselves.

It was clear from the outset that co-operation needed to be established at the highest government levels; the proposed exhibition was announced in a joint statement by the then British and Indian Prime Ministers at the end of a visit to this country by Mr Moraji Desai in 1978. The patronage of the Festival by Shrimati Indira Gandhi and the Rt Hon. Mrs Margaret Thatcher has been reflected in the full collaboration of Indian and British government departments, museums and scholars.

The organization of the Festival itself commenced in 1979 under the chairmanship of Sir Michael Walker, formerly British High Commissioner in India. The Festival of India Trust was established and a Festival Committee set up, which is matched in India by the National Advisory Committee under the chairmanship of Mrs Pupul Jayakar. Together the Indian and British committees and their Co-ordinators, Mr N. J. Singh and Mr Tom Petzal, have worked to present the fullest possible picture of Indian culture from the earliest times to the present day. Not only will the great historical past be represented through exhibitions of archaeology, sculpture, painting and manuscripts, but also the living traditions of craftsmen as well as the achievements of Indian contemporary artists and photographers, dancers and musicians. A further dimension will be provided by a presentation of Indian science and technology at the Science Museum.

The formation of the exhibition at the Hayward Gallery has been guided by Mr Robert Skelton, Dr James Harle, Dr Raymond Allchin of the Faculty of Oriental Studies at Cambridge University, Dr George Michell and Mrs Dalu Jones, co-editors of Art and Archaeology Research Papers, with Miss Joanna Drew and Miss Catherine Lampert of the Arts Council. The Indian advisers included Dr Kapila Vatsyayan, Joint Educational Adviser in the Ministry of Education and Culture, Sri C. Sivaramamurti and Dr N. R. Banerjee, former Directors of the National Museum, Delhi, and Mr B. K. Thapar, former Director of the Archaeological Survey of India, Mr H. S. Jassal, Under-Secretary in the Department of Culture, together with Dr Debala Mitra, Acting Director of the Archaeological Survey of India, and Dr I. D. Mathur, Acting Director and Mr Lala Aditya Narain, Keeper (Public Relations), at the National Museum. The collaboration has been whole-hearted and the Arts Council is greatly indebted to the many lenders, institutional and private as well as to the advisers and officials who have worked together to make this exhibition possible.

The assembly of information was a formidable task, to which was added the difficulty of organizing an exhibition mainly from collections spread across the Indian sub-continent. The British Council served as an indispensable link and our gratitude goes to Mr James Ure, Mr Bryan Swingler, present and former Representatives in India, and to Mr Peter Connell and Mr Robert Frost, former and present Education Advisers in Delhi. It has fallen to the permanent Indian representatives to maintain the channels of communication and to process with utmost tact and authority the requests from both ends. We are extremely grateful to Mrs Sushma Bahl in Delhi, and to Mr Foy Nissen in Bombay, for taking on this great responsibility and to those who have worked with them in India. In London the Council's South Asia Department has given continuous co-operation, in particular Miss Audrey Lambert and Mr John Lawrence, Mr Tony Davison, Mr Martin Ellis and Mrs Wendy Bednall.

Similarly, help at the diplomatic level in both countries has been crucial to the entire operation. The Indian High Commission in London have unsparingly offered their time and goodwill, especially the High Commissioner His Excellency Mr A. Goray and, since 1980, His Excellency Dr V. A. Seyid Muhammad. The support of the former Deputy High Commissioner, Dr I. P. Singh has been of inestimable value, as has that of Mr J. M. Gugnani, First Secretary, Education. In the later stages we have benefitted from the expert guidance of the Deputy High Commissioner, Mr P. Johari and of Mr N. Desai, Counsellor.

We have throughout been able to rely on the advice and assistance of the Foreign and Commonwealth Office and would particularly like to thank Mr John Macrae, head of the Cultural Relations Department, Mr W. T. Hull, Mr Leslie Buchanan, Mr Francis Sedgwick Jell and Mrs Sue Blackwell, present and former members of the Department. Particular thanks are also due to Mr John McGregor. From the moment of his appointment as Festival Director Mr Stanley Hodgson's guidance has proved invaluable.

From the outset it was known that the costs of air freighting exhibits would greatly exceed the sums available within the individual exhibition budgets. Fortunately, British Airways and Air India have provided most valuable assistance with the transport. We are immensely grateful for their support.

We have received generous financial assistance from Lazard Bros. and Co. Ltd to whom we are extremely grateful.

We would like to extend our warmest thanks to the Advisory Committees and organizers in both countries, in particular to those closest to the presentation of the Hayward exhibition – Dr Vatsyayan, Mr L. A. Narain, Dr George Michell, Mr Robert Skelton, Mr Ross Owen Feller, Dr Thomas Maxwell, Dr Linda Leach, and Mrs Dalu Jones. Their enormous expenditure of time and talent has made *In the Image of Man* possible. We are grateful also for the collaboration of Weidenfeld and Nicolson in the planning and preparation of the catalogue.

Our deepest gratitude is reserved for the people of India for they have been temporarily separated from a great many outstanding and beloved works of art. Along with the fine contributions of Indian painting and sculpture from British collections, these objects will undoubtedly enrich our understanding of India for many years to come.

KENNETH ROBINSON, *Chairman*, Arts Council of Great Britain
JOANNA DREW, *Director of Art*, Arts Council of Great Britain

FOREWORD

From the outset both committees agreed that it was important to consider the art of India from a non-sectarian and non-chronological point of view. The exhibition was intended to focus on concepts which were quintessentially Indian. Several of these have generally been thought difficult for a Western audience to grasp; for example, the Indian perspective which comprehends unity within diversity, and believes in the shared existence of the animal, vegetable, human and mythological worlds. The objects were thus selected not merely for their individual quality but also to demonstrate the cross-fertilization of cultural beliefs in the Indian sub-continent from ancient times to the nineteenth century. We hope that the beliefs which the art embodies will come alive to every visitor, including those who have never been to India, as well as to those who know India at first-hand, and especially to the post-Independence generation of British, many of Indian origin.

In June 1979 the Arts Council invited Dr George Michell and Mrs Dalu Jones to establish a thematic framework, keeping in mind the layout of the Hayward Gallery which they, like Mr Robert Skelton, knew well from their role in the Arts of Islam exhibition of 1976. Their initial outline has undergone continuous revision and improvement through exchanges between the advisers in both countries and in particular through the enlightened guidance of Dr Kapila Vatsyayan to whom we are enduringly grateful.

The first visits to establish possible loans were made in the winter of 1980 by Dr Michell and Mrs Jones accompanied by Mr Ross Owen Feller and Mrs Raimonda Buitoni, recording sculptures from 49 collections. This survey was accomplished with the aid of Kodak instant cameras and instant print film generously provided by Kodak.

Mr Robert Skelton and Dr Linda Leach, an American scholar presently cataloguing the Chester Beatty collection, made visits to India in 1980 to select the paintings. With the addition of works in British collections, the selectors sought to give a regional and chronological spread but not to attempt to chart every stylistic or iconographic classification. The stone sculptures selected were those largely intact, to enable a wide audience to recognize the subject matter. The paintings include many celebrated images as well as examples from less familiar areas. Needless to say a number of desired objects could not be borrowed, and the scale and profusion of temple decoration and large wall painting can only be sensed from the slide programmes and documentation which have also been designed to explain the ritual and social context of the works of art.

The theoretical structure has been necessarily interpreted and reconsidered by the advisers for the purposes of the installation. Apart from sensitively cherishing all five hundred objects, Mr Feller has attempted to suffuse the South Bank spaces with an Indian ambiance. Furthermore, he has sought to convey an impression of the Indian present through elements such as the modern South Indian chariot.

The catalogue is divided into two sections. The first is a reference section in which the function, history and salient features of Indian painting and sculpture are summarized. The two stylistic glossaries outline the chronological and geographical divisions. The second section follows the thematic structure of the exhibition moving from 'The Natural World' and 'The Abundance of Life' to 'The Four Goals of Life' and then to 'Devotion' and 'Enlightenment', and culminating in the 'Mythology of Vishnu and Shiva'. It begins with an introduction by Dr Vatsyayan who is herself a distinguished scholar and dancer as well as adviser to the Department of Culture, and who asks the reader to consider the Indian perception of the cosmos and its manifestation in the art seen at the Hayward. She also helps us to appreciate the universal nature of the imagery.

With the exception of Dr Leach's well-researched essays on 'Life at Court' the nine section introductions have been written by Dr Thomas Maxwell, a member of the Faculty of Oriental Studies, Oxford University, and Director of South Asian Religious Art Studies (SARAS). He has also followed the thematic structure of the exhibition and his identification with Indian concepts informs his approach to Indian art which is not primarily art historical or stylistic.

An exhibition of this scale and complexity depends greatly on the help of many people. The advisory committees and the Arts Council drew continually on the knowledge and generosity of specialists in the field of Indian studies. Their names are listed in the acknowledgements and we would like to record our appreciation of their help. We are deeply indebted to the many lenders to the exhibition who are listed elsewhere in the catalogue. Many others who have assisted in various ways are named in the acknowledgements. To those and to all who have supported us we extend our grateful thanks.

JOANNA DREW, *Director of Art*
CATHERINE LAMPERT, *Exhibition Organizer*

ACKNOWLEDGEMENTS

The Arts Council would like to thank the following individuals and institutions who contributed in many different ways to the organization of the exhibition and the preparation of the catalogue.

Government of India Ministry of Education and Culture: Shri A. S. Gill, Former Additional Secretary; Shri Mir Nasrullah, Additional Secretary; Shri P. Sabanayagam, Former Education Secretary; Dr K. Vatsyayan, Joint Education Adviser; Shri H. S. Jassal, Under-Secretary. Ministry of Information and Broadcasting: Shri A. K. Dutt, Former Secretary.

British Council James Ure, British Council Representative in India; Robert Frost, Education Adviser, Delhi; Mrs S. K. Bahl, Cultural Activities Officer, Delhi; Peter Connell, Assistant Education Adviser, Bombay; Foy Nissen, Assistant Representative (Cultural), Bombay; Mr M. R. Prabhu, Bombay; Mr S. N. Kumar, Madras.

New Delhi Dr Debala Mitra, Acting Director General of Archaeology, Archaeological Survey of India. National Museum: Shri I. D. Mathur, Acting Director; Shri L. A. Narain, Keeper (Public Relations). Mr O. P. Jain. Mr Nirmal Jeet Singh, Festival Co-ordinator.

Aihole Archaeological Museum. *Ahmedabad* L.D. Institute of Indology: Dr K. V. Sheth, Curator. Mr Surendra C. Patel. Mr Martand Singh. *Ajmer* Rajputana Museum: Ramdas Sharma, Curator. *Alampur* Archaeological Museum. *Bangalore* Government Museum and Venkatappa Art Gallery: Dr L. S. Krishnasastri, Curator. *Baroda* Museum and Picture Gallery: Dr S. K. Bhowmik, Director; M. N. Gandhi, Curator. *Bhopal* Shri M. D. Khare, Director of Archaeology and Museums, Government of Madhya Pradesh. Birla Museum: Mrs Manjushri Rao, Curator. *Bhubaneshwar* Orissa State Museum: Dr H. C. Das, Superintendent for Museums. *Bijapur* Archaeological Museum, Archaeological Survey of India: Shri M. K. Joshi, Assistant Superintending Archaeologist for Museums. *Bombay* J. P. Goenka Collection: Mr J. P. Goenka; Mr N. Haridas. Prince of Wales Museum of Western India: Shri S. Gorakshakar, Director. Ms Carmel Berkson. Mr Lance Dane. Weavers Service Centre: Mr Gautam Vaghela. Handicrafts and Handlooms Export Corporation: Mr D. R. Vincent; Mr R. Veeramani. *Calcutta* Asutosh Museum of Indian Art, University of Calcutta: Dr Niranjan Goswamy, Curator. Gurusaday Museum of Bengal Folk Art, Thakurpukur: Dr Asis Chakravarti, Curator. Indian Museum: Dr S. C. Ray. Suresh Neotia Collection:

Mr Suresh K. Neotia. State Department of Archaeology of West Bengal: Dr P. C. Dasgupta, Director. *Chandigarh* Government Museum and Art Gallery: Jagmohan Chopra, Director. *Deogarh* Shri J. P. Shrivastara, Superintending Archaeologist, Northern Circle, Agra. *Gauhati* Museum. *Gwalior* Central Archaeological Museum: R. P. Chaudhury, Curator. *Hampi* Archaeological Museum, Archaeological Survey of India: A. Satyanarayana, Assistant Superintending Archaeologist for Museums; K. M. Suresh, Curator. *Hardwar* Archaeological Museum, Gurukul Kangri University: Dr Vinod Chandra Sinha, Director. *Hyderabad* Jagdish and Kamla Mittal Museum of Indian Art: Shri Jagdish Mittal, Principal Trustee; Mr Naozar Chenoy, Trustee-Secretary. Dr N. Ramesan, Commissioner of Archives, Archaeology and Museums. State Archaeological Museum, Golconda: Mahan Shamsuddin, Curator. State Museum: Dr S. Ramakantham, Curator. *Indore* Central Museum. *Jaipur* Central Museum. Maharaja Sawai Man Singh II Museum: Dr Asok Kumah Das, Director. *Jhalawar* Archaeological Museum. *Jodhpur* Sardar Museum. Maharaja Museum, Umaid Bhavan Palace. Rajasthan Oriental Research Institute. *Khajuraho* Archaeological Museum, Archaeological Survey of India: Mr K. P. Padhy, Curator. *Kolhapur* Museum. *Konarak* Archaeological Museum: Mr V. N. Krishan Rao, Assistant Superintending Archaeologist for Museums. *Lucknow* State Museum: Dr R. C. Sharma, Director. *Madras* Archaeological Survey of India: Mr C. L. Suri, Superintending Archaeologist Southern Circle. Government Museum: Shri N. Harinarayan, Director. Tamil Nadu Department of Archaeology: Dr R. Nagaswamy, Director. Handicrafts and Handlooms Export Corporation: Mr A. G. Narasimha Sah. *Madurai* Thirumalai Nayak Palace Museum: Dr V. Vedachalam, Curator. *Mahabalipuram* Archaeological Museum: Shri Rajendram, Curator. *Mathura* Government Museum: A. K. Shrivastava, Director. *Mysore* Directorate of Archaeology and Museums, Karnataka: Dr M. S. Nagaraja Rao, Director. *Nagarjunakonda* Archaeological Museum, Archaeological Survey of India: K. Venkateshwar Rao, Assistant Superintending Archaeologist for Museums; J. Dawson, Curator. *Nalanda* Archaeological Museum, Archaeological Survey of India: Shri B. N. Prasad, Patna Sri Gopi Krishna Kanoria. Directorate of Archaeology and Museums, Bihar. *Ramvan Stana* Tulsi Sangrahalaya. *Sanchi* Archaeological Museum, Archaeological Survey of India: K. Purnima Iyer, Assistant Superintending Archaeologist for Museums. *Sarnath* Archaeological Museum, Archaeological Survey of India: Dr Arun Kumar, Assistant Superintending Archaeologist for Museums. *Simla* Himachal State Museum: V. C. Ohri, Curator; Ajit Singh, Assistant Curator. *Srinagar* Shri Pratap Singh Museum: M. Hussain Mokhdomi, Curator. *Thanjavur* Thanjavur Art Gallery: S. Rathnasabapathy, Curator. *Udaipur* Government Museum. *Varanasi* American Institute of Indian Studies, Ramnagar: V. R. Nambiar, Director; Dr M. A. Dhaky, Assistant Director. Bharat Kala Bhavan Museum, Banaras Hindu University: Dr O. P. Tandon, Deputy Director.

UK *Cambridge* Fitzwilliam Museum: Mr D. E. Scrase, Assistant Keeper, Paintings and Drawings. *Edinburgh* The Royal Scottish Museum: Miss J. M. Scarce, Assistant Keeper, Art and Archaeology. *London* The British Library: Mr J. Losty, Assistant Keeper, Department of Oriental Manuscripts and Books. British Museum: Dr David Wilson, Director; Miss J. M. Rankine, Deputy Keeper, Administration; Mr L. R. H. Smith, Keeper, Oriental Antiquities; Mr W. Zwalf, Assistant Keeper, Oriental Antiquities; Mr J. R. Knox, Assistant Keeper, Oriental Antiquities; Mr M. D. McLeod, Keeper, Museum of Mankind; Dr B. Durrans, Deputy Keeper, Museum of Mankind. India Office Library and Records: Mr B. C. Bloomfield, Director. Royal Asiatic Society: Mr A. S. Bennell, Director; Dr R. Pankhurst, Librarian. Victoria and Albert Museum: Dr Roy Strong, Director; Mr R. W. Skelton, Keeper, Indian Section; Mr A. S. Topsfield, Assistant Keeper, Indian Section; Miss B. Tyers, Senior Museum Assistant, Indian Section; Miss R. E. Stockley, Museum Assistant, Indian Section. *Oxford* Ashmolean Museum of Art and Archaeology: Dr J. C. Harle, Keeper, Department of Eastern Art. The Bodleian Library (University of Oxford): Mr E. R. S. Fifoot, Librarian; Mr A. D. S. Roberts, Keeper of Oriental Books.

EIRE *Dublin* The Chester Beatty Library and Gallery of Oriental Art: Dr Patrick Henchy, Chief Officer (Librarian); Mr David James, Islamic Curator.

USA *Philadelphia* Philadelphia Museum of Art, Mrs Eva Ray, Curator.

Mr Robert Alderman; Baron and Baroness Bachofen von Echt; Mrs Pat Bahree; Mr Douglas Barrett; Beck and Pollitzer Ltd; Mrs Wendy Bednall; Miss Virginia Casey; Mr John Cass; Mr Jean Claude Ciancimino; Mr David Cripps; Mr Peter Davidson; Mr Anthony Friedmann; Dr John Fritz; Mr Sven Gahlin; Mr Anthony Gardner; Mrs Melanie Gibson; Mr Howard Hodgkin; Mr Stanley Hodgson; Miss Tristram Holland; Mr Richard Lannoy; Dr Simon Lawson; Dr Heather Marshall; Mr Trilokesh Mukerjee; Mr Peter Mumford; Mr John Pannikar; Pitt & Scott; Miss Anna Plowden and Mr Peter Smith and their colleagues; Mrs Janine Schotsmans; Miss Carol Shields; Mr Snehal Shah; SINC; Mr Martand Singh; Miss Stella Snead; Miss Monique Vajifar; Mrs Muriel Walker; Mrs Hilary Westlake; Dr Clare Willington; Dr Mark Zebrowski.

PICTURE ACKNOWLEDGEMENTS

The colour photographs of objects in the exhibition are by David Cripps, assisted by John Pannikar.

The black and white photographs of objects in the exhibition, in addition to those supplied by the lenders, are by The American Institute of Indian Studies, Varanasi; Raimonda Buitoni; John Cass; David Cripps; Yolande Crowe; Ross Owen Feller; John Fritz; Jeffery Gorbeck; and Rodney Todd-White. A great many of the black and white photographs of the objects were printed by J. R. Freeman and retouched by Terry Boxall.

The drawings on page 15 are by P. J. Darvall from B. Rowland, *The Art and Architecture of India*, page 53, copyright © 1953, 1967 Penguin Books Ltd. The drawings on page 20 are by George Michell.

The exhibition organizers would also like to thank those who kindly made available photographs on the following pages:
23 (bottom) Ross Owen Feller; 26 (bottom), 27, 30 (top), 31 (bottom) Christina Gascoigne; 30 (bottom) A. F. Kersting; 16, 26 (top) David McCutchion archive; 15 (top), 18, 19, 20 George Michell; 17, 22 (bottom), 23 (top right and left), 29 Bury Peerless; 22 (top) Jan Pieper; 14 Christine Younger.

LENDERS TO THE EXHIBITION

Institutions

Aihole, Archaeological Museum: 56
Ajmer, Rajputana Museum: 431
Alampur, Archaeological Museum: 13, 55, 240, 452, 483
Bangalore, Government Museum: 70, 249, 347, 465, 468
Baroda, Museum and Picture Gallery: 54, 296
Bhopal, Birla Museum: 470, 471
Bhopal, State Museum: 87, 357
Bhubaneshwar, Orissa State Museum: 94, 95, 96, 340, 476
Bijapur, Archaeological Museum, A.S.I.: 11
Bombay, Prince of Wales Museum of Western India: 42, 97, 149, 157, 190, 197, 202, 209, 227, 377, 404. Loans by courtesy of the Trustees.
Calcutta, Asutosh Museum of Indian Art, University of Calcutta: 366, 407, 424
Calcutta, Gurusaday Museum of Bengal Folk Art: 27, 206
Calcutta, Indian Museum: 112
Cambridge, Fitzwilliam Museum: 38, 235
Chandigarh, Government Museum and Art Gallery: 148, 247, 283, 305, 401
Deogarh, Archaeological Shed, A.S.I.: 360
Dublin, The Chester Beatty Library and Gallery of Oriental Art: 151, 171, 201, 208, 212, 228, 236, 239, 264, 265, 297, 477
Edinburgh, The Royal Scottish Museum: 179, 217
Gauhati, Museum: 480
Gwalior, Central Archaeological Museum: 464
Hampi, Archaeological Museum, A.S.I.: 15
Hardwar, Archaeological Museum, Gurukul Kangri University: 369
Hyderabad, State Museum: 105, 123, 261, 308, 329, 449
Indore, Central Museum: 444, 445, 482
Jaipur, Central Museum: 462
Jhalawar, Archaeological Museum: 435
Jodhpur, Maharaja Museum, Umaid Bhavan Palace: 109, 110, 159, 367, 379, 447
Jodhpur, Rajasthan Oriental Research Institute: 408, 412, 414, 416
Jodhpur, Sardar Museum: 364
Khajuraho, Archaeological Museum, A.S.I.: 71, 83, 86, 119, 368, 370
Kolhapur, Kolhapur Museum: 205
Konarak, Archaeological Museum, A.S.I.: 25, 33
London, The British Library: 392
London, Trustees of the British Museum: 6, 14, 52, 74, 85, 106, 107, 116, 132, 143, 144, 150, 153, 154, 178, 194, 195, 198, 231, 232, 233, 244, 273, 275, 298, 299, 315, 334, 337, 341, 342, 353, 355, 359, 451, 467
London, India Office Library and Records: 46, 47, 131, 245, 274, 278
London, Royal Asiatic Society: 250, 317, 318
London, Victoria and Albert Museum: 24, 29, 37, 43, 48, 53, 58, 61, 76, 82, 88, 90, 101, 102, 104, 111, 134, 142, 170, 192, 204, 222, 229, 230, 243, 254, 263, 268, 277, 295, 314, 320, 327, 344, 356, 378, 380, 395, 405, 421, 443, 450, 456, 459, 460, 485
Lucknow, State Museum: 7, 80, 307, 324, 337a, 350, 426, 427
Madras, Government Museum: 98, 99, 253, 255, 262, 432, 481
Madurai, Thirumalai Nayak Palace Museum: 438
Mathura, Government Museum: 9, 59, 64, 66, 67, 115, 121, 256, 306, 321, 330, 349
Mysore, Directorate of Archaeology and Museum, Karnataka: 176, 326
Nagarjunakonda, Archaeological Museum, A.S.I.: 114, 319
Nalanda, Archaeological Museum, A.S.I.: 332
New Delhi, National Museum: 10, 12, 17, 18, 20, 21, 22, 28, 30, 31, 34, 41, 50, 51, 57, 63, 68, 69, 72, 73, 75, 77, 78, 79, 81, 85, 91, 92, 93, 103, 113, 116, 118, 120, 125, 130, 135, 139, 146, 152, 156, 161, 167, 169, 185, 187, 200, 203, 211, 219, 223, 224, 226, 241, 242, 246, 248, 258, 259, 271, 276, 281, 284, 302, 309, 313, 325, 328, 331, 336, 338, 343, 345, 346, 351, 352, 354, 358, 361, 365, 372, 373, 374, 375, 376, 381, 382, 387, 388, 397, 398, 400, 402, 403, 410, 419, 422, 423, 428, 453, 454, 455, 457, 458, 461, 464, 473, 475, 480, 484, 486, 487
Oxford, Ashmolean Museum: 32, 371, 434, 441
Oxford, University of Oxford, Bodleian Library: 127, 183, 189, 191, 193, 196, 225, 280
Patna, Directorate of Archaeology and Museums, Bihar: 60, 180, 348
Raipur, Archaeological Museum, A.S.I.: 339
Ramvan, Tulsi Sangrahalaya: 16, 65
Sanchi, Archaeological Museum, A.S.I.: 8, 62
Sarnath, Archaeological Museum, A.S.I.: 19, 117, 316, 333
Simla, Himachal State Museum: 442, 448
Srinagar, Sri Pratap Singh Museum: 363
Thanjavur, Thanjavur Art Gallery: 257, 440, 446
Udaipur, Oriental Research Institute: 384, 385
Udaipur, Zenana Museum: 126, 128, 215, 216, 301, 303
Varanasi, Bharat Kala Bhavan Museum, Banaras Hindu University: 3, 39, 89, 100, 122, 141, 163, 168, 175, 177, 184, 188, 199, 218, 234, 389, 391, 394, 406, 411, 413, 415, 420, 425, 437, 478

Private

Bombay, J. P. Goenka Collection: 165, 173, 181, 186, 288, 291, 294, 362, 390, 396, 418
Calcutta, Suresh Neotia Collection: 182
Hyderabad, Jagdish and Kamla Mittal Museum of Indian Art: 36, 44, 133, 140, 155, 162, 164, 172, 210, 213, 266, 279, 285, 286, 287, 292, 293, 300, 386, 399
Jaipur, Collection of Maharaja Sawai Man Singh II, Rajasthan: 436
London, Baron and Baroness Bachofen von Echt: 158, 174, 269, 417
London, Jean Claude Ciancimino Collection: 1, 2, 4, 5, 108, 311, 312, 409, 430
London, Spink & Son Ltd: 251, 252, 310, 335, 466, 474
Patna, Sri Gopi Krishna Kanoria Collection: 26, 35, 137, 145, 220, 221, 323, 393
Private Collections: 23, 40, 45, 49, 124, 129, 136, 138, 158, 160, 174, 207, 214, 237, 238, 246, 267, 269, 270, 272, 282, 289, 290, 304, 322, 383, 417, 429, 433, 439, 469, 472

The information supplied in the entries has been drawn from published and unpublished sources assembled by the British Advisory Committee with the assistance of scholars in both countries. If any of the entries is incomplete, it is because the relevant information was not available at the time the catalogue went to press.

All measurements are rounded to the nearest centimetre, height × width × depth. The measurements for paintings refer to the inside dimension, exclusive of border or frame. All paintings are in water-based colour on paper unless otherwise stated (European-style paper in the case of Company paintings).

Schools of painting are referred to by their type and where they were executed (e.g. Deccan school, from Bijapur).

Only rarely are the sculptures and monuments precisely dated by inscriptions; most are dated by an analysis of iconographic and stylistic features. The chronology of sculptures in India thereore is fairly broadly based. Only the century (or centuries) in which a sculpture is likely to have been produced is indicated here; there is little attempt to suggest a more accurate date unless reliable inscriptional evidence is available.

Sanskrit and Pali names and terms have been spelt to facilitate pronunciation by English-speaking readers: diacritical marks are used only for stressed vowels. With Persian and Urdu names and terms a similar system is adopted. Diacritical marks have not been used on geographical locations (such as Khajuraho, Rajasthan).

The translations of Indian literature (Sanskrit and Pali) within the second half of the catalogue are the work of T. S. Maxwell.

The glossary of terminology (including names of deities), the bibliography, the map showing the principle sculpture and painting sites, and the index of Indian deities are at the back of the catalogue.

The authorship of the individual themes is indicated by initials on page 89: TSM – T. S. Maxwell; LL – Linda Leach.

INTRODUCTION TO INDIAN SCULPTURE

by Dr George Michell

A sandstone carving of a meditating Buddha is not primarily a work of art; neither is a bronze image of the Hindu god Shiva pacing out the stages of creation to destruction. Seen in an exhibition, Indian sculpture is inevitably isolated from its original context – the sacred shrines and temples where men can communicate with the divine. The personalities and myths depicted in it belong to a world beyond that of man; they are visual interpretations of the pantheon of celestial beings. The great religious philosophies of India – Buddhism, Jainism and Hinduism – are all dedicated to the transcendence of the human condition through successive stages of enlightenment (*nirvāna, moksha*). Indian sculpture is the embodiment of this theme of enlightenment; its images voice the profound messages of the gods.

HISTORICAL PERSPECTIVE

Religious and artistic continuities in India can be traced back to the earliest phases of urban civilization. The oldest sculptures from the Indian sub-continent are the figurines, and faience and ivory seals found at Mohenjo-Daro and Harappa, key sites of the Indus Valley Civilization (3rd–2nd millennia BC). No historical records have survived from this early culture, and the writing on the numerous seals has yet to be satisfactorily deciphered. Although artefacts still cannot be identified precisely, it is possible to detect in them several themes familiar in later Indian art – the naked male ascetic seated in yogic posture surrounded by animals, the mother goddess, the phallic symbol (*linga*), and the humped bull with impressive horns. Whatever religious system operated at Mohenjo-Daro and Harappa, its expression in figural and animal art was partly to recur some two thousand years later in Buddhist and Hindu art.

By the middle of the 2nd millenium BC the power of the Indus Valley cities had declined. Successive waves of Āryan invaders swept across the sub-continent bringing with them a distinct language and a religion that were closely related to those of Iran and, more remotely, to those of the Aegean and eastern Europe at about the same time. Though they were nomadic, these peoples preserved some of their early traditions, which they later set down in a body of sacred writings, the *Vedas*. Though the religion contained in them is not to be identified with Hinduism, the *Vedas* are still regarded as the source for later sacred Hindu literature. The pantheon of deities they described is dominated by powerful male gods, the greatest of whom is Indra who is both war-god and weather-god. The *Rig Veda*, composed somewhere between 1500 and 900 BC, is the oldest of these texts. Its 1,028 hymns were intended to be used at the sacrifices performed by priests.

Certain elements of the culture that evolved over the centuries following the Āryan invasion bore little relation to the religion of the *Vedas*. These cultural manifestations can probably be traced to pre-Āryan times, and there are suggestions that by the time the *Rig Veda* was compiled the Āryans had already absorbed much of the ideology of the Indus Valley Civilization. As the Āryan people gave up their nomadic existence and settled down in the river plains of northern India they formed rural communities, some of which later developed into urban settlements. Changes in their patterns of living were accompanied by changes in their religion. The texts that were composed in the centuries following the *Vedas*, such as the *Brāhmanas* and the *Upanishads*, reflect the growing power of the priests who imbued the mystery of the sacrifice with a cosmic significance. From the pantheon of the *Vedas*, the creator came more and more to be seen as a single divinity or godhead. In the *Upanishads* this godhead is further identified with *ātman*, the 'self' or spirit, formless but all-powerful and ever-present. The cult of the ascetic who denies himself all material pleasures emerged as a reaction to increasing prosperity. The world of the senses was dismissed as unreal, and securing escape from temporal existence came to be seen as the chief purpose of living. This notion of escape or release (*moksha* or *nirvāna*) from the present world underlay the beginnings of the doctrine of transmigration (*samsāra*), according to which the soul of man returns to earth after death in an endless cycle of rebirths. The concept of *karma*, the idea that the actions of a human being in one life-span directly affect the rebirth that is to follow, is an important part of this doctrine.

It is in this religious context that Buddhism and Jainism appeared in the 6th century BC. Neither movement was these divinities rapidly evolved, while myths and popular legends flourished. By the beginnings of the Christian era, the major cults of Hinduism that were to dominate the beliefs and practices of Hindus for the next two thousand years had emerged.

The first monumental stone sculptures in India, and a number of miniature carved ivories and moulded terracottas, date from the 4th–3rd centuries BC, the period of the Mauryas – the first imperial rulers of India. Despite the archaeological evidence associated with the spread of the Āryans – pottery for example – no sculpture is known from that period. Maurya sculpture depicts male and female nature spirits – *yakshas* and *yakshīs* – as well as the naturalistic animals associated with Buddhist and Jain architecture. (The lion capital from Sarnath that once supported a cosmic disc now serves as the emblem of modern India.) This emphasis on folk deities and animals continued under the succeeding Shunga dynasty (2nd century BC–1st century AD); animated narrative reliefs illustrating episodes from the lives of the Buddha and Mahāvīra date from this period. These scenes are often set in naturalistic towns or villages, but the Buddha himself is never shown: an empty throne or riderless horse is sufficient to indicate the invisible presence of the Master. Absence of images of the Buddha is balanced by the importance accorded to emblems at this early stage of Indian sculpture: the trident, swastika and lotus, for instance, were all imbued with a distinct religious symbolism.

The first true cult images of Buddhism, Jainism and Hinduism date only from the 1st century AD, under the patronage of the Kushāna rulers of central and north-west India. The earliest seated and standing Buddhist and Jain figures belong to this period, as do images of Shiva, Vishnu, Krishna the pastoral saviour god, and other Hindu deities. The forms of these images are often clearly derived from earlier *yaksha* types, but they also incorporate foreign features such as costume akin to the Classical toga. Meanwhile narrative art, especially Buddhist, flourished, and folk deities continued to be represented. All these mixed religious images testify to the simultaneous, and sometimes competitive, existence of Buddhism, Jainism and the rapidly evolving Hindusim. Numerous brick temples were contructed to house these images, but only their basements now remain. Better preserved are the monumental Buddhist and Jain *stūpas*, some of which date back to the Maurya period. These were lavishly decorated with railings, gateways and free-standing columns of carved stone. The hemispherical solid *stūpa* is both a funerary mound, intended to commemorate the life and teachings of the Buddha or Mahāvīra, and a miniature representation of the circular form of the universe. Rock-cut temples from this time are also known, some of which incorporate small *stūpas* as the focus for rituals of devotion.

By the time the Gupta kings ruled north India (4th–6th centuries) monumental temple architecture in stone and brick was well established, particularly for Buddhist and Hindu cults, while *stūpa* building slowly declined. By this time the most important scriptures of popular Hinduism were already composed, and were available to all, not just the priests. The great epics (particularly the *Mahābhārata* and *Rāmāyana*), *Purānas* ('Ancient Stories') and numerous hymns brought together for the first time, the many legends and religious teachings that gave expression to the devotional theistic feeling popular in the early phases of Hinduism. Sculptures of the various divinities had already become fairly standardized by

More than 18 metres high, this colossal monolithic image of the Jain saint, Bāhubali, was carved in AD 981 at Sravana Belgola (Karnataka). Bāhubali is the first soul to attain enlightenment in this cosmic cycle: he stood lost in total meditation for so long that creepers wound themselves around his legs and arms.

originally concerned with an ultimate divinity; rather, they offered ethical philosophies of everyday life that were directed towards the transcendence of human existence. At the same time they concentrated upon the lives and teachings of actual personages, the Buddha and Mahāvīra, who came to be worshipped only in later centuries.

By the 3rd and 2nd centuries BC a new religion of devotional theism – Hinduism, as it is now known – had begun to emerge. It combined influences from both the north and south of India, and also probably from other people who continued to enter the sub-continent from the north-west. The central feature of Hinduism is the worship of a personal deity, who generally takes the form of a particular god or goddess, such as Vishnu the Preserver, or Shiva the Creator-Destroyer. The deities of this new religion were basically syncretistic creations; their mixed origins lay in the earlier pantheons of the *Vedas* and in various folk heroes, often regional gods or goddesses. At the same time there appeared a host of minor divinities and spirits who were no less important for human affairs. Elaborate rituals and ceremonies for the worship of

The *stūpa* serves both as a monument to commemorate the life and teachings of the Buddha and the great Buddhist teachers, as well as a diagram of the spherical form of the universe. Some of the oldest and simplest *stūpas*, dating back to the 3rd century BC are preserved at Sanchi (Madyha Pradesh). Here a hemispherical mound symbolizing the earth is elevated on a cylindrical base; above is a tiered umbrella-like finial representing the various heavens. Stone gateways mark the cardinal directions, and are covered with carved scenes from the life of the Buddha, and emblematic motifs associated with Buddhism – the wheel, column and trident. A stone railing around the *stūpa* defines the path of circumambulation followed by devotees as they walk around the solid dome in a clockwise direction, thus worshipping the *stūpa*.

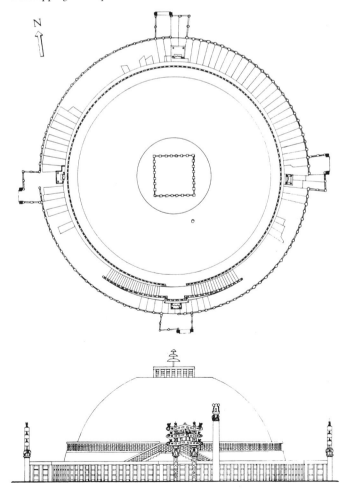

Gupta times, though there was some development of Hindu images illustrating the myths associated with the varied aspects of Shiva and Vishnu.

The succeeding centuries witnessed the waning of Buddhist sculpture, as the appeal of Buddhism lessened and became partly merged with Hindusim. Nevertheless, Buddhism and its art survived in eastern India well into the Pāla and Sena periods (8th–12th centuries). Thereafter, it was preserved only on the peripheries of India – Nepal, Tibet, Assam, Burma and Sri Lanka – though it spread to the Far East and south-east Asia, together with the Buddha image of Indian inspiration. By contrast, Jainism was to have little appeal outside India but continued to survive within the country, even to the present day, especially in the western regions and the peninsula. Jain sculpture is largely restricted to the depiction of saints (Tīrthankaras) but Jain images are known from all periods of Indian art. Even after the Muslim invasions, Jain art and architecture continued to flourish, particularly in Gujarat.

Following the Gupta period there was an efflorescence of Hindu sculpture that reflected the widespread appeal of the syncretistic Hindu deities. Hinduism was to remain the dominant religion of India, surviving the impact of Islam, and even that of colonial rule, until the present day. It is the religion practised by the majority of Indians today (though some 70 million are Muslim). It is with the temple that Hindu sculpture is inextricably associated and temples became increasingly elaborate in order to house more and more images within their dark sanctuaries and columned halls, and on exterior walls and soaring curved towers. The large number of sculptural panels reflects the proliferation of Hindu deities in their numerous aspects and emanations, as well as the large range of semi-divine beings, attendant females, guardians, mythical beasts and other animals.

In northern India the evolution of Hindu temple art was largely interrupted by the Muslims from the 11th century onwards. Though smaller and more modest temples continued to be built, little large-scale temple building was attemped after the Muslim invasions. Southern India, by contrast, did not experience effective Muslim influence until much later. Temple architecture and art in the south were therefore able to preserve a relatively unbroken tradition, which has continued to this day.

Despite the enforced iconoclasm of the Muslims, Indian sculptors were able to make a considerable contribution to Indo-Islamic architecture. Mosques, tombs and palaces are often embellished with superb stone carving, and inlay work in different coloured marbles and sandstones. Despite the popularity of Islamic calligraphic and geometric decorative motifs, more traditional Indian themes frequently reassert themselves, in particular the lotus in its multiple forms.

THE FIGURE

Indian sculpture is essentially a representation of the sublime – gods, goddesses, demons and innumerable semi-divine beings in visible form. These images draw upon human as well as animal and bird forms; species are frequently combined to create composite creatures. Of great significance in India is the belief that outer forms can be assumed at will: divinity expressed as a transient form is a fundamental concept of both art and mythology. In sculpture this means that the same deity may be depicted in a number of different ways, often simultaneously. Major divinities appear in a wide variety of guises, expressing their multiple roles and moods. This is true both for the saviours and saints of Buddhism and Jainism and for Hindu gods and goddesses. Indian sculpture consists, therefore, of countless images communicating different aspects of the divine. At the same time, however, there is always the notion that truth lies beyond the world of appearances, that these multiple images are but illusory manifestations (*māyā*) of a single ultimate reality.

The human figure is the inspiration for much Buddhist, Jain and Hindu sculpture. Sacred images were required to be beautiful as it was believed that the deities would then be persuaded to inhabit their outer forms. As a result, Indian sculpture has evolved distinct physical types as definitions of divine beauty. In sculptures of gods, the shoulders and chest are broad, the waist slim, the stomach slightly overhanging the belt, and the limbs solid and almost cylindrical. In sculptures of female divinities the essential features are an elaborate headdress and jewellery, heavy spherical breasts, a narrow waist, ample hips and a graceful posture. Indian figurative art displays only rudimentary attempts to portray musculature; rather, it conveys the idea of inwardly held breath. This breath (*prāna*) is identified with the essence of life, the control of which is the aim of all religious discipline. Sculptures of gods and goddesses, saints and saviours, often have their bodies tautly drawn as if containing a pressure from within.

Standing figures, with their hands displayed in various gestures, form an important category in Indian sacred sculpture. An inflexion is usually given to the body by tilting the axis; the favourite composition employs three bends (*tribhanga*) at the neck, shoulders and hips. There are also numerous examples of seated images in 'lotus' posture with the soles of the feet turned upwards, as in the meditating Buddha or Jain saint, or with one or both legs down, and hands decorated with symbolic emblems. In order that these images may express superhuman qualities, Indian art frequently adopts the simple device of multiplying the heads and arms of figures. Images with more than four arms have them outstretched in a variety of positions. A few divinities are shown reclining, such as the celebrated icon of Vishnu on the serpent, or the image of The Goddess as a mother accompanied by a child. In mythical episodes, images have more varied postures, especially when destroying or hunting. Provocative postures expressive of an undisguised sexuality are present throughout Indian figurative sculpture, particularly in the depiction of youthful females. Often in Indian sculpture there is an emphasis on postures derived from dance positions, the arms thrown out in different directions, the legs kicked up or bent, the heels rythmically beating the ground. This close connection between sacred sculpture and dance is traced back to the temple itself, where the gods were entertained by temple dancers, themselves 'married' to the god. Exquisitely poised stone and bronze figures represent a moment in the dance removed from time; implied are the musical rhythms, voiced syllables and narrative gestures of Indian dance.

The significance accorded to the gestures of the hands (*mudrās*) is one of the distinctive characteristics of Indian sculpture. It was Buddhist art that first developed a vocabulary of allusive hand gestures, but Hindu art subsequently adopted the system. The position of the fingers and thumbs of the

The doorway of the Hindu temple is carved with motifs that have a particular protective function. In this 5th century temple at Nachna (Madhya Pradesh) guardian figures with tridents, embracing couples, river goddesses, flying figures and lotus decoration are combined to create a complex ornamental doorway.

hands expresses the character of gods and goddesses in both their benign and fearsome moods. The uplifted outward-facing palm bestows grace upon the worshipper, while the downward palm signifies charity; other gestures indicate meditation, teaching or protection, for example. Like the different postures of the body, these hand gestures relate closely to dance: every hand and body movement is imbued with meanings to create a language of motion by which sacred myths and stories are told.

The facial features of the majority of sacred sculptures conform to a sterotype that has survived numerous stylistic variations. Both gods and goddesses have a full face with fish-shaped eyes, eyebrows fashioned in the contour of an arched bow, a sharply defined nose and full lips. The facial expression of these figures is mostly inward-looking, detached and other-worldly; only occasionally do cult images express the momentary glances of human beings. A calm expression is sometimes retained even when the deities are engaged in violent pursuits, curiously contrasting with the energetic posture of the body. However, fearsome facial expressions are also utilized in Indian sculptures for the portrayal of the terrifying aspect of gods and goddesses, such as Bhairava and Kālī. Here the eyes protrude in a demonic stare, the mouth has fangs and the tongue drips blood.

Identification of particular deities relies heavily upon recognition of the emblems that symbolize their power and nature rather than their physical appearance. In their quasi-human forms Hindu deities are often provided with characteristic weapons, illustrating the association of these divinities with war and hunting. Among the most popular emblems are ritual rosaries, ladles and water pots; musical instruments, both stringed and percussive; objects concerned with beauty, such as jewels and mirrors; natural motifs like flowers and shells; and an enormous range of weapons, including bows and arrows, swords, spears, clubs and tridents.

The emblems are themselves sometimes personified by the addition of human features. In the cult of Shiva, the Hindu god of Creation-Destruction is symbolized by the phallus (*linga*) indicating divine procreative energy. In general the *linga* is preferred to an image of Shiva for purposes of worship. Some versions of the Shiva *linga* are provided with faces of the god, symbolizing the divine energy radiating outwards. These 'face-*lingas*' illustrate well the fluid relationship between representative and symbolic forms.

One of the special features of sculptures of almost every divinity is the animal or bird 'vehicle' (*vāhana*), which distinguishes one deity from another. This vehicle is more than a means by which the god or goddess is transported, for it symbolizes an essential aspect of the divine personality. Thus Nandin, the humped bull, is fully expressive of Shiva's sexuality; the lion or tiger mount of Durgā, the fierce Hindu goddess, embodies her aggressive nature. In Buddhist and Jain sculpture the many-headed serpent appears as a protector at the crucial moment of enlightenment, rearing up and over the head of the saviour. Even without their quasi-human counterparts, animals and birds are able to suggest the deity to whom they belong and are themselves worshipped.

There is also a remarkable series of hybrid creatures in which human, animal and bird features are combined. Numerous figures have animal heads (boar and man-lion incarnations of Vishnu), or human heads have animal bodies (Garuda, the eagle mount of Vishnu). Animals and birds, too, are combined into composite fantastic creatures.

Gods and goddesses are often depicted in scenes from myths and legends. Prominent among such scenes are those showing the deities in terrifying postures slaying their enemies. As the man-lion, Vishnu savagely rips open the demon's body in order to devour the entrails; Krishna subdues the serpent by dancing upon his cobra hood; Durgā violently slays the buffalo. In other myths the moment of rescue or miraculous manifestation is chosen for the depiction of the god – thus Shiva appears from within the fiery *linga*. Stories of creation, especially associated with the mythology of Vishnu, are also illustrated – Vishnu sleeping on the serpent and, as the tortoise, supporting the axial world mountain in the churning of the cosmic ocean.

There are also portraits of celestial 'family groups' in which the gods are shown together with their various consorts, children, attendant figures and animal or bird vehicles. Shiva and his wife Pārvatī, with Ganesha and Kārttikeya, often considered to be their children, are depicted in their mountain home, for example. Inspired by the epic stories of the *Rāmāyana* and *Mahābhārata*, narrative friezes illustrate forest and battle scenes. Depictions of the Krishna legends, especially episodes from his childhood and his youthful dalliance with Rādhā, are noted for their liveliness and humour.

The multi-headed cosmic serpent, the guardian of the treasures of the earth, rears up to protect the *linga*, emblem of the Hindu god Shiva. This monolithic sculpture is found at Lepakshi (Andhra Pradesh).

In the sculptures associated with Buddhism and Jainism, figures gaze inwards as if in a trance; here they draw together their powers of concentration, conquering the duality of human existence. Scenes from the life of the Buddha focus on particular incidents – birth, departure from the palace, the first sermon, various miracles, and the great 'death' (*parinirvāna*). Often these episodes are brought together into a long narrative frieze. In comparison, Jain sculpture is limited to the depiction of saintly heroes as youthful ascetics.

RITUAL AND ARCHITECTURE

Many of the sculptures shown in this exhibition were once housed in the sanctuaries of Buddhist, Jain and Hindu temples. These sanctuaries are the ritual focus of elaborate architectural complexes where priests and devotees can commune with the divine. The Indian temple – whether Buddhist, Jain or Hindu – is an abode of the gods and seeks to recreate the celestial environment of the gods, particularly the cosmic mountain, the axis of the universe. Some gods are said to live in mountains; Shiva, for example, usually resides on Mount Kailāsa in the Himalayas. After the 6th–7th centuries the form of the temple was rapidly evolved, and despite some regional variation, the principles of its construction and its

THE HINDU TEMPLE

Essentially the temporary abode of the gods on earth, the Hindu
temple is also a re-creation of the celestial environment of the gods.
Thus the mountain-like tower of the 11th-century Rājarājeshvara
Temple at Thanjavur (*above*) refers to the mythical mountain on
which Shiva lives, while the 6th-century rock cut sanctuary dedicated
to Vishnu at Badami (*right*) evokes the natural caves in which the
divine presence is manifested. Both the exterior of the temple,
especially the towering superstructure, and the interior elements –

columns, brackets and ceiling – are covered with sculptured images
and decoration. In the Badami cave temple a major composition
forms the focus of a long colonnaded aisle; at Thanjavur carved icons
are positioned in outside wall niches.

A visit to the temple reveals its fundamental role – linking the
world of the gods to the world of man. Here man may contact the
gods. Devotees or pilgrims are regular visitors, and the columned
halls and porches of Hindu temples are places where they can pay respect
to the deity, thus achieving their heartfelt desires.

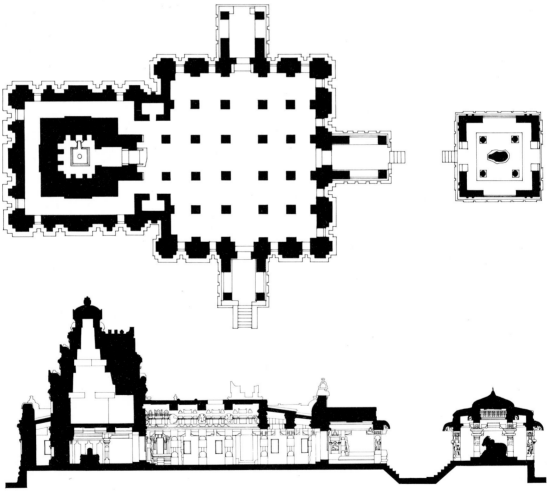

Pattadakal (Karnataka) is a ceremonial coronation site associated with the early Chālukya rulers. The Virūpāksha temple, dedicated to a form of Shiva, was erected in the early 8th century by a Chālukya queen to commemorate the victory of her royal husband over the neighbouring Pallava kingdom. This is one of the earliest coordinated temple scenes developed in India. The temple itself consists of a sanctuary surrounded on three sides by a narrow circumambulatory passage; the columned hall is divided into aisles and has three doorways with elaborate porches. In front is a detached open pavilion housing a gigantic image of Shiva's bull, Nandin. The outer walls are divided into bays and sculpture niches by slender pilasters. The tower rises above the sanctuary in a series of stepped, diminishing, storeys.

complex symbolism were to remain constant. Essentially, the temple is a massive structure deep within which is the cave-like sanctuary, the 'womb-chamber' (*garbha-griha*), approached through a sequence of columned halls, open verandas and flights of steps. Characteristic is the progression from light to darkness, from open spaces to confined chambers, from rich ornamentation to unadorned simplicity. Above the sanctuary the temple rises in a series of towers; this is the mountain-like superstructure, the 'peak' (*shikhara*). Northern India temple towers are curved and clustered, reproducing the effect of a chain of peaks; in the south, temple towers are storeyed and crowded with multi-coloured deities vividly evoking the mountain of the gods.

Direct worship of images (*devapūja*) forms the focal point of religious activities embraced by the temple: ritual and ceremonies that include image worship are intended to promote the manifestation of the divine. According to Hindu doctrine, the performance of ritual earns merit for the worshipper and can lead to the union of self and godhead. Hindu rituals of devotion for different cult deities follow a basic pattern. Worship is conceived as the paying of royal honours – evocation, reception and entertainment of the god or saviour as a royal guest. Before ceremonies can begin the priests first bathe and purify themselves. At the ceremony there is no need for a congregation to be present as rituals are performed by priests on behalf of the community.

Temple rituals for an ordinary day usually consist of several celebrations, which depend upon the size of the temple but usually take place at sunrise, noon, sunset and midnight. Ceremonies begin with the reverential opening of the sanctuary door: the powers guarding over the door are saluted, and there is the ringing of bells and the clasping of hands. The priest then expresses his intention to worship, and hymns are recited to persuade the deity to take visible form by inhabiting the image or symbol. Various verbal formulae (*mantras*), sacred syllables (*bījas*) and symbolic hand gestures (*mudrās*) are then employed to concentrate the power of the god or goddess, and to allow the priest to draw himself into contact with the divine. In this context, the image acts as a meditational focus for the priest.

Worship consists of the awakening of the god or goddess who is considered to have been asleep. Due attention is paid to the comfort of the divine presences, so the preparation of necessary vessels and ingredients, bathing and dressing the sacred image, and offering refreshments, form significant parts of the ceremony, which all take place in front of the deity. The image is anointed with oils, camphor and sandalwood; it is then garlanded, and entertained with moving flames. The offerings presented next vary considerably but usually include rice and betel leaf. Several circumambulations in a clockwise direction (*pradakshinā*) are then made around the image, and sometimes round the sanctuary as well. The priest bows and offers a handful of flowers; finally the sanctuary door is closed as the deity is considered to be asleep.

In addition to these daily ceremonies there are also opportunities for private worship by individuals, who make offerings to the symbol or image of the deity and recite prayers. The making of vows and presentation of offerings are an important part of private devotion and form part of birth, marriage and death ceremonies as well as the taking of oaths for civil cases. Some forms of worship are more congregational in character – public performances of sacred songs and dance,

recitals of ancient texts. Many of these activities take place in the columned halls in front of the image or symbol in the sanctuary.

Not all sculptures, however, are housed in the temple sanctuary: doorways, columns, ceilings and outer walls are often richly carved, and some temples have their exterior surfaces completely covered with sculptures of deities, semi-divine beings, animals and birds. Despite this profuse imagery, a precise relationship is always maintained between architecture and its surface sculpture. For example, guardians with weapons, alluring females, amorous couples and entwined serpents are often positioned at gateways and doorways where they magically protect the temple and its deity. Rows of elephants, lions and mythical beasts at the base 'support' the temple, while birds appear above. Columns are usually richly carved with monster masks, flowers and foliage, garlands and jewels. Brackets carrying beams or overhanging eaves are deeply carved with seductive females or couples. Even ceilings have their special motifs – lotus flowers or 'flying' divinities. Balustrades flanking steps, or spouts carrying away liquid offerings, are also fashioned into particular forms, especially mythical beasts.

Panels in niches running around the outer walls of temples are carved with various divinities. The multitude of deities found here – cult gods and goddesses in their numerous guises, their consorts and children, guardians of the directions of space, and protectors of the sanctuary – affirms the temple as the terrestial abode of the gods. While walking around the temple as part of devotional ritual, the worshipper pays reverence to all these deities. (Narrative sculptures, which are not normally worshipped, are usually confined to horizontal friezes carved on beams, wall bases and tops of railings.)

Processional images, usually fashioned in metal or clay and made to be seen in the round, are the focus of public festivals associated with many shrines and temples throughout India. During the festivals the images, or their substitutes, are brought outside so that they may be seen by all and be presented with flowers, fruits and other offerings. They are elaborately dressed and then placed in a swing, carried on a float, or transported in a wooden chariot. Great attention is lavished on the throne, mount or vehicle bearing the image; wooden chariots, for example, are covered with carved panels, including diverse deities and rearing mythical beasts.

Small sculptures of divinities that protect the family are usually associated with domestic shrines – sometimes elaborate niches or even a small room. Daily homage is paid to these images made of stone, metal or terracotta, by members of the household; sometimes a local priest is in attendance.

PATRONS AND CRAFTSMEN

Stone and bronze sculptures in India are closely linked with sacred architecture and royal patronage. In fact, the beginnings of monumental stone architecture and sculpture are directly connected with the patronage of the emperors of the Maurya period, particularly Ashoka, in the 3rd century BC. Building in stone was always a costly undertaking: the material had to be cut and transported, workmen of different skills employed, and supervision of the project maintained. The craftsmen responsible for sculptures were highly paid and, if

RITUALS OF WORSHIP

Direct worship of gods and goddesses forms the focal point of religious activities that take place within the Indian temple. The various rituals of worship permit an identification of the devotee with the godhead; those who are able to achieve a unity of self and godhead gain merit and access to the path that leads to ultimate liberation. Worship is conceived as an evocation, reception and entertainment of the god or goddess as a royal guest. The rituals are performed by priests on behalf of the community, and often in the presence of devotees. Hymns are recited in front of the image housed in the temple sanctuary, persuading the deity to take visible form by inhabiting the image. Once this takes place the priest is able to converse with the divine by means of magical syllables, verbal formulae and symbolic hand gestures. The deity is then awakened and due attention is paid to the divine presence – the preparation of vessels and ingredients necessary for worship, the bathing and dressing of the sacred image, and the offering of refreshments. The image is then anointed with oils, camphor and sandalwood, garlanded, and entertained with moving flames. Offerings usually include rice as the principal meal of the divinity, and flowers. Circumambulations are sometimes performed around the image when it is free-standing.

Practices of temple worship generally follow the same basic pattern in Hindu and Jain temples. In the latter, the twenty-four saviours (Tīrthankaras) are sometimes shown together in meditation postures, and the priest moves from one image to the next with offerings and oblations (*left, below*). Always there is an emphasis on brightly coloured garlands, costumes and jewels, whether the images are of gods and goddesses in quasi-human forms (*right, centre*) or in animal form like Nandin, the bull mount of Shiva (*far right, below*).

Festivals are an important part of temple worship and at these times performances of sacred music, drama and dance are given in honour of the god or goddess. During festivals children sometimes take the parts of divine personalities. Here (*far right, above*) children are dressed up as Krishna and Rādhā, precisely imitating the traditional costumes of the divine images. Festival activities usually take place in front of the temple or sanctuary where the deity is housed. If the image is free-standing, it is sometimes carried outside to be publicly displayed so that the whole population can participate in the celebration. The chariots that transport the deity through the town are themselves mobile temples and reproduce, in bamboo and coloured canvas, the permanent forms of a stone building (*left, above*).

necessary, were brought from other artistic centres.

Patronage of monumental architecture and art seems to have been a sincere expression of piety as well as a means of communicating the power and wealth of the patron. Not only did the ruler commission the building with all its sculptures, but he also contributed money, treasure or income from agriculture towards the upkeep of the temple, and for the performance of certain rituals. Following this royal example, many wealthy individuals also acted as patrons.

Building a Buddhist *stūpa* to commemorate the life of the Buddha or Jain hero, or erecting a Hindu temple to house a deity, was sometimes undertaken in celebration of an important political event such as a military victory; occasionally such buildings were intended to be the settings for ceremonies of coronation and honour. Little wonder, then, that sacred monuments in India incorporate much sculpture that is distinctly courtly in spirit. Even gods and goddesses (Shiva and Pārvatī, for example) are often depicted as royal figures, complete with crowns, jewels and richly ornamented costumes; narrative episodes take place in palace settings and reproduce contemporary courtly life. In addition, the royal couple is sometimes considered an earthly reflection of the celestial couple. Thus royal patrons were able to identify themselves with the temple deity; such an identification is suggested by the fact that patrons and temple divinities often shared the same name – the early 11th-century Rājarājeshvara temple of Thanjavur is one example.

Courtly activities are often incorporated into religious art. Processions of elephants and horses, soldiers, warriors, and armed guards, hunters, courtly women, musicians and dancers are found on the gateways of Buddhist *stūpas* or on the bases of Hindu temples. Sometimes there is the actual depiction of the royal figure as the patron of the temple, usually shown in a devotional attitude. On the 13th-century Sūrya temple at Konarak, the king sits with the chief *brāhman* priest – the meeting of the twin heads of secular and religious power. The tendency to depict royal devotion is imitated in the images of saintly figures shown with their hands clasped together.

Indian society makes little allowance for the pursuit of self-expression; only rarely does a craftsman sign his work. The traditional role of the artist in India is to give visible form to things higher and greater than himself. The sculptor considers his work a means of access to the divine, and before beginning his work he has to undergo mental preparation and ritual purification. Only in this way can the sculptor identify himself with the transcendental principles to which he attempts to give outer form in stone, metal or wood.

Like architects and other artisans and workmen, sculptors working on a sacred monument were generally organized into groups which functioned somewhat like the guilds of medieval Europe. The traditions of these groups were mostly preserved orally, the groups being extensions of family units in which techniques were handed down from one generation to another. Family and individual craftsmen were thus united into a corporate body that fixed rules of work and wages, and set standards for work completed. Frequently such organizations became wealthy and were themselves able to make charitable donations.

Stone sculptors (*shilpins*) were engaged on all portions of buildings and their services were required at many stages in the construction. Sculptured work was usually assigned on the basis of contracts for separate operations. Leading master sculptors worked on the principle images of the sanctuary and outer walls, while other craftsmen were responsible for carvings on beams, brackets, columns and bases. Though the master sculptors probably worked with assistants, the designs and compositions of major pieces were almost certainly the inspiration of a single artist. Metal workshops, especially for bronze-casting, and terracotta craftsmen, were sometimes also closely connected with the building of the temple.

The close relationship between artists and priests was important in the evolution of Indian sculpture. In order that certain theological ideas be successfully translated into images, priests set out rules governing all details of making sculptures. The earliest records of these iconographic prescriptions occur as sections in the epics and mythological collections (*Purānas*) already written down by the Gupta period; later they were gathered together in the *Shāstras* and *Āgamas*. These texts on image-making attempt to codify all aspects of sculpture: they describe in great detail the appropriate costume, ornament, facial expression, posture, hand gesture and emblems for divinities, their consorts and animal vehicles, and even their correct location on temple walls. The systematic ordering of icons according to the measurements also forms a large part of these texts, and here the proportions of figures are precisely laid out. As one ancient text warns, 'the image not made with the prescribed rules is fruitless and its worship is without any effect'.

The history of Indian sculpture well illustrates the increasing dependence of artists upon *brāhman* priests for suitable forms for sacred sculpture. For example, the varied sculptures from earlier periods (before the 7th and 8th centuries) are replaced in later periods (9th–12th centuries) by more standardized images as the disciplines of iconography and iconometry were increasingly applied. This continuing relationship of artists and theologians clearly demonstrates the underlying purpose of Indian sculpture: to render in visible and accessible form the world of the gods.

INTRODUCTION TO INDIAN PAINTING

by Dr Linda Leach

The miniature paintings in this exhibition represent an extraordinarily varied experience of Indian life, and yet they are drawn just from the small proportion that have survived and can be moved. The historical and artistic background of these particular works is complex and in order to fully appreciate the context from which they derive, it is also necessary to understand the earlier traditions of Indian wall painting.

EARLY PAINTING TRADITIONS

The tumultuous world perceived by the Indian wall painter is controlled by organic patterns of growth and dissolution, the forms of which are at first difficult to identify. Human figures of varying scales are arranged without reference to ground planes or to spatial conventions, as if the personalities they represent are appearing and disappearing in the flux of reincarnation.

Most of the information we have about this vision of the world comes from the remaining fragments of dry fresco on the walls of some of the Ajanta caves. This complex of Buddhist assembly halls and monasteries in western India was excavated in a semicircular ravine some distance from any urban settlement as a habitation for monks during the rainy season. The paintings, which date from the 1st century BC to the late 5th century AD, were created by artists who probably worked in guild-like organizations. The smoothed walls were plastered and the underdrawings or plans made before earth pigments, such as ochre, or the rarer mineral pigment, lapis lazuli, were applied.

In many cases, the wall paintings serve as background scenes for sculptured deities that were themselves once painted. Many of the wall scenes are elaborately shaded and modelled so that the distinction between two-dimensional and three-dimensional forms is blurred. Wall paintings at later sites, such as Kanchipuram and Ellora, show that there was a traditional correlation between painting and sculpture. However, it is apparent at Ajanta that illusionistic painting techniques were particularly suitable for showing crowds, buildings and vegetation – all the details of genre that cannot be conveyed so well in the less pliant materials of sculpture. The Ajanta painters were expert at depicting complex groups of people and could even treat them in motion.

The environment glimpsed in the Ajanta paintings is a warm and open one, with man shown in an unselfconscious manner as an element of nature. Little social artifice or formality is revealed by narrative scenes; instead, gracious and humanistic values are expressed by figure grouping and gesture, supported by the choice of earthy colours and the broad, generous rhythms of the compositions. Kings are atttended with little ceremony by peoples of various racial types, while women in relaxed, graceful poses express great freedom as well as a feminine serenity.

Although Gupta wall painting can be related to sculpture, the Mughal epoch, when the majority of miniature paintings were produced, comes well after the major period of sculptural creativity. Thus there is a curious dichotomy between miniature painting and sculpture that represents a far greater gap than necessarily arises between two different media. This divergence results from man's altered attitude to the world and his increased self-awareness, signalling a change in his previous relationship to nature.

Early palm-leaf book paintings and wooden book covers, some dating from the 10th century, reflect the style of the wall painting tradition: figures, for example, are plastic and skilfully modelled. Since many of the subjects are Buddhist, it is to be expected that their style of illustration should follow that developed in murals at Buddhist sites. However, in other medieval paintings, strong, wiry outlines replace the soft, coloured modelling characteristic of Ajanta. This style of illustration comes to be associated particularly with Jain scriptures, produced in vast numbers from about the 12th century. The Jain faith, with its carefully observed ritual worship of Tirthankaras, or saints, occasioned an art governed by strict conventions with lively, though formally regulated, designs.

By the 12th century the task of the book painter had become quite divorced from that of the sculptor, and new artistic concepts suited to a miniature format were well-developed. Concern with an enjoyment of line, colour and two-dimensional pattern had entirely replaced the earlier desire for plasticity.

AJANTA

Between the 2nd century BC and the late 5th century AD the rocky ravine at Ajanta in the Deccan was utilized by Buddhist monks as a place of retreat, particularly at monsoon time. Here craftsmen created accommodation and temples for the monks by excavating directly into the cliffs (*above*). These artificial caves were adorned with carved images as well as frescoes; the latter covered the walls and ceilings, both inside and outside. Remarkably well preserved by the remoteness of the site, the Ajanta paintings form the most complete record of an artistic tradition that has almost completely disappeared elsewhere in India. The lively and crowded compositions, the rich colouristic effects, and the sensitive drawing are a vivid testimony to an inventive and varied painting tradition that was to influence much of Asia. Not only did the painters at Ajanta visualize the many Buddhas that were worshipped by the monks in their rituals (*left*), they were also able to depict the sensuous pleasurable atmosphere of contemporary courtly life. Refined and elegant attendant women (*opposite*) form part of large-scale narrative compositions that illustrate scenes from the life of the Buddha or from the Jātaka folk tales adopted by early Buddhism.

MUSLIM-HINDU INTERACTION

Book painting associated with both Buddhism and Jainism pre-dates the Islamic period, yet its importance was reinforced after the 12th century in areas ruled by Muslim dynasties. Because of the severely limited use of iconic forms in Islamic painting (which were viewed as a counterfeit of Allah's true creativity), illustration was restricted to inconspicuous dimensions, and only developed by secular patrons bold enough to interpret iconic limitations in liberal terms. Since the energies of the Muslim artist had been focused for many centuries on small book illustrations, imaginative and refined forms of miniature painting had evolved which gradually stimulated the popularity of this medium at an increasing number of native Indian artistic centres.

The successive Muslim sultans of India encountered an intricate social network, strengthened by centuries of custom and supported by religious justifications concerning caste differentiations. The Hindu Rājput nobles, who ruled the states and small territories across much of north India, were members of the *kshatriya* (warrior caste). They had themselves been invaders of India in about the 6th century AD and were subsequently absorbed into the Hindu system. These chieftains, living in fortified palaces, maintained themselves with the aid of their extended families and numerous retainers. They were governed by a chivalric code that required fierce clan loyalty, constant skirmishes between rivals, harsh revenges for betrayals, passionate ardour in romance and bitter death in the face of defeat.

The Muslims often attempted to despoil the Rājput strongholds, either asserting themselves as overlords or jostling for positions as neighbours. Both Muslim and Hindu patrons during this period commissioned illustrated manuscripts, and there was some interchange between their characteristic styles. Muslim manuscripts included epics, poetical works and astronomy texts in debased Persian styles, while Hindu painters concerned themselves with chivalric romances and devotional works. Particularly popular was the ecstatic devotional poem the *Gīta Govinda*, or 'Song of the Cowherd', (a title refering to Krishna's occupation in adolescence). This intense allegorical description by Jayadeva, a 12th-century Bengali court poet, of the union between the soul and God, which is dramatized as a union between the lovers Rādhā and Krishna, expresses the deepest beliefs of Jayadeva's period. The ardent and mystic deification of Krishna, eighth incarnation of Vishnu, was adapted by the Rājputs as a focus for both their symbolic literature and their painting.

Krishna became the central object of a Hindu longing for personal devotion, and the cult of *bhakti* or salvation through passionate adoration grew up especially around him. The moral values attributed to Rāma, the seventh incarnation of Vishnu, were seen in relation to the *Rāmāyana* narrative, which was often illustrated as an epic, but Rāma as an independent deity did not have as much attraction as Krishna. Krishna, embodying all the warmth and fallibility of a human being, was accepted as an anthropomorphic god because of his egoistic will. While the heroic Rāma was self-effacing, Krishna had the egocentric personalities of a mischievous child, demon-killing herdboy, lover and warrior, which demanded adulation. His capriciousness intensified his attraction; Rādhā and the *gopīs* could search and yearn for him, yet he manifested himself only when he desired. This elusiveness made it possible for Krishna to represent the unobtainable ideal in any romantic scene.

The use of metaphor in romantic paintings allowed the artist to project his thoughts through nature – two birds might exemplify his sense of completeness while one bird signified unutterable loneliness. Though this kind of emotional symbolism was part of earlier poetry and painting, the inhibitions and self-conscious artifices of courtly love introduced a new intensity. The competitive pride of chivalric warriors, the female purdah restrictions introduced by Muslims, and the discord between Hindus and Muslims, all combined to restrict the openness of the social environment and to heighten the emotional qualities expressed in art.

THE MUGHAL PERIOD

In 1526, after a decisive battle on the plains of north India, Bābur, a young monarch who had lost his own small kingdom in Afghanistan, entered Delhi and became the first of the Mughal emperors, so-called because of their descent from the Mongol line of Genghis Khan. Bābur's four years of rule in India were apparently insignificant – he was simply another of the military adventurers to come to the subcontinent – yet he bequeathed his grandson Akbar a wealth of personal qualities which insured the boy's success. Akbar was crowned in 1556, at the age of thirteen, after the accidental death of his father Humāyūn, who had introduced Persian painters to the court shortly before. Within a few years, the new ruler proved to be extraordinarily logical, dynamic and fair-minded with ideas well in advance of his times. His personal courage and diplomacy enabled him to found an empire unprecedented in India for over a thousand years. He created a stable administrative bureaucracy and promoted religious toleration (Hindu and Muslim artists worked together in the imperial studio).

Akbar, who was illiterate, immediately understood the communicative power that lay behind manuscript illustration. Under his patronage the decorative and symbolic Persian style of painting that had been a hallmark of taste was superseded by one more suited to his personal vitality and to his court. By altering both style and content, he broadened the appeal of the art.

Except for some poetry illustrations, the miniature paintings of Akbar's reign generally express populist ideals. Packed with assertive forms principally relevant to everyday life, they are the products of the activist rather than the introvert, and their subjects – such as conquests or building projects – are those of cooperative rather than individual activity. The emperor wanted historical paintings that would communicate his powerful dynastic ambitions, and he also commissioned paintings of the Hindu religious epics in order to demonstrate to his own followers the stimulative value of the ancient Indian tradition.

Because of his father's political competence, Akbar's son Jahāngīr was able to lead a cultivated and somewhat irresponsible life. He enjoyed paintings and began to patronize artists while still a prince. By the time he came to the throne in 1605, at the age of 35, his interest both in refined Persian miniatures and 'exotic' European works was highly developed.

The tomb of the *sūfi* saint Salīm Chishti who prophesied the birth of Akbar's three sons, is near the Buland Darwaza Gate in Fatehpur Sikri, the capital city that Akbar had built over Salīm's village.

He commissioned paintings not as a political leader but as someone who was exploring his own tastes from a position of unique power. These paintings are both beautiful and intellectually satisfying; since Jahāngīr was an amateur naturalist he passionately desired that depictions of the birds, animals and flowers he had seen during his travels should be accurate.

The courtiers surrounding the emperor were constantly involved in political intrigue that Jahāngīr observed but – unlike Akbar – could not accurately assess or control. Perhaps for this reason, the emperor became obsessed with commissioning character studies. Contemporary portraiture, of both humans and animals, was based upon a knowledge of European art that arrived in India through contacts with Jesuits, traders and emissaries to the Mughal court.

Under Akbar the large Mughal painting studio included about 150 known artists who illustrated the pages of the volumes he commissioned. The artists worked under a librarian, with the emperor examining and rewarding their work weekly. The more accomplished executed the designs of the scenes, while less capable artists were responsible for the slower job of colouring. Mineral pigments, such as malachite, lapis lazuli and cinnabar, were laboriously ground and mixed with gum arabic. The paints were then applied in layers and the miniature repeatedly burnished on the reverse side with an agate so that the surface became dense, glossy, and enamel-like. The great care with which this process was completed distinguishes early Mughal painting.

As Jahāngīr was more interested in individual masterpieces than in large numbers of manuscript illustrations, he required fewer but more original artists. Although their working environment may have been less regulated than in Akbar's reign, they must nevertheless have found Jahāngīr an extremely demanding patron. From his own account it is clear that artists were on call whenever he wished to have a scene recorded and that some were required to accompany him on his frequent travels.

In 1627, Jahāngīr's son Shāh Jahān (who built the Taj Mahal) succeeded to the throne, and although not interested in natural history he otherwise continued the general style and direction of painting favoured by his father. However, the miniature tradition gradually suffered as various emperors failed to maintain the leadership Akbar and Jahāngīr had provided. After the early years of the 17th century, the Mughal empire and its artistic life began to be strangled by the prevailing confused materialism. Courtly splendour and extravagance consumed the fabulous wealth provided by the country, while the emperors failed to develop industry or trade either internally or with other nations. The isolation created by the court's wealth, its rigid ceremonies and intrigue, seemed to stifle initiative as well as constrict opportunities. The social system provided few alternatives to the coveted but highly insecure positions of the feudal hierarchy. If comparison is made between the easy, informal life revealed in the Ajanta paintings and that of Shāh Jahān's time, the differences are startling. Despite its rich beauty, the latter environment appears to be stilted and to offer fewer social amenities for all those within it, including the emperor himself.

RĀJPUT PAINTING

Akbar's conquests and diplomacy forced the Rājputs in the strategic area of Rajasthan to take some stand in relation to the pressures he imposed. Although others allied themselves with the emperor and were influenced by Mughal culture, the rulers of Mewar continued their resistance until the middle of Jahāngīr's reign. These rulers, who were the foremost clan of Rajasthan and considered themselves descendants of the sun, had been humiliated by the overthrow of their great fortress of Chitor and carried on a bitter guerrilla struggle with the Mughals.

The symbolic and intense paintings of Mewar reflect the very essence of Rājput life. Mughal influence only spasmodically penetrated the painting studios of the state until the early 18th century. Rajasthan is a dry region with reddish-brown fields, hilly jungles covered in grass and small trees, and a large desert region in the west. The human elements of culture, such as architecture and costume, contrast vividly with the somewhat stern landscape that during much of the year forms a monochromatic background for man's activities. The villages, temples and palace or fortress comprised most men's environments, with few urban centres to diversify interest. Mewar painters captured the harsh concentration as well as the vitality of this lifestyle, along with certain artists from Bundi, Kotah, Marwar, and the central Indian state of Malwa.

By contrast, courts such as that of Bikaner, whose rajas were in the Mughal armies and who looked to the central government for support, tended to be receptive to Mughal painting styles. One means of assessing Rajasthani paintings is by determining the amount of stylistic borrowing from the Mughal court. In addition to the desire of patrons to imitate the Mughals, Mughal-trained artists often left the imperial atelier for various reasons and went to work in Rajasthan so that there was a degree of cross-fertilization.

The studios maintained by the Rājputs differed in character, and though most were small, states like Mewar produced large

MUGHALS AND RĀJPUTS

The Hindu and Muslim rulers of northern India built sumptuously
appointed fortress palaces which were virtually self-sufficient; as well
as private quarters for the ruler's extended family, there were sections
for governmental and ceremonial functions, and for the manufacture
of certain household necessities. At Udaipur in Rajasthan (*above*) an
artificial lake surrounds a 17th-century island pleasure palace,
communicating something of the sense of fantasy also beloved by the
Rājputs. Building on a grander scale at Delhi and Agra, the Mughal
emperors constructed huge fortresses surrounded by massive stone
walls, and entered by well-guarded gateways. Within these walls,
gardens, apartments, reception halls, mosques, stables, bath-houses
and a host of accessory structures were linked together in formal axial
arrangements. The marble interiors of the 17th-century mosque at
Agra Fort (*left*) illustrates the refined decoration and delicate
manipulation of light and space characteristic of Mughal architecture.
The carved and inlaid decoration of Shāh Jahān's buildings in the
fort (*right*) includes coloured semi-precious stones. The floral motifs
are closely related to contemporary textile designs and miniature
paintings.

numbers of illustrated religious manuscripts. The existing records show that Rājput paintings were done in domestic environments and presented to the ruler for approval; however, artists were still commanded by the court rather than operating independently. In many cases, masters supervised apprentices, probably family members, who merely completed their works. The tendency was for an eminent court artist to set a style that was assimilated by the other painters of the state. While Rājput artists often possessed considerable talent, the pigments and materials at their disposal were inferior to those of the Mughal court, and paintings were less carefully prepared.

In certain cases, Rājput pictures were also produced in temple environments as, for example, at Nathadwara, a town devoted to the worship of Shrī Nāthjī, a special form of Krishna requiring the services of artists who specialized in cloth cult paintings and religious souvenirs.

While art became a status symbol, it was not necessarily rajas at the largest courts who sponsored the most paintings, or the only good ones. Small *thikanas* (fiefdoms) under the control of the larger states often produced miniatures. One example of a prolific *thikana* studio is that of Devgarh, under the protection of Mewar, whose painters worked in an offshoot of the Mewar style. The Devgarh artist Chokhā is one of the most original and significant of Rajasthani painters.

The Rājputs in the Himalayan foothill region, the Pahari hill area, ruled smaller, less strategic states, and were therefore not exposed as quickly or as strongly to Mughal influence. Although painting of the pre-Mughal type known in Rajasthan was probably also produced in this region, the examples that are considered to initiate the Pahari Rājput schools date only from the mid-17th century, by which time Rajasthani studios were already flourishing. Early Pahari paintings are of two major types: one is influenced by Mughal painting; the other is highly coloured and symbolically conceived. In regard to the latter style, it can be said that the hill area, somewhat removed from the rest of India and cut off by winter snows, developed its own Hindu customs of worship, whose beliefs became emphasized by isolation. In the symbolic paintings of Devī, the Goddess, and Krishna, the lover, yellows, reds and pinks leap out with astonishing vibrancy. The glances of the figures and their taut bodies seem to demonstrate the tensions of a godlike energy. This style is especially represented by the states of Basohli, Mankot and Kulu.

Oddly, the greatest development in later Pahari painting is almost antithetical. Artists who were familiar with the Mughal painting of the 18th century created a naturalistic but rhythmic lyrical style of drawing that became associated particularly with the states of Guler and Kangra. The scenery of the Pahari region, with its lush tree-covered areas, its flowers and many cool greens was an ideal backdrop for the pastoral and love scenes connected with the Krishna cult. The miniatures of Krishna, who supposedly grew up far to the south in the Mathura area, are entirely convincing because the Kangra artists have perfectly captured the rural life of India.

THE END OF THE MUGHAL EMPIRE

The Deccan plateau of peninsular India was subject to Islamic rulers who, during the Mughal period, maintained their kingdoms in a precarious fashion by adroit juggling of alliances and the payment of large sums of money. Mughal pride was provoked into determined opposition because these rich states always appeared to be on the verge of downfall, and yet contrived to remain tantalizingly out of reach. The final Mughal victories towards the end of the 17th century were Pyrrhic ones, for after decades of frustrating struggles they only emptied the coffers of the central government and contributed to the downfall of the Mughal empire.

The Deccani rulers, intent on enjoying their span of comfort, commissioned elegantly sensitive paintings that blended Islamic and native Indian qualities. This mixture is quite different from that in Mughal miniatures, which include Akbar pragmatism and European naturalism. The evocative and symbolic aspects of Persian painting, rather than being submerged as in north India, were combined with Indian hedonism. Colour is a strong, sensuous element with pinks, oranges and violets often used in rich combinations. Deccani paintings are preserved mainly from the kingdoms of Bijapur and Golconda.

The long fight for the Deccani kingdoms had the effect of tearing the Mughal empire asunder since, in 1680, Aurangzīb (ruled 1658 to 1707) elected to move his capital close to the area of battle, leaving a power vacuum in the north. During the 18th century, the most powerful Mughal officials began to look to their own interests and to make the provincial cities of the north their centres of influence. These *de facto* rulers actively sponsored painters, though never on an imperial scale. Artists were thus forced to seek patronage from other nobles and members of the wealthy class. During this period there is discernible Mughal influence in the Pahari area as well as interchange with Rajasthan due to the migration of artists seeking work.

Although painters were continually in search of stimulus, their inspiration and artistic opportunities were generally underdeveloped because their patrons had inadequate initiative or resources. The British assumption of power brought an entirely different class of confident, sometimes overbearing, patrons to the fore. These men and women, and the European criteria of art that they brought with them, challenged the Indian painter, rousing him to fresh observations of the houses, festivals and landscapes around him. British patrons preferred paintings in soft watercolour tones, which were 'exotic' to the Indian artist. Readily, perhaps even gratefully, responding to this new aesthetic, painters expressed themselves with great dignity, and sometimes with much exuberance. Thus the Indian artist, adapting his talents to foreign demands, once more demonstrated his extraordinary ability to grasp novel ideas, and to endow them nevertheless with a distinctive Indian spirit.

GLOSSARY OF SCULPTURE STYLES

by Dr George Michell

---

1 NORTH AND NORTH-WESTERN INDIA

Maurya and Shunga periods (3rd century BC–1st century BC)
7, 8, 12, 19, 22, 26, 28, 59, 62, 64, 65, 117
India experienced its first political unification under the Maurya kings who ruled from Patilaputra in the 3rd century BC. The earliest stone sculptures – easily recognizable for their finely polished surfaces, a technique derived from Achaemenid Iran – date from this period. The sandstone columns, capitals and other architectural fragments associated with the imperial Buddhist monuments patronized by the emperor Ashoka (272–232 BC) are meticulously carved with naturalistic animals and birds.

The sculpture of the succeeding Shunga dynasty, also in

22

22 Shunga period, 2nd century BC
Elephants with riders and dancing girls (*see p. 101*)

sandstone, is concentrated on railways and gateways of the great Buddhist and Jain *stūpas*, as at Sanchi and Barhut. Here are depicted folk deities and guardians as well as scenes from the life of the Buddha (though the Buddha himself is absent), and a variety of ornamental motifs – lotus flowers, animal friezes and miniature architectural compositions with columns, windows and roofs. Vitality of expression and precision of detail in costumes and headdresses is immediately evident in the friezes and fully rounded figures, as well as in miniature terracottas and ivories.

Kushāna period (1st–4th centuries)
9, 29, 66, 67, 68, 77, 91, 115, 118, 121, 122, 307, 310, 313, 321, 328, 331, 426
The Kushānas, who arrived in India from the north-west in the 1st century BC, rapidly spread their rule across northern and central India. Under their patronage, artistic traditions from the north-west Gandhara region, and beyond, became blended with the central Indian idiom that had evolved during the Shunga period. Ruling for a time at Mathura, the Kushāna kings constructed monuments dedicated to various Buddhist, Jain and Hindu cults, and the first depictions of the Buddha, Mahāvīra and Hindu divinities date from this period. Though central Asian and Roman influences – details of costume, headdress, emblems, etc. – were often incorporated into

figurative art, an essentially Indian expression always
predominated. Invariably in red sandstone, figures are fully
rounded and solid, bodies tautly drawn even when covered
with loose garments, and postures and gestures clearly
displayed. Characteristic of the sculpture of this period is a
monumental vigour, sometimes achieved with fairly crude
carving.

Folk deities, especially *yakshīs*, are found on the railways
and gateways of *stūpas*. Here there is an emphasis on rounded
limbs, prominent breasts and sensuous smiles. A courtly
element is also detected in 'toilet scenes', sometimes showing
drunken revellers. But it is in Buddhist and Jain art that
Kushāna sculpture is most innovatory. The iconographic
models developed here are clearly defined: standing and seated
figures of the Buddha have flowing robes, the palm of one
hand is raised in protection, and the fully rounded head with
staring eyes is dominated by a large halo. Similar conventions
are found in sculptures of the Jain saints and in the royal
portraits, particularly those of standing kings, such as
Kanishka (2nd century AD). Naturalistic illustrations of animal
and vegetable life were often incorporated into figural
compositions though there is an emphasis on the fantastic in
the depiction of beasts.

Gandhara (1st–4th centuries)
53, 58, 61, 251, 252, 314, 320, 322, 325
Forming part of present-day Afghanistan and north-western
Pakistan, the Gandhara region was an important meeting place
of different artistic traditions. From here come terracotta
figurines of the 'mother goddess' type, known in India from
the time of the Indus Valley cities (3rd–2nd centuries BC). The
archaic forms and simple outlines of these figurines represent a
style almost untouched by historic evolution, and still found in
the tribal art of India today.

Following the invasion of Alexander the Great (4th century
BC), Gandhara came into contact with Classical Mediterranean
culture. The influence of provincial Graeco-Roman art was
such that it resulted in a style sometimes known as 'Indo-
Greek'. Sculpture in blue-grey schist was used to ornament
Buddhist *stūpas*, shrines and monastries dating from the time
1st century AD, some of which were erected by the Kushāna
rulers. The Graeco-Roman origins of Gandhara Buddhist
icons are seen in the classical draperies and architectural
settings. By the 2nd–3rd centuries AD this hybrid style had
become completely Indianized, and the forms of Buddhist
narrative scenes and cult icons were well established. From the
Gandhara regions artistic influences travelled to Central Asia,
and from there to China by way of the silk routes.

Gupta period (4th–6th centuries)
31, 89, 124, 254, 256, 330, 333, 349, 350, 360, 381, 394, 427,
428, 437, 474, 492
Rulers of central India during the 4th–6th centuries AD, the
Guptas were responsible for a cultural efflorescence in all the
arts. Deriving from Kushāna traditions, and justly celebrated
for its monumental simplicity and refined carving, Gupta
sculpture developed its own distinctive style, especially at
Sarnath and Mathura, as well as at the rock-cut sites of Ajanta
and Ellora. This style was to influence all subsequent artistic
developments throughout northern India.

Both Buddhist and Jain sandstone figures are noted for their
mood of calm achieved through an expression of inner

68 Kushāna period
2nd century
Shālabhanjikā (see p. 112)

328 Kushāna period
2nd century
Maitreya *(see p. 190)*

320 From Gandhara
3rd–5th century
Head of the Buddha *(see p. 188)*

324 Gupta period
5th century
The Buddha *(see p. 189)*

363 From Kashmir
11th century
Vishnu on Garuda *(see p. 200)*

363

455 From Himachal Pradesh
10th century
Consort of Sadāshiva
(see p. 220)

455

tranquillity: delicately modelled oval-shaped heads have their eyelids gently lowered; standing figures in subtle robes reveal gracefully posed bodies, softly modelled almost in the round. Typical of Gupta sculpture are the great halos ornamented with lotus flowers and other plants, and the hand gestures carved with utmost precision. Depictions of the life of the Buddha also became standardized – usually reduced to a limited number of scenes, sometimes arranged vertically.

Figurative art associated with stone Hindu temples also developed during the Gupta period. One-faced and four-faced *lingas* are characterized by swelling forms and subtly carved Shiva heads. Narrative scenes from *Rāmāyana* and Krishna legends are also found, particularly as temple friezes (at Deogarh, for example). Decorative motifs, especially at doorways, include subsidiary imps, mythical beasts and foliage panels. The carving is always fluid and supple, the figures and animals gracefully posed.

Another important series of Buddhist and Hindu Gupta monuments executed in brick with terracotta ornamentation were plaques showing mythological scenes, divinities, and holy men and devotees in a crude but vigorous style. Some plaques show evidence of the use of moulds.

Kashmir (8th–12th centuries)
323, 337, 363, 429, 430
The isolated valley of Kashmir preserved cultural and artistic traditions long after they had disappeared elsewhere. Sculpture in Kashmir is associated with both Buddhist and Hindu temples. The impact of the neighbouring Gandhara style, surviving for a longer period in Kashmir, is clearly seen in small Buddhist ivories of the 8th century, where the meditating Buddha, dressed in a toga-like costume, is surrounded by a crowd of animated figures in a miniature pseudo-Classical frame: the oval face, pronounced nose, arched eyebrows and fat chin are typical. The same features are found in larger stone sculptures (particularly of Vishnu riding on Garuda), which are also characterized by their smooth surfaces and rounded forms.

Kashmir artists worked in a variety of other materials too. Their bronzes of the 10th–11th centuries, both Buddhist and Hindu, are superbly cast with silver and copper inlay, and the fully modelled figures with delicately incised details are often shown in elegant, swaying postures. Terracotta plaques and pavement slabs around *stūpas*, and carvings on wooden temples, depict a variety of subjects including representations of ascetics, usually in a vigorous and animated style.

Himachal Pradesh (8th–12th centuries)
455
In many respects the stone sculpture of the valleys of this Himalayan region is closely related to the artistic traditions of central India during the Gurjara-Pratihāra period. Bronzes of Hindu divinities are cast almost in the round, often with elaborate frames. Icons of Durgā and Kālī in energetic postures and carrying a large number of weapons are particularly vivid. Wooden carvings are also known from temples in this area.

2 THE DECCAN

Sātavāhana and Ikshavāku periods (1st–4th centuries)
6, 17, 51, 52, 114, 205, 308, 309, 315, 319, 329
Because the principal artistic centres of the Deccan at this period were at Buddhist sites such as Amaravati and Nagarjunakonda, the first stone sculptures in the Deccan are linked with the adornment of *stūpas*. Railing slabs from the 1st and 2nd centuries display a variety of decorative themes (lotus panels, attendant figures) and commemorative emblems (wheels, depictions of the *stūpa* itself), while 3rd–4th-century panels concentrate on narrative scenes from the life of the Buddha. Carved in the characteristic local limestone the figures are modelled with a remarkable delicacy and softness. Later phases show contacts with Kushāna artistic traditions of northern India – as in the iconography of the Buddha figure – as well as direct influences from the Mediterranean world – as in the Graeco-Roman dress of the Buddha and his followers and in the pseudo-Classical compositions. The crowded and animated scenes, with subtle perspective effects, and the pronounced realism of the figures are outstanding features. Three-dimensional stone figures are also noted for their delicate modelling and serene expressions.

Early Chālukya period (6th–8th centuries)
13, 55, 56, 240, 365, 452, 481, 483, 486, 487
Under the patronage of the Early Chālukya kings, Hindu art in the Deccan received enormous impetus: both excavated and free-standing temples at Badami, Aihole, Pattadakal and Alampur are covered with a wealth of carvings. Maintaining artistic contacts with both northern and southern India, Early Chālukya sculpture evolved its own unique style: figures have dynamic but elegant postures, they are carved deeply in red, yellow or grey sandstone, and display a wide variety of icongraphic models. The rounded figures are often delicately carved. Principal cult icons of Vishnu, Shiva and The Goddess are sometimes large-scale compositions integrated into the walls or ceilings of temples. Mythological episodes, too, are found on temple walls, as well as on columns in friezes.

Rāshtrakūta, Late Chālukya and Western Ganga periods (8th–12th centuries)
97, 326, 334, 342, 344, 449, 468
These later dynasties continued the artistic traditions established by the Early Chālukyas. Flourishing more or less at the same time in the Deccan, the rulers of these kingdoms promoted their own closely related sculpture styles. Rāshtrakūta sculpture is usually associated with Hindu and Jain rock-cut temples, as at Ellora, excavated in coarse-grained trap rock. The monumental carvings at Ellora, for example, are characterized by their deep modelling and dynamic composition – features also imitated in smaller panels. Late Chālukya sculpture is distinguished by static postures of figures, usually in combination with delicately carved costumes, jewellery and ornamental frames. Black granite, often highly polished, is the usual medium for cult icons.

The Western Gangas were great patrons of Jainism, as can be seen in the colossal monolithic sculpture of the saint Bahubali (*see p. 14*) at Sravana Belgola. But small Jain and Buddhist bronzes are also known from this period, and are celebrated for the delicate modelling of the saviour in human form. Elaborately cast frames are occasionally added.

452 Early Chālukya period
8th century
Durgā (*see p. 220*)

326 Western Ganga period
c. 11th century
A Jain Tīrthankara
(*see p. 189*)

450 Hoysala period
Early 13th century
Durgā (*see p.219*)

Hoysala and Kākatīya periods (12th–14th centuries)
70, 105, 123, 361, 450, 465, 467
Sculptures from these periods generally serve as wall panels or brackets on Hindu temples, as at Halebid, Belur, Somnathpur and Palampet, for example. Deriving from late Chālukya traditions, Hoysala sculptures are characterized by a preoccupation with carved detail that frequently dominates the central fully modelled figure. Durgā, Bhairava and other divinities are surrounded by frames, delicately carved with prolific foliage; even the costumes, jewellery and headdresses of figures are elaborately carved with minutely observed detail. Green chlorite schist is the usual medium.

Kākatīya sculpture is distinguished for the elegant postures of its figures, especially female dancers and musicians. Typical characteristics are tall slender bodies, angular limbs and refined elegant faces with curious bun-like coiffures.

3 CENTRAL AND WESTERN INDIA

Gurjara-Pratihāra period (8th–10th centuries)

24, 74, 87, 92, 351, 355, 357, 372, 431, 435, 436, 444, 445, 451, 461, 464, 467, 476, 482

Following the disintegration of the Gupta empire there was a period of considerable confusion, but the rulers who established themselves at Kanyakubja in central India eventually gained control of most of northern India. The most powerful of these were the Gurjara-Pratihāras, who ruled an area from Sindh to Bengal and were great patrons of temple architecture. Sculptures from this period originally came from a large number of Hindu temples, where they were installed in niches on the outer walls, around doorways and on columns and brackets. Many, of course, remain *in situ*. Almost all the principal Hindu divinities, and the myths connected with their cults, are represented, usually in fairly conventional iconographic forms. Almost always executed in sandstone, Gurjara-Pratihāra sculptures continue the Gupta artistic tradition. There is the same delicate modelling and refinement of carving, but the figures are fuller and more rounded, and the postures pronounced. Attendant females, for example, are sensuously depicted in lyrical poses with full breasts. An increased preoccupation with detail is evident in the richly jewelled costumes and headdresses. Facial features are clearly sculpted, especially the eyebrows, eyes and nose; and the hair is sometimes meticulously depicted. Crowded compositions are popular; accessory figures are often grouped close together, forming frames for principal images or architectural friezes. In addition to figurative art there is a proliferation of decorative motifs – pots, bells, lotus flowers, foliage, monster masks, mythical beasts, etc. Several small bronzes are also known from this period.

Maitraka and Solankī (Chaulukya) periods (7th–12th centuries)

325, 343, 377, 384, 441, 464

Under the rulers of Gujarat a distinctive western Indian style emerged for the first time, linked with Hindu and Jain temple building. The earlier Maitraka phase shows a predominance of Gupta features, though there is an increased emphasis on fullness of form, particularly in the schist sculptures from sites such as Samlaji. Bronzes, especially the small Jain images from Akota, also have gently rounded figures.

Sculptures from the later Solankī (Chaulukya) period include carvings set into wall niches and covering ceilings, brackets and columns. The preferred material was marble, which permitted an astonishing degree of finely-cut detail, resulting in figures in angular postures and faces with sharply defined profiles. The lace-like texture of the carving increased in intricacy as the style progressed.

Chandella and Paramāra periods (10th–11th centuries)

71, 83, 85, 86, 100, 119, 177, 368, 370

Numerous temples were erected by the Chandella and Paramāra rulers of central India, of which probably the most famous examples are at Khajuraho. Sculptures from this period include a large range of Hindu divinities, accessory female figures and important depictions of courtly life – processions, hunting, building, etc. Sandstone is the usual medium for these carvings, distinguished by their deep modelling and pronounced sensuality. Swaying postures, sharply incised detail of costume and facial expression, and crowded compositions are typical features. The Khajuraho temples in particular are completely covered with gracious figures on the outer walls. Unusually prominent are the many panels of seductive females and embracing couples.

445 Gurjara Pratihāra period
10th century
Pārvatī *(see p.218)*

71 Chandella period
11th century
Girl *(see p. 113)*

69 Solankī period
11th century
Girl playing with balls
(see p. 112)

4 EASTERN INDIA

Pāla and Sena periods (8th–12th centuries)
14, 75, 88, 104, 256, 327, 332, 336, 338, 371, 433, 439
Deriving from the traditions of Gupta art in central India, the sculptures of Bihar and Bengal first evolved a distinctive stylistic expression during the reign of the Pāla and Sena kings. Beyond India, this style had a profound impact on the art of south-east Asia and the Far East. Highly accomplished technically, eastern Indian figurative sculpture is characterized by clear outlines, smooth surfaces and formal postures. Under the Pālas, large numbers of sculptures were produced for both Buddhist and Hindu cults; prominent among artistic centres was Nalanda, the most important Buddhist university in India.

The early phases of the style, in both sandstone and bronze, show a dependence on Gupta prototypes, particularly for standing Buddhist figures. There is, however, an emphasis on rigid postures. Bronzes, often inlaid with silver or copper, display a preference for soft modelling of figures, in contrast to the sharply delineated ornamental frames. The superlative technique can be seen in the casting of fine details.

Typical of the more developed Pāla style are large relief sculptures in black basalt, with smooth and sensual modelling. Both seated and standing Buddhist and Hindu divinities are set in high relief against a vertical slab covered with accessory figures, monster masks and flame-like foliage in shallower relief. The richly jewelled deities often wear high crowns and sit on thrones supported on double lotus flowers.

Eastern Ganga period (11th–14th centuries)
25, 33, 94, 95, 96, 106, 111, 341, 359, 469, 476
In Orissa the eastern Indian style is well illustrated in the carvings that adorn a superb group of Hindu temples dating from as early as the 8th century, and spanning the whole history of the eastern Ganga kings to the 14th century. Perhaps most striking is the vitality of the figurative and animal carvings, the range of images, and the transition from small wall panels to monumental free-standing sculptures.

Most of the panels from Orissa temples are still *in situ*. Made from green chlorite and red sandstone from Bhubaneshwar, they are delicately executed with very precise detail. Richly decorated frames surround figures that are sometimes carved so deeply that they are fully three-dimensional, and whose gentle facial expressions contrast with their dynamic postures.

Associated with the 13th-century Sūrya temple at Konarak (one of the largest of all Hindu temples, but now mostly ruined) are a great number of carved panels, many of which are preserved on the basement of the building. Coarsely-grained khondalite has been used for most of the architectural relief sculpture – hence the massive modelling and general lack of detail. Nevertheless, the lyrical poses of female figures and their gently sensual expressions are remarkable. There is an emphasis on musicians, dancers, erotic couples, animals and mythical beasts. Chlorite panels, also incorporated into the temple decoration at Konarak, depict important cult images of the sun god and his planetary 'retinue' as well as significant portraits of the royal patron.

Hindu Revivalism (17th–19th centuries)
27, 366, 400, 407, 424, 460
After the Muslim invasion of Bengal, there was a period of Hindu revivalism there that concentrated on the cult of Krishna. Narrative scenes from Krishna's life and from the *Rāmāyana*, together with the whole range of Hindu divinities, are found on the celebrated terracotta panels that cover the outer walls of the brick temples of Bengal. Typical of the plaques, which form bases and cornices, columns and arches, is their small scale, the vitality of the modelling and the sharply cut detail. Stylistically they are related to contemporary Bengali wood carving, painted scrolls and book covers.

By the end of the 18th century the impact of European artistic forms had been thoroughly absorbed into the Bengal idiom. Terracotta plaques, and wood and ivory carvings from this period onwards display rounded modelling, a preference for European costume and furniture, and a fascination with Neo-classical settings.

88 Pāla period
Late 12th century
Pūrneshvarī *(see p.119)*

III **Eastern Ganga period**
13th century
King Narasimha *(see p.128)*

460 Hindu Revivalism
19th century
Durgā *(see p.220)*

5 THE SOUTH

Pallava period (7th–9th centuries)

79, 354, 438, 446

The beginnings of stone sculpture in south India go back to the period of the Pallava rulers who adorned rock-cut sanctuaries with numerous Hindu deities. The fluid modelling of these early carvings is associated with the characteristic medium, granite. Free-standing sandstone temples also incorporated carved panels noted for their massive but graceful figures. Deeply cut panels illustrate a wealth of images and narrative events drawn from Hindu mythology. Typical features of the Pallava style include varied postures of tall elegant figures, high crowns, and often crowded and animated compositions. Temples at Mahabalipuram and Kanchipuram, for example, are covered with figures as well as fantastic lions on columns.

354

354 Pallava period
8th century
Vishnu (see p. 198)

374 Vijayanagara period
15th century
Narasimha (see p.203)

257 Chola period
10th–11th century
Tamil saint (see p. 169)

374

257

Chola period (9th–13th centuries)

241, 242, 255, 257, 259, 353, 356, 380, 402, 432, 440, 446, 453, 479, 481

Under the Chola kings, an empire was established in the lush river valleys of Tamil Nadu. Continuing the sculpture traditions established under the Pallavas, the Cholas were great patrons of sacred art, and were responsible for the largest Hindu temples of their time – as at Thanjavur and Gangaikondacholapuram. Chola stone sculpture is closely linked to earlier Pallava models, the granite medium lending a characteristic soft modelling to massive figurative forms. Postures are generally formal, though always tall and elegant with delicately incised detail of costume, jewellery and headdress. Other than the usual range of Hindu divinities, there are fierce door-guardians, their legs wrapped around large clubs, a host of mythical beasts, and even royal portraits. Especially interesting are the depictions of worshippers in the act of devotion, sometimes offering their own cut-off heads! Modelled in the round, these sculptures were probably employed as accessory figures in altarpieces.

The glory of Chola sculpture is seen in the superb bronzes housed deep within the temple sanctuary, sometimes serving as processional images. Both technically and artistically, these bronzes are acknowledged to be among the greatest of all Indian sculptures. The most notable features of the figures are their large scale (often more than 75 cm high), the subtle and fluid modelling, the graceful postures, and the supremely refined expression. The whole range of Hindu deities is to be found here, though there is an emphasis on Shaivite themes – Shiva seated with Pārvatī and their son Skanda, and Shiva dancing the steps of creation-destruction. The detached inward-looking expression of Shiva is remarkable. Other Chola bronzes of dancing figures include Krishna subduing the serpent demon. The same preoccupation with posture and balance is seen in the bronze images of Shaivite saints, often holding their hands above their heads in salutation.

Vijayanagara and Nāyaka periods (14th–18th centuries)

15, 116, 217, 243, 258, 262, 374, 378, 380, 443

Battling against the Muslim incursion into south India for more than two centuries, the Vijayanagara empire of south India maintained traditional Hindu cultural and artistic forms. The imperial style of the Vijayanagara period borrowed many features of Chola sculpture. In bronze casting, for example, there seems to have been a direct continuity; late Chola bronzes are almost indistinguishable from early Vijayanagara examples, though there is a general reduction in both scale and fineness of casting. Larger stone sculptures, in granite, are monumental in expression, but lack the precision of detail and subtlety of modelling associated with Chola times. Nonetheless, Vijayanagara sculptures are noted for their distinctive vigour – in images of such guardian figures as Hanumān, for instance. Huge rearing horses, both naturalistic and fantastic, are found in the great columned halls erected during this period, as in the temples at Vijayanagara and Srirangam. Even bronze models of these sculptured columns exist: an example is the columned hall from the Madurai temple dating from the later Nāyaka period. Also preserved from the Nāyaka period are ivory plaques and innumerable wooden panels, the latter coming from festival chariots. Here animated divinities and beasts are carved in a distinctive angular and energetic style.

GLOSSARY OF PAINTING STYLES

by Dr Linda Leach

1 PRE-MUGHAL PERIOD
Jain 11th–16th centuries
Sultanate 14th–16th centuries
Early Hindu 16th century

2 MUGHAL PERIOD
Akbar 1556–1605
Jahāngīr 1605–27
Shāh Jahān 1627–58
Aurangzīb to Muhammad Shāh mid-17th–
mid-18th centuries
Provincial Mughal Style second half of the
18th century
Company Style 18th–19th centuries
The Deccan c. 1560–1850

3 RAJASTHAN AND CENTRAL INDIA
Ajmer c. 1630–1800
Amber/Jaipur c. 1640–1850
Bikaner c. 1600–1800
Bundi c. 1590–1800
Kishangarh c. 1720–1850
Kotah c. 1630–1850
Malwa c. 1620–1750
Marwar c. 1600–1850
Mewar c. 1600–1900

4 HIMALAYAN FOOTHILLS (PAHARI REGION)
Basohli c. 1660–1850
Bilaspur c. 1660–1800
Chamba c. 1660–1860
Guler c. 1690–1850
Jammu c. 1690–1850
Kangra c. 1760–1850
Kulu c. 1690–1800
Mandi c. 1660–1850
Mankot c. 1650–1800
Nurpur c. 1660–1800

---

1 PRE-MUGHAL PERIOD

Jain (11th–16th centuries)
35, 317, 318

The strongest and most continuous tradition in India during the Sultanate era is that of the Jain religious centres in the west. The earliest Jain book paintings were done on palm leaves and date from the 11th century; wooden book covers survive from the 12th century, while paintings on paper became common in the 15th century. The earliest Jain illustrations have shading and floral elements reminiscent of Ajanta, but they also have an exaggerated linear quality of their own: facial outlines are accentuated, noses are long and sharp, eyes are finished with long tails and the further eye often projects beyond the outline of the face. Hands and feet are placed in elaborate angular poses defined by many linear flourishes. The backgrounds are clear blue and red, with green and yellow used to a limited extent for costumes and accessories. As the Jain style matures, elaborate patterns evolve for architecture, tilework and textiles, and small scenes become increasingly crowded with refined detail. Compositional formats remain limited, with figures or objects generally arranged in horizontal bands. Jain illustrations are usually devoted to depicting the lives of the 24 Tīrthankaras.

Sultanate (14th–16th centuries)
131, 202

The history of Sultanate painting traces the disparate styles patronized by the Afghans, Turks, Persians and other Islamic peoples who established power alongside Hindu Rājputs. Since the artists who worked for these patrons came from different backgrounds, there is little stylistic continuity during this period. The best documented Muslim paintings of the time are from the kingdoms of Malwa in central India and Gaur in Bengal. Persian characteristics are common: these include carpet-like backgrounds with tufts of grass or stylized flowers at regular intervals, as well as flowering trees, decorative tiles and curling cloud forms. The *Ni'mat Nāma* cookbook produced at Malwa is interspersed with Indian textiles and poses, demonstrating the conjunction of diverse elements in the Muslim kingdoms. Paintings were undoubtedly produced during this period at other Muslim centres, such as Jaunpur and Delhi; there are also many manuscripts that cannot be definitely ascribed to a particular locale, and it is questionable whether some are in fact Indian rather than provincial Persian. Some illustrations of Islamic stories show few traces of Muslim artistic influence, but are closely related instead to Jain manuscripts of western India, again revealing the early association of Islamic and native Indian traditions.

Early Hindu (16th century)
218, 396, 478
The earliest manuscripts of Hindu devotional and romantic
literature are often referred to as the *Chaurapanchāshikā* group
after a spectacularly illustrated poetry manuscript that
epitomizes the type of style. Although their relative chronology
has been generally agreed upon, their exact dating, which
extends into the Mughal era, remains controversial.

While these manuscripts are varied, they have enough
common characteristics to be unified as a group. Among their
stylistic traits are flamboyantly curvaceous women with
pendulous breasts wearing checked Indian textiles, elaborately
stylized transparent veils, and black tassel ornaments. All the
figures have large eyes and exaggerated profiles. The style
clearly evolves from Jain illustration; a few late 15th-century
Hindu manuscripts are very similar to Jain scenes. The
treatment of faces and of blue or red backgrounds in particular
confirms this debt to the past, though the compositions are
freer (most are no longer in horizontal bands) and show
increased action. Although the various Islamic styles of the
pre-Mughal era generally faded out, Hindu painting exerted a
great influence on the formation of the Mughal school under
Akbar's policy of religious tolerance.

396

396 Early Hindu school
c. 1570
Detail from Krishna
breaking the cart
(see p. 207)

134 Jahāngīr period
c. 1620
Muhammad Qutb Shāh
(detail)
(see p. 135)

142 Akbar period, *c.* 1570
Detail from the birth of
Prince Murād
(see p. 136)

134

2 MUGHAL PERIOD

Akbar (ruled 1556–1605)
39, 142, 183, 204, 228, 230, 234, 235, 236, 237, 248, 265, 267,
268, 274, 277, 395
Painting of Akbar's period is much more unified than that of
the previous era, reflecting the new political situation. The
miniatures are full of action, depicted in a rather crude and
unbalanced manner if judged by Persian standards. Artists
arranged forms in bold diagonals and sweeping lines that
convey strong, unified movement. Scenes generally include
many figures, and these are realistic in style although few of
the court history scenes include actual portraits. Poses,
modelling, and facial features were influenced by European art
that was mainly brought to the court by Jesuit missions.

The most significant early works are from the *Hamza
Nāma*, which originally comprised about 1400 illustrations
painted on cloth. These scenes include turbulent natural
features as well as violent human action to heighten the
narrative. The histories and religious manuscripts which were
the main commissions during the middle of Akbar's reign are
more sophisticated in their expression of dynamic movement.
Colours are generally bright in these works, but more muted
tones were introduced towards the end of the period.
European influence can be detected in style as well as in
costumes and religious symbols, especially at the close of the
era.

Jahāngīr (ruled 1605–27)
37, 38, 48, 134, 191, 192
Figures in the paintings of Jahāngīr's time are generally larger,
fuller and more peacefully posed than in Akbar's era. Colours
are muted and portraits more accurate, so that, by about 1615,
scenes resemble European works more closely than before,
despite the fact that naturalism had been the intention of
Akbar's artists.

Connoisseurs have long regarded Jahāngīr's reign as a
period of superb taste: the emperor was a discerning aesthete
who sponsored works combining compositional simplicity,
great richness of detail and perfect technical control; their
polished surfaces, either of a lustrous or a milky appearance,
testify to Jahāngīr's liking for opulence. While the emperor
often requested miniatures to be painted from life, some works
nevertheless have a static quality. He himself noted that artists
found it difficult to capture motion.

142

Shāh Jahān (ruled 1627–58)
141, 171, 193, 201, 219, 297
Artists of Shāh Jahān's era continued the styles developed under Jahāngīr; indeed there are many impressive works from his time by painters who had worked throughout much of Jahāngīr's reign. However, Shāh Jahān was less interested in his artists' work than his predecessor had been and, gradually, the human dimension in art became somewhat eclipsed. The courtier portrait, for example, clearly a status symbol, was often stiffly posed and was reproduced in countless copies. Backgrounds began to be enlarged so that they dwarfed the subjects; techniques are drier. While such tendencies did not prevent beautiful miniatures being produced, some lack of inspiration is apparent, attributable to the stifling conventions of the court as well as to a detached patron preoccupied with other art forms.

Aurangzīb to Muhammad Shāh (mid-17th–mid-18th centuries)
129, 147, 196, 212
Although this period was to mark the end of truly centralized Mughal rule, and throughout it the stature of the rulers was being steadily diminished by corruption and intrigue, certain emperors nonetheless obtained good work from their painters, among them Aurangzīb (ruled 1658–1707) and Muhammad Shāh (ruled 1719–48).

Several of the surviving paintings from the early part of Aurangzīb's reign are refined, original in treatment and human in feeling. In 1680, however, through stricter adherence to Islamic orthodoxy, Aurangzīb became generally antagonistic to the arts and dismissed his painters. The dispersal of these artists created a wave of Mughal influence at Rājput courts.

After about 1680, Mughal naturalism, including painterly modelling, was superseded by more decorative work of various types. One of the most common conventions was a clean, rhythmic drawing method used especially by Muhammad Shāh's artists; it smoothed away all awkward angles and imperfections so that only the ideal was transmitted.

This style is exemplified by the paintings of Muhammad Shāh dressed in white against a white architectural backdrop, a fashion that set a trend followed by the later provincial Mughal and Rājput painters.

Provincial Mughal Style (second half of the 18th century)
43, 173, 184, 189, 245, 295
Provincial Mughal is the term used to describe works done after the mid-18th century in the provincial cities, mainly Lucknow and Murshidabad, where Mughal officials had attained near-independent status following the losses in imperial power. Although ruling nawabs sponsored paintings, Mihr Chand, the best known artist of the period, and a few others managed workshops that were also commercial. Mihr Chand typifies this period in that his versatility enabled him to copy miniatures of other eras though unconsciously adding stiff details from his own time. Like him, other artists preferred to imitate earlier styles and adapted their work to suit their different patrons rather than evolving a single distinctive style of their own.

Certain subjects were especially popular among contemporary patrons, with the result that compositions were repeatedly copied in the originating workshop and, additionally, pirated by artists elsewhere. Stock scenes are portraits on white marble terraces and paintings of the zenana

297 Shāh Jahān period
c. 1640
Elderly *yoginī* and princess
(see p. 180)

196 Mughal school
c. 1740
Muhammad Shāh with courtiers *(detail)*
(see p. 150)

173 Provincial Mughal school
c. 1760
Princess with attendants in the garden *(detail)*
(see p. 143)

297

196

173

233

210

233 Company school,
c. 1830
Horse merchants
(see p. 161)

210 Deccan school,
c. 1590
Cock fight
(see p. 155)

187

187 Deccan school,
c. 1660
Prince with musicians
(see p. 147)

or women's quarters. Hindu romantic themes also began to be produced in Mughal styles despite general superficiality of literary subject matter. Though large areas of white were frequently used in miniatures, in other cases colours tend to be murky; figures are often squat with large heads.

Company Style (18th–19th centuries)
45, 46, 47, 229, 231, 232, 233, 238, 250, 290
This style was inspired by the British who were its main patrons. Among the best-known centres were Madras and Thanjavur in the south, Delhi in the north, and Lucknow, Calcutta and Patna in the east, all major areas of British influence. Many Indian artists who were hired for practical work, such as drafting, learned to use perspective and other techniques required to meet European demands.

British customers wanted mainly souvenir paintings of India usually of trade, caste groups or festivals. More ambitious patrons requested large series of flora and fauna, etc. Technique was freely adapted from European watercolours, the chief borrowed features being transparency of texture, soft tones and modelling in broad strokes.

The Deccan (c. 1560–1850)
41, 49, 127, 132, 162, 187, 210, 214, 225, 266, 271, 273, 291, 352
The Deccan plateau was the site of a Muslim state that split into several separate kingdoms. Throughout the Mughal period, these kingdoms maintained independent ties with Persia, Turkey and other Muslim areas that contributed to painting styles. The three kingdoms known to have produced miniatures are Ahmednagar, Bijapur and Golconda. Of all Indian artists, those of the Deccan most successfully combined a feeling for the sensuous beauty of objects with extraordinary technical ability.

The few existing works from the short-lived kingdom of Ahmednagar depict similar figure types wearing transparent *jamas* and elaborate gold belts. Bijapur and Golconda have longer traditions that can be more fully documented. Golconda painting evolved in the reign of 'Abdullāh Qutb Shāh (ruled 1626–72). Early works are closely related in style to the cotton hangings produced in the area and often include identical features: background patterns, costume patterns, and elongated figures with round pop-eyes who are found in the same pose.

Bijapur subjects include portraits, illustrations of romantic adventure and idealized princes or *yoginīs*. The most important patron of the school was the aesthete Ibrāhīm 'Ādil Shāh II (ruled 1580–1626) who promoted the development of several different styles; under him, Bijapur painters became more sophisticated and cosmopolitan than, and distinct from, other artists in the Deccan. One style that he sponsored had a soft, misty quality; after his rule, however, artists went back to harder, flatter and more stylized designs.

Painting in the Deccan continued to flourish despite subordination to the Mughals towards the end of the 17th century. The best documented works are those from the city of Hyderabad which superceded the old palace fortress of Golconda. Hyderabad paintings often use beautiful deep greens and blues and are rather flat in appearence, with much finely controlled detail.

3 RAJASTHAN AND CENTRAL INDIA

Ajmer (c. 1630–1800)

40, 137, 186, 211, 220, 221, 383, 393

Although little is known about the development of painting in Ajmer, existing works dating from the first part of the 17th century suggest a clumsy, popular Mughal style; later works have more charm, combining Rajasthani and Mughal features with more ease and assurance. At least one talented Ajmer artist produced pictures of elephants, passing the style on to Kotah; and paintings in a more folkish manner, of horses and elephants, continued to be produced in Ajmer in the 18th century. Many of these have been specifically attributed to the fiefdom of Sawar. The usual Sawar or Ajmer style of the 18th century is somewhat childlike, spritely and mildly humorous. Compositions are often laid out in orderly rows, and a clever, rhythmic manner of drawing is used to outline doll-like figures and objects.

Bikaner (c. 1600–1800)

158, 200, 207, 269, 298, 418

The earliest known paintings from Bikaner, dating from about 1600, already show the Mughal influence that is characteristic of the Bikaner tradition throughout its development. Though the desert kingdom was in western Rajasthan, far from the imperial court, it was economically and politically linked with Mughal rule. Bikaner painting is extremely soft in colour with few contrasts and rather melting forms. Many compositions are devoted to women, demure in character and based on Mughal models. When the Bikaner rajas fought in the Deccan with the Mughal armies during the 17th century, Bikaner artists began to employ Deccani colour schemes and lyrical touches. Many of the figures in Bikaner miniatures are small, proportioned like children. The subjects are generally romantic and Krishna themes very popular. Like Mughal works, Bikaner paintings are often inscribed with dates and artists' names so that a better record of court painters exists than for other Rājput states.

Bundi (c. 1590–1800)

146, 165, 168, 174, 420

Bundi painting begins very early: the first dated Rajasthani manuscript – a *Rāgamāla* of 1591 – is in the Bundi style. It combines Hindu and Mughal features, and elements of both its style and its composition were employed by artists throughout the next century. 17th-century paintings from the Bundi school are animated but nevertheless gentle, lyrical and dignified; many court scenes give indications of the grace of Rājput manners. Backgrounds are filled with varieties of blossoming trees, illustrating nature's abundancy. Verdant nature is a particular feature of *Rāgamāla* compositions, which were the most often repeated Bundi subjects and were commonly produced from tracings. Until about 1685, the Bundi style continued to alter and develop sufficiently to exercise the painters' creative talents; contacts with the Deccan during the Mughal wars were particularly stimulating. However, by the early 18th century, figures tend to become heavy and inexpressive while compositions are generally staid.

40 From Ajmer, *c.* 1660
Horse and groom
(*see p. 106*)

298 From Bikaner, 18th century
Yoginī waters a *tulsī* plant
(*see p. 181*)

420 From Bundi, *c.* 1695
Rādhā and Krishna in a pavilion (*detail*)
(*see p. 212*)

298

420

150

300

150 From Kishangarh
c. 1760
A raja approaching the
zenana *(see p.137)*

300 From Kotah
c. 1670
Women worshipping *āmlā*
trees *(see p. 181)*

163 From Malwa,
c. 1640
Āsāvarī Rāginī
(see p. 140)

163

Kishangarh (c. 1720–1850)
125, 145, 150, 284
The earliest paintings of Kishangarh, mainly portraits, are
only slowly being distinguished from those done at the Mughal
court. The miniatures for which the state is well known derive
from this stylistic association but are much more
conventionalized. They are elegant imitations of an 18th-
century Mughal style that accentuated elongated bodies, stiff
postures and wide eyes with long slanting curves. The
Kishangarh adaptation of such elements is credited to an artist
named Nihāl Chand who expressed the ideals of the
Vaishnavite devotee and poet Rāja Sāwant Singh (reigned
1748–64). The artist created delicately passionate symbols of
Sāwant's relationship with a court slave girl, often depicting
the two as Rādhā and Krishna gazing into each other's eyes.
The ruler and his consort left the state in the last years of the
Rāja's reign and wandered together through the territory in
which Krishna is supposed to have lived. The Kishangarh
miniatures inspired by Sāwant Singh often include extensive
landscape vistas with huge white palaces and all the rich
trappings of an idealized court life. Moody blue-green colour
tones are typical. More lively styles of Kishangarh painting
include caricatures and religious scenes.

Kotah (c. 1630–1850)
156, 164, 199, 208, 209, 285, 286, 300
Kotah, in southern Rajasthan, was permanently separated
from her sister state of Bundi in the early 17th century.
Nevertheless for a number of years the paintings
commissioned by Kotah rajas followed Bundi prototypes,
though they include more lively details. Some of the Kotah
Rāgamāla scenes are clearly copied from Bundi compositions.
Rāgamālas and royal portraits were early common subjects.
  The most exciting works from Kotah are the hunt sketches
and paintings dating from about 1720 to 1870. During much
of this period, they form the main artistic output.
  Groups of painters must have attended large hunts,
probably sketching at the site before returning to a studio to
complete the work. Careful observation of animals as well as
terrain is evident from these miniatures. The Kotah painters
were better able to capture the characteristic movement of
animals than any other artists in India.

Malwa (c. 1620–1750)
163, 203, 389, 391   *Ragogarh:* 136, 289
Accomplished Sultanate manuscripts are known to have been
executed in Mandu, the capital of Malwa. Although the
Mandu court was overthrown early in Akbar's reign, the state
was so remote that it was never greatly influenced by Mughal
customs. Post-Mughal paintings, dating from about 1630, were
probably produced as part of a continuous Hindu tradition.
They do not follow Mandu Sultanate styles but instead
preserve archaic conventions that derive from Jain painting:
for example, colours are mainly blue, red and white. Figures
and pavilions relate to paintings of the *Chaurapanchāshikā*
group with a slight Mughal influence.
  This 17th-century Malwa style was very slow to change and
is rightly considered to be a pure, classic statement of Indian
abstract shapes; compositions are simple, controlled and yet
intense. This conservative style began to decline by about
1690, and with a few exceptions, later paintings are
comparatively weak.

Marwar (c. 1600–1850)
42, 109, 110, 159, 195, 197, 198, 367, 379, 447; Nagaur: 138
A broad spectrum of styles evolved in the courts and towns of
the large desert state of Marwar, ranging from the rough or
folkish to very controlled work of the Mughal type. The latter
paintings, usually refined portraits, were mainly done for the
Jodhpur court that controlled part of the state, although
sophisticated artists also worked for the *thikana* of Ghanerao
on the Marwar border. The more folkish styles were used for
the illustration of local chivalric legends. Common elements of
many 18th-century Marwar paintings are the elaborately
arranged and extravagantly high turbans worn especially by
central figures.

In the late 18th and early 19th centuries many lavish
devotional or epic manuscripts were illustrated for the Jodhpur
court.

385 From Mewar, *c.* 1650
Bhārata meeting Rāma
and Lakshmana *(detail)*
(see p. 205)

385

Mewar (c. 1600–1900)
36, 126, 128, 149, 157, 161, 169, 175, 185, 215, 216, 301, 302,
303, 305, 362, 384, 385, 392, 408, 410, 412, 414, 416; Devgarh
148, 155, 160; *Sirohi* 172; *Aghatpura* 246
The Mewar school made an enormous contribution to Indian
painting during its long history. Some early works continue
the *Chaurapanchāshikā* style, indicating that painters were
already working in Mewar during the pre-Mughal era. By the
mid-17th century, a fairly large team of artists was producing
religious manuscripts, mainly illustrations of the Krishna story
executed for the most devout and perceptive of Mewar
patrons, Rāja Jagat Singh (ruled 1628–52). These paintings,
from the state with the strongest tradition of chivalric pride,
epitomize Rajasthan itself, expressing much that can only be
understood from exposure to the intense and austere
environment. Colour schemes are pungent and often
superficially discordant; forms are vibrant but harsh,
mirroring man's relationship with nature in this area.

421

After Jagat's death, there was little originality in painting
until, in the late 17th century, Rāja Amar Singh (ruled
1698–1710) ushered in an era of court portraiture that inspired
new developments. Artists began to paint larger scenes, some
involving as many as 400 figures, with backgrounds showing
the palace and environs of Udaipur, the capital. These palace
settings have arbitrary perspectives, but are otherwise quite
accurate, as a visit to the present-day town will attest. The
depictions of successive rajas participating in festivals, hunts or
military manoeuvres afford an excellent view of 18th-century
Rājput life.

421 From Basohli, *c.* 1680
Rādhā swooning *(detail)*
(see p. 212)

423 From Bilaspur, *c.* 1690
Detail from Krishna on a
lotus bed
(see p. 212)

226 From Guler, *c.* 1750–60
A begam hunting *(detail)*
(see p. 159)

423

226

Amber/Jaipur (c. 1640–1850)
130, 140, 283
Although the most powerful Rājput during Akbar's and
Jahāngīr's time came from Amber, the state itself did not
become particularly significant until the accession of Rāja
Sawai Jai Singh II (ruled 1699–1743); he moved the capital
from the old palace of Amber to the planned city of Jaipur in
1728. Jaipur painting tends to be flat, with black detailing that
gives it a rather harsh appearence. After about 1760, figure
work and other aspects of Jaipur painting were influenced by
the provincial Mughal style. Artists of the Jaipur school
continued to produce rather hard-edged paintings far into the
19th century, some of which have interesting genre subjects
illustrating Rājput life.

4 HIMALAYAN FOOTHILLS (PAHARI REGION)

Basohli (c. 1660–1850)
170, 273, 358, 406, 421

Basohli was a small Rājput state in the midst of mountains, of little political importance. The earliest work is refined, with clean, hard contours and sophisticated colour combinations, yet it has an almost unparalleled ferocity that denotes a primitive influence. Paintings of Krishna and Devī, for example, express an elemental energy. Colours in Basohli painting are vibrant (red, pink, yellow, deep green), while patterning, especially of rugs and architectural features, is florid. The figures are often elongated, with oblong heads. Although painting continued to flourish here for about two centuries, the designation 'Basohli style' is used exclusively to refer to early miniatures with vivid colours and expressionistic shapes. The term is significant as it is often generically used to characterize similar miniatures from such states as Kulu or Mankot that partly owed their inspiration to Basohli. One of the distinguishing features of paintings actually from Basohli is the use of blue-green beetle wings for jewellery.

By 1730, figures are fuller and more realistically proportioned, and the harsh rhythms and patterns have become subdued. While some exciting paintings were produced in Basohli after this date, they represent the influence of creative periods in neighbouring states especially Guler.

Bilaspur (c. 1660–1800)
144, 279, 287, 373, 423

Bilaspur, the capital of the state of Kahlur, in the undulating hills cut by the Sutlej river, was the home of a prolific group of painters. The first extant works which reflect Mughal influence, they are among the earliest known from the Pahari region. Though there are several concurrent styles of painting, typical Bilaspur work has figures with large square heads and wide open eyes. Scenes tend to be vividly colourful, with ornate detail, especially of architecture and vegetation. After about 1750, however, painting became less inventive and distinctive.

Chamba (c. 1660–1860)
133, 247, 275, 459

Chamba, a large state in a dry, barren part of the Himalayan foothills, was the home of one of the earliest schools of Pahari painting, particularly specializing in portraiture. Chamba painters generally, however, seem less self-assured than those from other states, such as Basohli. Forms are tentatively drawn and colours more subdued. Several styles appear to have been concurrent, but a typical feature of Chamba work is the short, cherubic figures with large heads and puffy cheeks.

A change takes place in the painting of Chamba, as in other states, from about 1760; figures grow taller and more naturally proportioned. In the late 19th and early 20th centuries, the Kangra style becomes popular in Chamba in a stylized form.

19th-century Chamba painters are also credited with drawing many caricatures.

Guler (c. 1690–1850)
188, 226

From its beginnings in the late 17th century, the Guler tradition inclined towards Mughal naturalism and included precise, though rather dry, portraits. It was a combination of Mughal drawing techniques and Pahari lyricism that gave this school a genuine identity. The extraordinarily accomplished mid-18th century miniatures are an ode to nature and to the loveliness of woman. The benign climate and graceful manners of the Pahari area are reflected in the simplicity and freshness of the painters' approach.

Artistically Guler was the most influential state of the Pahari region from about 1740–80, during which time Govardhan Chand (ruled 1741–73) was the school's most active patron. Among notable artists were members of Nainsukh's family, some of whom were responsible for spreading the Guler style to the larger, politcally more important state of Kangra.

Jammu (c. 1690–1850)
190, 222, 272

The early paintings of Jammu are dignified and quietly expressive, usually executed in rather pale colours. They are stylized but not as exaggeratedly as Basohli miniatures. One of the most important groups of Pahari pictures are those of Balwant Singh, youngest son of a Jammu raja. From around the time he was 20 until his death in 1763, aspects of Balwant's daily life as a country gentleman were recorded by the artist Nainsukh, a member of the Seu artist family of Guler, who also helped to alter painting styles throughout the hill region. These miniatures, and the circumstances behind them, are quite distinct from the development of Jammu painting generally, but can best be discussed under this classification. With particular attention to detail, they show Balwant Singh with the barber, pondering his letter writing and wandering through his house. The warmth and sympathy with which his moods are captured show the deep understanding that existed between artist and patron. Nainsukh was very skilled at turning movements into dancelike poses; many artists, especially other members of his family, imitated his repertoire of poses.

Kangra (c. 1760–1850)
175, 223, 397, 398, 417; *Garhwal* 304, 477

Kangra, a large state with a massive fortress, was the focus of Mughal attempts to subdue the Pahari region, and until the late 18th century there was little opportunity for art to flourish. Sansār Chand (ruled 1775–1823) was an ardent patron, however, and stimulated the development of a school of painting founded on his devotion to Krishna, commissioning many large series based on Krishna literature.

Much Kangra painting is almost indistinguishable from that of Guler, from which it derived. However, the Kangra style became one of refinement and detailed execution; Guler miniatures, in general, are slightly simpler and broader. Artists in both states accentuated the beauty of the landscape and the natural poise of Pahari women. Among the numerous important miniatures dealing with feminine subjects that were commissioned by Sansār Chand, the Krishna scenes evoke the rapture of the *gopīs'* meetings with the god in dreamlike river and forest landscapes.

Kulu (c. 1690–1800)

44, 143, 386, 388, 399

Painting in the remote state of Kulu was strongly influenced by Basohli, with which it had a clan association. Kulu paintings are florid, colourful and energetic, more ebullient than those in Basohli and figures are stockier, with angular limbs. The largest and most exciting Kulu series known is the Shangri *Rāmāyana* manuscript (c. 1690–1710). Various sections of the story were illustrated by different artists, and four semi-independent styles, all charming and intensely dramatic, appear in the volume in succession. One of the most accomplished Kulu artists, whose work evolved from Shangri conventions, has left many biting caricatures, an unusual genre in India.

Mandi (c. 1660–1850)

292, 293, 403

Mandi painting probably began at the end of Shāh Jahān's reign, with refined works showing Mughal influence. However, the Mandi tendency towards folk culture and a folkish Shaivite devotion produced many compositions depicting Shiva and Pārvatī. 18th-century Mandi work can be distinguished from all other Pahari painting by its rather crude though pleasing stylistic features: drawings are often executed with thick black outlines and dark washes; paintings, also heavily outlined in black, are coloured dramatically in dense, muddy tones such as browns and dark blues. A complete change, however, occurs in the early 19th century, when a decorative version of the feminine Kangra style is introduced.

Mankot (c. 1650–1800)

181, 227, 270, 288

Only a formidable palace that remains shows that the small state of Mankot may once have been powerful. The Mankot school is the one most likely to be confused with Basohli, and it is helpful to compare the two for purposes of definition: Mankot work is blunter and somewhat coarser; its forms tend to be larger; fewer elaborate decorative patterns are employed and backgrounds are frequently empty. Mankot painters make franker, less sophisticated statements, using reds, yellows and oranges rather than the range of pungent reds, pinks, greens and blues of Basohli work. Portraits are the earliest and among the most numerous as well as significant productions.

Nurpur (c. 1660–1800)

167, 299, 390, 456

Early Nurpur artists experimented with a variety of styles: that used for illustrating most of the extant poetry and epic texts bears some relation to Basohli painting but is nevertheless quite distinctive. Compositions are simpler, purer and more restrained; the artists have shown great skill in arranging designs to convey abstract values. Human figures have squarish heads and long, upturning eyes. While later Nurpur work loosely resembles Guler or Kangra miniatures, female figures in particular have more heavily stylized faces.

399

292

399 From Kulu, *c.* 1710
Cowherds wrestling around Krishna
(see p. 208)

292 From Mandi, *c.* 1725
Rāja Sidh Sen as an ascetic
(see p. 179)

182 From Mankot, *c.* 1710
Krishna and Balarāma
with musicians
(see p. 145)

167 From Nurpur, *c.* 1720
Waiting heroine
(see p. 141)

182

167

7 Palm leaf capital *(see p. 96)*
Pre-Kushāna period, 3rd–1st century BC
80cm high
Lucknow, State Museum, J.584

437 Shiva *(see p. 217)*
Gupta period, 5th century
14cm high
Varanasi, Bharat Kala Bhavan Museum, 1605

59 Mother Goddess *(see p. 110)*
Shunga period (?), 2nd century BC
26cm high
Mathura, Government Museum, 66.2

118 **Courtier and courtesan with attendant** *(see p. 130)*
Kushāna period, 2nd century
101cm high
New Delhi, National Museum, 2800

67 *Shālabhanjikā (see p. 112)*
Kushāna period, *c.* 1st–2nd century
77cm high
Mathura, Government Museum, SO.IV.27

LEFT
86 Mithuna couple *(see p. 118)*
Chandella period, 11th century
47cm high
*Khajuraho, Archaeological
Museum, 1342*

RIGHT
83 Flying female warriors
(see p. 117)
Chandella period, 11th century
33cm high
*Khajuraho, Archaeological
Museum, 1821*

296 Devotee holding a *chaurī* (fly whisk)
(see p.180)
Maitraka period, 8th century
24cm high
Baroda, Museum and Picture Gallery, AR547

69 Girl playing with balls *(see p.112)*
Solanki period, 11th century
101cm high
New Delhi, National Museum, 71.L/5

120 King Narasimha on a swing *(see p. 130)*
Eastern Ganga period, 13th century
87cm high
New Delhi, National Museum, 50.185

262 Worshipper *(see p. 169)*
Vijayanagara period, 15th–16th century
46cm high
Madras, Government Museum, 2544

307 Cosmic diagram *(see p.185)*
Kushāna period, 1st century AD
89cm high
Lucknow, State Museum, J.250

30 Mythological horse and rider *(see p.103)*
Gupta period, 5th century
93cm high
New Delhi, National Museum, 49.115

LEFT
309 *Stūpa* **and figures** *(see p.185)*
Sātavāhana period, 2nd century
151cm high
New Delhi, National Museum, 50.25

RIGHT
333 **The Buddha** *(see p. 191)*
Gupta period, 6th century
105cm high
Sarnath, Archaeological Museum, 5512

LEFT
377 Vaikuntha (composite head of Vishnu) *(see p.203)*
Solanki period, 11th century
36cm high
Bombay, Prince of Wales Museum of Western India, 95

RIGHT
370 Varāha *(see p. 202)*
Chandella period, 11th century
145cm high
Khajuraho, Archaeological Museum, 861

440 Shiva and consort *(see p. 217)*
Chola period, 11th century
108cm high and 93cm high
*Thanjavur, Thanjavur Art
Gallery, 86/87*

66

LEFT
428 One-faced *linga (see pp. 214–5)*
Gupta period, 5th century
96cm high
New Delhi, National Museum, 76.223

RIGHT
473 *Gana (see p. 224)*
Gupta period, 5th century
85cm high
New Delhi, National Museum, L.77.2

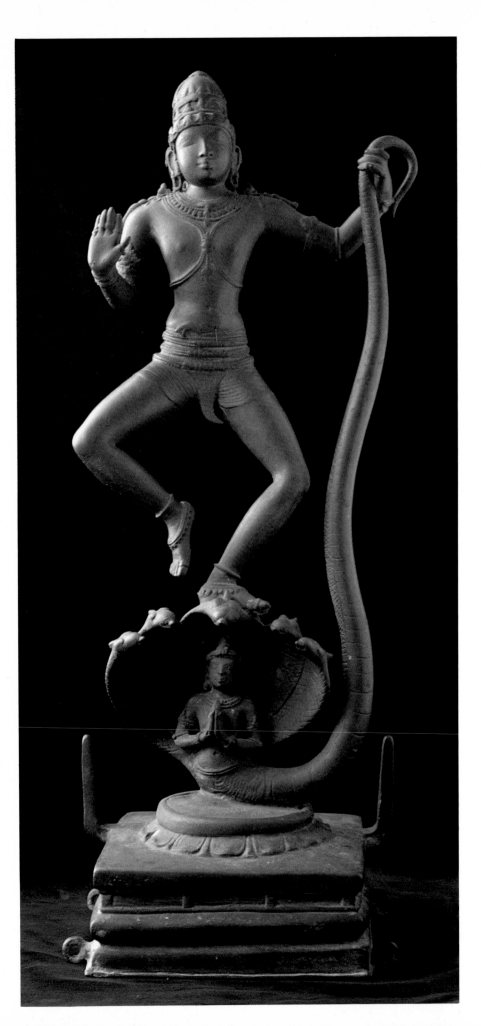

LEFT
**402 Krishna subduing the
serpent demon, Kāliya** *(see p.209)*
Chola period, 10th–11th century
59cm high
New Delhi, National Museum, 70.11

RIGHT
455 Consort of Sadāshiva *(see p. 220)*
10th century
37cm high
New Delhi, National Museum, 64.102

386 Test of Sītā *(see p. 205)*
From Kulu, *c.* 1720
18 × 26cm
*Hyderabad, Jagdish and Kamla Mittal
Museum of Indian Art, 76.222*

202 Lāur in armour *(see p. 152)*
Pre-Mughal school, *c.* 1520
21 × 15cm
Bombay, Prince of Wales Museum of Western India, 57.1/8

41 Prince with rose *(see p. 106)*
From Golconda, late 17th century
31 × 20cm
New Delhi, National Museum, 58.39/5

42 Rāja Bijay Singh of Marwar with his decoy buck *(see p. 106)*
From Marwar, *c.* 1720
44 × 24cm
Bombay, Prince of Wales Museum of Western India, 57.7

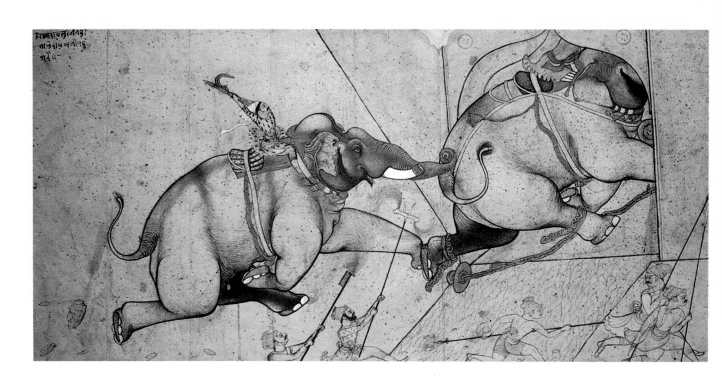

209 Two elephants running out of a tent *(see p.154)*
From Kotah, *c.* 1720
24 × 49cm
Bombay, Prince of Wales Museum of Western India, 55.96

213 Thakur Akshay Singh hunting *(see p. 155)*
From Bednour, *c.* 1810
23 × 44cm
Hyderabad, Jagdish and Kamla Mittal Museum of Indian Art, 76.200

तुंगपवलंधनिघ दगाग:शोलञक गोलिनधोलगाक्रावगाभ्मावनि वरुधध्रानिरोत्
कुर्भा लका लपेन्दम

214 Ruler with falcon *(see p. 155)*
Deccan school, *c. 1725*
29 × 12cm
Private collection

203 A hero at war, from a *rāgamāla, Nat Rāginī (see p. 152)*
From Malwa, *c. 1730–40*
21 × 15cm
New Delhi, National Museum, 63.1696

412 Krishna bathing with the *gopīs*
(see p. 211)
From Mewar, *c.* 1630–40
*Jodhpur, Rajasthan Oriental Research
Institute*

39 The bears in the burning desert
(see p. 106)
Artist: Shankar
Mughal school, 1596
Varanasi, Bharat Kala Bhavan Collection, 9069/18

382 Rāma and Sītā in the forest *(see p. 205)*
Sub-imperial Mughal school, *c.* 1600
New Delhi, National Museum, 56.114/5

125 **Rādhā and Krishna in front of**
palace buildings *(see p. 133)*
Artist: Nihāl Chand
From Kishangarh, *c.*1750
New Delhi, National Museum, 63.793

168 Heroine in a pavilion *(see p. 141)*
From Bundi, *c.*1770
Varanasi, Bharat Kala Bhavan Museum, 8872

157 Rādhā and Krishna in a bower
(see p. 139)
c. 1700
22 × 16cm
Bombay, Prince of Wales Museum
of Western India, 52.18

85

403 Krishna swallowing the forest fire *(see p. 209)*
From Mandi, *c.1660*
20 × 29cm
New Delhi, National Museum, 62.2375

397 Krishna subduing the serpent *(see p. 208)*
From Kangra, *c.* 1775
23 × 29cm
New Delhi, National Museum, 58.18/19

160 Krishna and Rādhā lost in admiration *(see p.139)*
Attributed artist: Chokhā
From Devgarh, *c.*1810
22 × 16cm
Private collection

THE CATALOGUE

Introduction to the Exhibition
by Dr Kapila Vatsyayan

INTRODUCTION TO THE EXHIBITION

by Dr Kapila Vatsyayan

Within its deep infinity I saw ingathered, and bound by love in one volume the scattered leaves of all the universe.
The universal form of this complex whole I think that I saw, because as I say this I feel my joy increasing.

Dante, *La Divina Commedia : Il Paradiso*

The theme of Indian art, in essence, is the universe in all its abundance and multiplicity of life and form. Yet, within and behind the complex whole, is that omniscient, omnipotent and transcendental spirit which permeates forms and which is itself, in the last analysis, without form (*arūpa*).

Life on earth, as in the Biblical stories, emerges from the eternal waters that hold the potency of fire : the two together change into the forms of the world, mineral, plant, animal, human and divine. In India, this evolutionary pattern is traditionally couched in a language of myths and symbols.

From the primeval waters emerge stones in many shapes – ovoid pebbles and spheres with ammonites going back millions of years. They are *bāna-lingas* and *shālagrāmas*, worshipped as the self-shaped deities. The exhibition opens with a display of these ammonites and pebbles from the beds of the Narmada and its tributaries. The earliest Indian writing conceives of life emerging from these rivers and oceans, and also from the *anda*, the cosmic egg of all creation. As the *Chāndyoga Upanishad* (3.19. 1–2) explains:

In the beginning this world was merely non-being. It was existent. It developed. It turned into an egg. It lay for the period of a year. It was split asunder. One of the two eggshell-parts became silver, one gold.

That which was of silver is this earth. That which was of gold is the sky. What was the outer membrane is the mountains. What was the inner membrane is cloud and mist. What were the veins are the rivers. What was the fluid within is the ocean.

From the primeval waters also emerges the lotus, the most important of vegetative forms born of the waters, connected to the mythical centre of the earth through its stem, and always above the waters, blooming with the beauty and fragrance of the flower. Both physically and mythically, the lotus assumes the greatest importance in Indian cosmology, speculative thought and art. The lotus and its petals are the multiplicity of form : its centre corresponds to the centre of the universe, the navel of the earth, all is held together by the stem and the eternal waters. From this first awareness of the lotus as the symbol of life and supporter of the universe, the Indian mind conceives of all nature as an aspect of that universal spirit of which Dante speaks. But nature, vegetation and foliage, are more than a mere aid or background for the human world. The life of nature is indispensable to the human world – the two are interrelated, interdependent and always transmutable. The world of vegetation has inspired a great variety of motifs throughout Indian art. These are naturalistic, beautiful and spontaneous on one level, and imbued with symbolic significance on another level : the two move concurrently, distinguishing this approach from pantheism. At Mathura and Amaravati, this Indian characteristic finds its finest artistic expression in the coping stones with flowing swags, vertical stone columns, and trees with abundant foliage.

The life of water and plants is intrinsically related to the first creations of nature, the reptiles. Like the lotus, they too represent a moment of transition. As in other ancient religions, India has given a special significance to the snake. The coiled and intertwined snake represents a moment in the undifferentiated condition of creation (*pralaya*) on which human life rests. By the first century AD, the motif of the snake pervades Indian art, both in the coiled and intertwined form, and also as the many-headed serpent. Later it represents cyclical time without beginning or end, and ultimately crystallizes into the motifs of the 'line of eternity' or the labyrinth. From ground to ceiling, from outer walls to inner sanctuaries, the snake is carved in stone and wood in permanent structures ; it is also painted on walls and drawn on floors for ephemeral magic ritual. Sometimes, the snake and the fish coalesce, at other times the heads of some divinities are protected by 'cobra hoods', finally a group of part-human, part-serpent images – the *nāgas* and *nāgīs* – proliferate. Contemporary India perpetuates these traditions in a variety of cult-paintings, dance and music forms.

The snakes and reptiles, in a dramatic moment of biological mutation, acquire wings and become birds. Intuitively the Indian seer knew the process : both Indian myth and art provide significant examples of reptiles changing to birds, or coalescing into conjoined images. This is a pervasive theme and provides Indian art with an opportunity for the creation of some of the most fantastic images in stone and wood. The animals follow suit, and the entire range of evolution, from the hare to the lion, from the rodent to the primate, is vividly represented. They crowd the outer walls and lower lintels of Indian *stūpas* and temples by the hundred, sometimes in processional rows, in pairs, or yet again in conjunction with trees, floral motifs, and as conjoined images of fantasy. Occasionally they are aquatic, as in the mythical crocodile (*makara*) who is the vehicle of Gangā; at other times, they are of the earth, or the desert, as are the elephants and lions; while others are monkeys who befriend man. Amongst the creations of fantasy are the mythical lion or tiger, the *shārdūla*; more fearsome is the *vyāla*, the vicious beast. These mythic animals appear either in isolation or in conjunction with dwarfs and women on temple walls, guarding sanctuaries. There are also the many-winged animals called *suparnas*. Each animal acquires its own symbolism, and by the fourth century they develop into a systematized pantheon closely related to the world of humans and celestials. Most Indian sculpture is structured to comprehend the world of the aquatic, plant, animal, and human life. Each is an aspect of the other; superficially they appear as decoration, yet at a deeper level, the aquatic, vegetative, and animal elements represent aspects of the human psyche. Metamorphosis and transmutation is logical and traditional. This rich abundance of nature, its manifold creations and organic coherence, logically culminates in the universal fertility theme known to all ancient religions.

The fertility of Mother Earth is symbolized through the image of brimming vase, the bowl of plenty. Foliage and the lotus emerge from it: the waters below represent the life-giving forces of regeneration and energy surges out through the vegetation as the sap of life (*rasa*). Water, earth, plant, animal, human and the divine come together again to form the image of the goddess of fecundity, Lakshmī. She sits on a lotus, holds a lotus in her hands, and is sustained by the life-giving waters of protection, poured over her by two elephants.

More primary is the symbolism of the mother goddess. Mother goddesses persist in Indian sculpture in many shapes and forms, dating back some four thousand years. They appear as ring stones, as parallels to the primeval spiral-stone ammonite with spherical exteriors, or as the standing figurines of the Indus Valley Civilization, or as the fecundity figures of Hindu India.

These mother goddesses are related to another group of female figures, the *yakshīs*, along with their male counterparts, the *yakshas*. They too symbolize the fertility of water and earth. They stand against trees, embrace them, and thus become an aspect of the tree, articulating the interpenetration of the plant and the human. The tree is dependant upon the woman for its fertility, as is the woman on the tree. The *yakshīs* also punctuate the walls of all Indian architecture – Buddhist, Hindu, and Jain. The motif is expressed in innumerable forms, grouped together into eight or nine basic categories, each pointing to the special characteristics of the woman and the tree, and also to the animal below and the flying figure above.

It is the *yakshīs*, essentially representing the water and earth principle, which culminate in the image of the river goddesses, principally Gangā, Yamunā and Sarasvatī. In geographical terms, these are three important rivers of the Indo-Gangetic plains, in mythical terms they are the principle of eternal sustenance. They represent the stream of the waters, which mothers the children of the soil. In their human forms, Gangā and Yamunā are symbols of auspiciousness, they are the guardians of sanctuaries, and of the portals of the gods. Throughout the subcontinent, Indian shrines portray mighty figures of Gangā and Yamunā standing on their respective vehicles guarding the sanctuaries and preparing the devotee for the inner journey, Sarasvatī, the third river, has now run dry, but is remembered as the goddess of speech and learning and also of music. The three together led to another statement of the same principle of abundance in the form of Shrī – or Lakshmī – the radiant goddess of the lotus representing both the mother and prosperity. The binary opposite of Shrī is the goddess of sloth, Jyeshthā, representing inertia and grossness.

But the female principle, although fundamental, is never independent of that other principle which is indispensable to the creation of life on earth. If the *yakshīs*, the mother goddesses and the rivers represent energy, vitality and diversity of form – that is *prakriti*, and nature in its manifold aspects – the *purusha*, or male principle, is just as essential. Throughout Indian thought and art, and in all the philosophical systems, the two are interdependent and indispensable to each other. In some philosophical schools, the male principle (*purusha*) is still and eternal, while the female principle (*prakriti*) is changing and dynamic; in others, it is the opposite. The concepts of *prajñā* (knowledge) and *upāya* (manifestation) pervade Indian thought in all periods, regions and religions. In art, these complex speculations find the most charming and sensuous expression in the motifs of the tree as male and *yakshī* as female, or more explicitly, as man and woman, in war or love, confronting or co-mingling, and ultimately in consummation in the motif of the couple, the *mithuna*. As an artistic motif refined to an indescribable degree of stylization, the *mithuna* is unique to the history of world art. Again, as in the case of the *yakshīs*, the range is wide. Men and women are represented in rows, holding implements, fighting or dancing, in pairs or groups, in a variety of poses and movements. Walls of *stūpas*, and Hindu and Jain temples, are peopled by these *mithunas*, which have attracted – and bewildered – uninitiated spectators. The couples stand, sit, run, dance or fly, but in each case the linear flow of the female passes to the male, and the bodies interlock to provide one beautiful design where mass and volume merge. Many explanations ranging from the purely erotic to the spiritual have been advanced to explain these figures. Even those who disapprove of the theme are attracted by the sheer beauty of line and rhythm. The mother and child provides another eternal theme which reminds us of the culmination and also of the continuity of life.

Nature as *prakriti* provides one central theme in Indian art. Man as *purusha* provides the second, complementary theme. The Indian mind conceives of the cosmos as a man standing within a circle. Space, directions, the planets, the sun and moon, and the elements surround him. This concept is also known to other ancient religions. In India, it constitutes the basis of a massive body of myth, legend and art motifs. The segments of the circle are four or eight. They are personified as the guardians of directions of space. The elements are five: water (*varuna*), air (*vāyu*), fire (*agni*), space (*ākāsha*) and earth (*prithvī*). Then there are the signs of the zodiac, and the planets. The sun is the centre and in a commanding position.

Man as the microcosm and the macrocosm is mentioned in Indian literature and art from the earliest times. The *Rig Veda* provides the basis of the concept of *prithvī* (earth) – *prakriti* and *purusha*. Indian art takes the theme and the symbolism further once again in all schools and art forms ranging from architecture to music, in all ages. Man as *purusha* is portrayed as containing within himself the whole universe of mineral, plant, animal and human life, the sun and the planets, the quarters and directions, the elements and the psychical states. Paintings, especially of the Buddhist, Jain, Hindu and Tantric cults, portray this macrocosm as Man in the Universe.

Man in space and man in relation to the cosmos, imbued with breath (*prāna*) and encompassed by the elements, quarters and planets, is one aspect. The other is his relation to Man and the course of his life. As life on earth is comprehended as one form transmuting into another, the goals of life are also not world denying, but world transcending. Man comprises the physical, the emotional, the mental and the spiritual. He is a composite of the gross and the subtle body and his senses and his emotions are the driving forces. They are called the 'horses' of his actions and his body must be harnessed to goals of beauty, power, wealth, and, ultimately, emancipation and liberation. The body, intellect and spirit are essential, but are always seen in a balance and in an ascending hierarchy of values. According to the *Katha Upanishad* (3.3–4, 10–11):

> *Know thou the soul (ātman) as riding in a chariot,*
> *The body as the chariot.*
> *Know thou the intellect (buddhi) as the chariot-driver,*
> *And the mind (manas) as the reins.*
>
> *The senses (indriya), they say, are the horses;*
> *The objects of sense, what they range over.*
> *The self combined with senses and mind*
> *Wise men call 'the enjoyer' (bhoktri).*

and again:

> *Higher than the senses are the objects of sense.*
> *Higher than the objects of sense is the mind (manas);*
> *And higher than the mind is the intellect (buddhi).*
> *Higher than the intellect is the Great Self (ātman).*

Naturally, such a world view leads to the articulation of the conception of the four goals of life, all of which require discipline and balance. Likewise, man can achieve enlightenment and liberation, here and now, from the 'so muchness' of life, through a balanced cultivation of the life of the senses – the life of action with duty and power – and he can will it through the life of negation by being an ascetic. The ordinary man follows the goals through the four stages of his life (the student, householder, the itinerant or forest dweller or ascetic *sannyāsin*). The exceptional man adopts the lone journey of an ascetic. Both paths are valid; each has its own system of rules, regulations and methodologies. The nature of the journey is different, but the ultimate goal, that of a state of bliss (*ānanda*), of liberation (*moksha* or *nirvāna*) and of release from life here and now, is the same.

Indian aesthetic theory derives directly from this world view. The content of art is the world of sense perceptions – the pursuit of duty, power, pleasure – all in harmonious balance, always keeping in view that these are multiple forms also of the one indivisible unity. In artistic terms, life is divided into a spectrum of the rainbow, comprising different colours and patterns, but never oblivious of the white luminosity which is

the source and to which it must return. There are seven or eight basic moods (*rasas*), ranging from love, heroism and valour, to pathos, compassion, humour, laughter, fear, disgust and wonder. There are the eight types of hero (*nāyaka*), heroines (*nāyikā*), the principal modes of music (*rāgas*), and the changing seasons of the annual cycle (the twelve months). This impersonalized typology provides for a fantastic variety of themes, forms and techniques. From the earliest times, Indian sculpture and painting portray domestic life in simple homes or courts, wars, battles, heroic tales, romantic stories, as lovers in separation and union, all within the framework of the typology of the mood or states, heroes, heroines, modal or melodic forms (*rāgas*) and seasons. This typology accounts for the easy assimilation of many new themes and techniques, some indigenous, others foreign. Gradually but surely, they fell into place in the fundamental paradigm of the four goals of life, the four stages of life and the two paths of knowledge (*jnāna*) or devotion (*bhakti*).

The division of life and art into categories based on binary opposites is only one dimension of the Indian world view. The sacred and profane, celestial or terrestrial, the religious or mundane, are differentiated categories, but are always viewed in a relationship of complementaries rather than polarities. Thus one element can be transmuted into the other and vice-versa. The sensuous can become devotional, the devotional spiritual, the physical metaphysical. Understandably, the *mithuna* as a motif is multi-dimensional, representing both the human and the divine.

The ascetic life of renunciation, bar a few exceptions, was nevertheless fundamental to the Indian world view. Great spiritual leaders appeared on the Indian subcontinent who renounced the world and transcended the first three goals to follow only the last. There is the path of enlightenment (*jnāna*) through disciplined asceticism. This path of knowledge was followed by some, called the saviours. Historical characters soon became deified; Buddha and Mahāvīra belong to this group. Others, perhaps mythical or historical, such as Rāma and Krishna, followed the path of action (*karmayoga*), and there was a third group of devotees who through personal devotion (*bhaktiyoga*) also attained liberation. The ascetics, Buddha and Mahāvīra, transcended joy and sorrow, pain and pleasure, and attained liberation on earth – *nirvāna* in one case and *kaivalya* in the other.

Indian art incorporates the theme of the ascetic saviour and the three paths (*mārga* or *yoga*) in both sculpture and in painting. Neither Buddha nor Mahāvīra were represented in human form in the earliest phases of Indian art. The lotus and the tree, the feet and the intertwined line (*svāstika*) were their symbols. In due course, the figure of Buddha appeared as one of the Bodhisattvas. He is Padmapāni, holder of the lotus, and as Buddha he sits on the lotus seat and is in *padmāsana*. A figure of the Buddha standing or sitting, or of Mahāvīra standing, manifest the human ascension to the path of enlightenment. The path of devotion (*bhakti*) provided the opportunity of equalization and catholicity of spirit and approach, for release through devotion knew neither caste nor creed, nor a central monolithic church or sect. The *sūfis* attained a state of beatitude through *zikr* (invocation), the *bhaktas* a state of ecstasy through song and dance. The one experienced the mystical state *hāl*, the other *ānanda*. In *karmayoga* (path of action), the ascension was through detached action, in order to restore balance.

But, in the *Bhagavad Gītā*, (x, 5–9; xi, 5–6), Krishna declares to Arjuna:

> *I am the one source of all: the evolution of all comes from me. I am beginningless, unborn, the Lord of the worlds. I am the soul which dwells in the heart of all things. I am the beginning, the middle and the end of all that lives.*
>
> *I am the seed of all things that are: and no being that moves or moves not can ever be without me.*
>
> *By hundreds and then by thousands behold, Arjuna, my manifold celestial forms of innumerable shapes and colours.*
>
> *Behold the gods of the sun and those of fire and light: the gods of storm and lightning and the two luminous charioteers of heaven.*
>
> *See now the whole universe with all things that move and move not and whatever thy soul may yearn to see. See it all as one in me.*

This is the cosmic man, symbol of the universal order (*rita*) in its unending rhythm, evolution and devolution, creation and destruction, comprising time past, present and future (the three *yugas*), its space consisting of the netherworld, earth and sky, the forces of inertia, action and release, the states of sleep, dream and awakening, the five sheaths of consciousness and the three phases of the day. The Vishvarūpa mentioned in its incipient form in the *Upanishads* is articulated powerfully in the *Gītā* and in turn becomes the theme of powerful Indian sculpture, where Vishnu is seen in his multi-forms with teeming life around him, containing all manifest diversity and symbolizing unity. The binary opposites, or the complementarity of *purusha* and *prakriti* finds another statement, and now it is the principle of the many and the one, the diverse manifest and the unmanifest or uncreate. The triads, or the multiples of five, provide the other paradigm, for there are three worlds (*triloka*), the three orders of time (*trikāla*), the three phases of day (*trisandhya*), and the three faces (*trimūrti*), and the three mighty steps (*trivikrama*), along with the three inner states of consciousness (*triguna*) and the five sheaths (*avasthā*).

From the fourth century onward, Indian art incorporates these postulates through an extensive body of mythology revolving around the three principle deities: Brahmā, Vishnu and Shiva, particularly the latter two. The pattern of the myth, however, is clear and unequivocal in each case. It begins with the unmanifest or water principle, the aniconical stone, column or tree, and gradually develops into multiple forms called incarnations (*avatāras*), as in the case of the principal deities, or personifications of other natural phenomena.

The myths of Vishnu and Shiva are fundamental. In the case of Vishnu, the evolutionary process is the model. The primeval waters of the universe are churned: the elixir of life is obtained, but not before the deadly poison, *kālakūta*, surfaces and the dross is destroyed. Many sculptures and innumerable paintings depict this episode of the churning of the ocean (*amrita-manthana*), where a column is shown as the churning rod, symbolizing the centre of the earth. Vishnu also slumbers on the never-ending coils of the snake Shesha, representing time and eternity, causation and effect. In either case, Vishnu restores imbalances and rescues the world from recurring disaster. As the fish (Matsya) he rescues the *Veda*, as the tortoise (Kūrma) he upholds the earth; as the boar (Varāha) he rescues her; as the dwarf (Vāmana) he covers her in his three steps, and thus is known as the Trivikrama. As the divine in

human form, Rāma or Krishna, he relieves the world of its misery and restores balance, harmony and peace.

He rides the eagle, Garuda, and dances on the hood of the snake, Kāliya. Above all, he is the supreme dancer, the man of the wheel, whose movement is the balanced and dynamic rhythm of the universe. Indian art is fascinated by each of these themes, and, whether as a narrative or dramatic portrayal, or as an icon for worship, Vishnu appears in a number of forms. Perhaps the most powerful expression of the theme of multiplicity and unity is the dancing Krishna at the centre of a wheel of *gopīs*. The multiplicity and unity inherent in both Vishnu and Shiva is often conveyed by portraying the deities with one body and several arms or legs.

Shiva is the last in the trinity. Like Vishnu, he too is sentient and omniscient, mundane and transcendent, manifest and unmanifest, with energy for creation and destruction.

Unlike the evolutionary model followed in the myth of Krishna, the myth of Shiva moves from the unmanifest uncreate, to that of bi-unity, and ultimately to multiplicity and oneness. The *linga* is the primary aniconic form and in some ways corresponds to the column, post or pillar of the Vishnu myth. This stone phallus is also the counterpart of the primordial stone seen at the beginning of the exhibition. The *linga*, symbol of the conservation of energy, has the power to withhold and to give, to create and destroy, and to transmute the dross into the sublime. The three states of consciousness, the three orders of the universe (*triloka*), and the three orders of time (*trikāla*) are contained in him, as they are in Vishnu in his aspects of Trivikrama. The *linga* sometimes has one face, at other times four, facing the four quarters. The four faces are the directions of the compass, and the fifth is the unmanifest *linga* itself. The principle of bi-unity is seen in Indian sculpture revolving around the Shiva myth, as the androgyne images of Ardhanārīshvara. In this form, as half man and half woman, Shiva is the symbol of sexual bi-unity, and therefore beyond the duality of Shiva and Shakti corresponding to the *purusha* and *prakriti* (man and nature), for both are within him. Not only do Shiva and Shakti combine into one, but also Vishnu and Shiva, in the conjoined image of Harihara.

But Shiva, like Vishnu, has many other forms, and he looks at the play of the world (*līlā*) in these many forms. Sometimes alone and aloof as the *yogin* teacher, emaciated as the cursed beggar (*bhīkshātana*), or fearsome and full of terror as *Bhairava*. At other times, he is accompanied by Pārvatī and Ganesha (the elephant-headed god), or by his eternal companion Nandin, who is none other than his own ego, and Kārttikeya or Kumāra, the son born out of the waters again to rescue the world. Like Krishna he is the musician *par excellence*. He plays on the lute (*vīnā*) and not on the flute (*venu*). Like Krishna, but more so, he is the supreme 'Lord of the Dance' (Natarāja). Krishna dances on the hood of the snake, or against the wheel as *chakra-purusha*. Shiva is Natarāja, symbolizing the dance of the cosmos, the rhythm of the movement of the sun and moon, the earth, the wind and the skies, and the pulsation of time: past, present, and future. He dances accompanied by the 'Seven Mothers' (Saptamātrikās) or alone; he rides on the bull Nandin, his own ego, which leads him and the world to the final liberation of *moksha*. The dance of Shiva is the unique plastic statement of this universal complexity, where all forms manifest dissolve into the moment of eternal stillness through disciplined ceaseless movement.

प्रकृतिमण्डल

I

THE NATURAL WORLD

There is no natural world set apart from man. True, in the very distant past the Vedic fire god, Agni, was praised in ritual chants for destroying the great forests – for the invading forefathers used him to clear areas in which to settle. But they praised, too, the mighty 'Lord of the Forest', Vanaspati, tallest of trees; and those few trees spared at the outskirts of the settlement were sacred, standing between bright heaven and this world, between the circle of civilization and the savage tribes of Rudra deep in the dark forest beyond. The sacrificial stake was hewn from a felled tree and resurrected upon the ritual arena, on sacred ground, as the direct link between the eternal unitary sun and this world – haunted transiently, yet continuously, by the generations and tribes of man. He who separates himself from all this life is a shadow, he neither knows nor is known; he is the outsider, feared and spurned. Exile from the community in the midst of life is a living death. Thus, in India all life is embraced. It is the same life current which flows from the sun, and from the rivers, which courses through all that lives: rock, earth, wood, water, fire, cloud, air, light and dark.

Life has a symmetry which sages, self-exiled from man but not alone have perceived. Fearless and naked in the dark forest where all this life was one with them, such men are living links with the teeming flow of life, with the wind and the stillness, the drought and the flood, the agile and the unmoving, that which climbs and that which crawls, the predator and the prey. They have experienced life, alone and still in the wild, and they have fathomed its secret ways, its patterns; and they have returned to tell us, to explain. In the footsteps of these travellers flowers grow, and through their perceptions the world is viewed; but they have known through their entire being. Out of these generations of seers (*rishis*) has grown the communal understanding of all life, its balance: through them is glimpsed, beyond the self-perpetuating fabric (*prakriti*), beyond the semblance of reality (*māyā*), the one Being through Whom all live (*purusha*), Who is sacred (*brahman*), and to Whose myriad appearances and manifestations is returned His share in the ritual of the sacrifice. For the balance (*rita*) is always to be renewed, restored, confirmed.

IN THE BEGINNING

Man has always sought to understand the conditions which obtained before the world evolved and the origins of his own existence. Every society has its religious creation myths; and the search for this understanding continues today, in our technological age, through scientific means. Scientific theory frequently finds conceptual parallels in mythological systems which are very old, a fact which may indicate that man's basic perceptions have altered very little. Hindu thought postulates perpetual regeneration as opposed to the Biblical concept of creation. It follows that time and existence are conceived of as a system of interconnected cycles, not in linear terms starting from one specific divine act of creation. Indian cosmogonic imagery tends therefore to be circular or ovoid. Certain natural forms are seen as reflecting and confirming this continuum. The most highly venerated of these are egg-shaped stones found along the river beds of the Narmada and its tributaries, and ammonite fossils found in the Himalayas which were once sea-creatures before the mountains were forced up between one and two million years ago.

Their aquatic origin is significant: in Hindu mythology, evolution stems from 'the waters', the horizontal oceanic state called *pralaya* in which there is no polarization. It is said in one Sanskrit account that the eternal, unborn, the Self Existent (Svayambhū), wishing to create, meditated intensely; from his sweat and semen there appeared an egg floating upon the waters. Within this Golden Egg (Hiranya-garbha) the unborn was born. He stood, and this first vertical movement separated the halves of the egg into earth and heaven, still upon the watery fundament. Being himself now created, he made all things from the contents of the egg. All this came from himself; there was no creation out of a void.

The active vertical movement of separation is contemplated in these stones when set upright as the *linga* or phallus of the god Shiva, when they are termed *svayambhū-lingas* or *bāna-lingas*. The natural coloured markings are taken to represent the energizing female energy which stimulates the erection of the masculine urge to create, or the three strata of the universe, depending on their shape. Man-made *lingas*, imitative of these stones of enormous age, are painted with

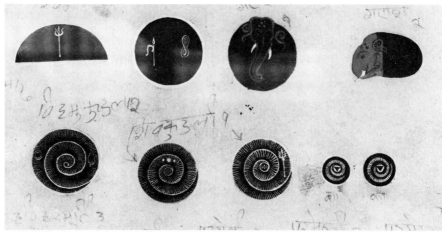

1 *Shālagrāmas*
Provenance unknown
Stone containing ammonite fossils
Each 5–7cm across
*Jean Claude Ciancimino collection
and Ross Owen Feller*

three horizontal lines to complete the original symbolism. These stones are brought out of the rivers deliberately so that they may be worshipped. The symbolism of their association with water is thus clearly understood: as well as being painted, man-made *lingas* are also perpetually lustrated with river water in their artificial temple settings.

The ammonite fossils, however, come from the mountains. Spiral, with radial lines and a projecting centre, these *shālagrāmas* are primarily associated with solar energy and often with the sun god Sūrya. But more widespread is their connexion with the god Vishnu, who in temple sculpture personifies the horizontally floating Golden Egg, lying upon an undulating serpent which represents the inexhaustible, primordial ocean of *pralaya*. One of Vishnu's primary emblems is the disc (*chakra*) which has solar and fiery associations, and these fossils seem to represent its archetypes. The fire rising from the waters, or the sun rising from the ocean, is a symbol of the eternal being and life-giving power emerging from the unpolarized fundament. Contemplation of the spirals may lead to a comprehension of the continuous evolution/devolution process of all time and existence, and the *shālagrāmas* are used in ritual to represent Vishnu who sustains this cosmic rhythm.

2 **Catalogue of** *shālagrāmas* *(detail)*
18th or 19th century
From Jaipur (Rajasthan), 164 × 44cm
Jean Claude Ciancimino collection

3 **Egg of Brahmā** *(not illustrated)*
Pahari school, 1730, 17 × 28cm
Varanasi, Bharat Kala Bhavan Museum, 240

4 *Svayambhū-linga*
Age unknown
From northern India
Stone, 25cm high
Jean Claude Ciancimino collection

5 *Svayambhū-linga*
Age unknown
From eastern India
Stone, 30cm high
Jean Claude Ciancimino collection

TREES, FLOWERS AND FOLIAGE

In the creation of a sacred Buddhist enclosure at Sanchi, on a hilltop overlooking the great north Indian plain, the architecture was made to harmonize with the unending pulse of the force that flows through all living things. The rhythmically undulating lotus stalk, burgeoning with buds and blossoms (8), is more than decoration. This fragment contains many of the deepest preoccupations of the Indian imagination of more than 2,000 years ago. Through the natural symbolism of the lotus stalk, the sculptor reveals his concern that the generations of man should flourish in unbroken continuity; and in so doing he re-creates in stone the ancient hallowed environment of the forest inhabited by his ancestors who knew the essence of life as an ever-flowing unity.

Nature triumphs in the artificial shrines of all Indian religions, embowering the gods in all the exuberance of the wild, which is yet controlled, for it has a place of equal importance alongside the creative genii – personifications of this seeming riot of growth and perpetual change – at the entrances to the temple. This need to sanctify religious experience by placing it within the embrace of nature is reflected, too, in the scriptures: illuminated manuscripts enclose the sacred word in a forest of fantasy.

More intimately, Indian sculptors remembered the tree as holy in its own right. The apotheosized Hindu hero Balarāma, elder brother of Krishna, was symbolized by the palmyra, stylized for the sake of symmetry. The tree trunk carved in stone as a sacred pillar derived its sanctity from the sacrificial post, hewn from a tree trunk, of the ancient Vedic ritual (7). Early Hindu attempts at expressing cult philosophies through complex images were artistically controlled and religiously validated by the holiness of the tree. For those creeds which were founded upon notions of multiple evolutionary phases stemming from a single source – the 'unity in diversity' for which Hinduism is renowned – the ramifying imagery of a spreading tree provided the ideal controlling pattern. The emanatory hexad of goddesses (personifying diverse energies driving this multifarious existence into being from a static and unitary source), on one side of a panel for example, was both sanctified and explained to the worshipper by the depiction of an *ashoka* tree on the back (9). The trunk stands for the main figure while the branches symbolize the five other goddesses who stem from it. The force of life is naturally symbolized by the growing configuration of a tree, and the naturalism was preserved, to balance and lend credence to the anatomical unnaturalism of the multiple image itself, even to the extent of rendering the tree slightly asymmetrically and portraying a squirrel swarming up the trunk, symbolically ascending the axis of creation.

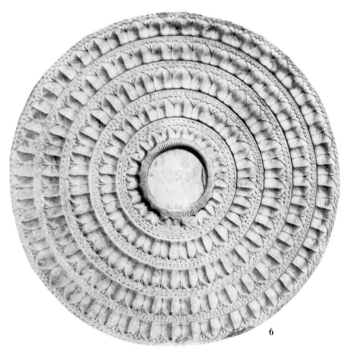

6

6 Lotus
Ikshvāku period, 3rd century AD
From Amaravati (Andhra Pradesh)
White limestone, 82 × 94cm
London, Trustees of the British Museum, 1880.7–9.6

7 Palm leaf capital (*see p. 49*)
Pre-Kushāna period, 3rd–1st century BC
From Mathura (Uttar Pradesh)
Yellow sandstone, 80 × 52cm
Lucknow, State Museum, J.584

8 Frieze of lotus stalk and flowers
Shunga period, 2nd century BC
From Sanchi (Madhya Pradesh)
Sandstone, 25 × 165 × 27cm
Sanchi, Archaeological Museum, 2712
Both this coping stone and the lotus medallion (6)
were associated with the decoration of Buddhist *stūpas*.

8

9

9 *Ashoka* **tree**
Kushāna period, 2nd century AD
Provenance unknown
Red sandstone, 66 × 89 × 25cm
Mathura, Government Museum, F.2

10 Column with pot, foliation and monster mask
10th century
From Sagar (Madhya Pradesh)
Sandstone, 157 × 58 × 40cm
New Delhi, National Museum, 78.996

11 Koranic inscription with foliage
ʿĀdil Shāhī period, 17th century
From Bijapur (Karnataka)
Basalt, 149 × 46 × 13cm
Bijapur, Archaeological Museum, A.1
Despite the Koranic inscription, the lotus
ornament is traditionally Indian

10

11

12

13

14

12 *Nāga* beneath tree
Shunga period, 2nd century BC
From Pauni (Maharashtra)
Sandstone, 104 × 53 × 48cm
New Delhi, National Museum, L.77.1
Beneath the *bodhi* tree, the multi-headed
cobra king, Muchilinda, rises up to protect
the seated Buddha, here represented by an
empty seat; *yakshas* on either side hold their
hands together in reverential salute.

13 Coiled *nāga*
Early Chālukya period, 7th–8th century
From Alampur (Andhra Pradesh)
Red sandstone, 125 × 85cm
Alampur, Archaeological Museum, 9

14 Manasā, goddess of snakes
Pāla period, *c*.750 AD
From eastern India
Bronze with inlay, 46 × 18cm
*London, Trustees of the British Museum,
1969.1–15.1*

SNAKE DEITIES

Beneath the tangled roots of trees lie the subterranean waters,
the haunt of serpents. Here are the hidden treasures of the
earth – precious stones and metals – and it is from this
darkness that the tree and all terrestrial life arises. The
multiform, colourful world of man grows out of the uniform
dark, the formless waters. Inhabiting both these worlds,
gliding from one to the other, symbol of their interconnection,
is the snake, swift and silent, limbless and deadly. This sign of
transition is vital to man, who must be assured that his world
is a cohesive unity; he cannot exist in chaos. Just as the tree
trunk, felled and lopped, was erected upon the Vedic sacrificial
arena as a ritual connection between his world and heaven, so
the snake connects the world of man with the netherworld:
this is the *triloka*, the triple-world, its three strata linked by
the axis of tree and snake.

So it was in ancient times, and the survival of this element
in the pattern is evident everywhere in later religious art,
cosmology and philosophy. In images of the Hindu god
Vishnu at the moment before the creation of the universe, he
is depicted lying in a yogic sleep upon the serpent Ananta,
'Endless', with its multiple cobra-heads forming a canopy
above him. This serpent represents the oceanic,
undifferentiated condition of the raw material of creation
(*pralaya*) before it is polarized and developed through a series
of transformations stimulated by the female energy of the god.

Nāgas – cult figures of the serpent-rulers of the underworld
– whether depicted alone or dominated by the high gods in
composite images, assume a standard form which was created
for Buddhist sculptural panels as long ago as the 2nd century
BC. This form consists of a human head and torso with a
serpentine extension below the waist, and a canopy of either
five or seven cobra-heads above the human face. In early
Buddhist art, *nāgas* appeared in human form with a group of
snakes rearing above their heads, submerged up to the waist in
a river or lake; the serpentine body below the waist, to
symbolize their aquatic origin, was a later development which
enabled the sculptor to depict them in any architectural or
natural environment.

Both *nāgas* and *nāgīs* (the former masculine and the latter
feminine – despite the difficulty in sexing snakes, the
differentiation of gender was known very early in India) appear
as cult figures in their own right, most frequently integrated
into the iconographic schema of a temple dedicated to one of
the high gods. There are exclusive *nāga* shrines, too, and some
in which snakes are encouraged to live, being fed regularly

15 *Nāgī*
Vijayanagara period, 14th–16th century
From Vijayanagara (Karnataka)
Whitish granite, 285 × 50 × 21cm
Hampi, Archaeological Museum, 622

16 *Nāga* (not illustrated)
Shunga period , 2nd century BC
From Barhut (Madhya Pradesh)
Sandstone
Ramvan, Tulsi Sangrahalaya

17 Muchilinda, the *nāga* king
(not illustrated)
Ikshvāku period, 2nd century AD
From Amaravati (Andhra Pradesh)
Soapstone, 108 × 87 × 22cm
New Delhi, National Museum, 63.1535

15

with offerings by the priests. As a sculpted image, the *nāga* presence in a temple is always auspicious, being a part of the ancient pattern of natural phenomena which imitates the wild and so sanctifies all holy places. It also invokes human and agricultural fertility and at the same time, paradoxical as this may seem, protects the worshipper from snakes. For while the *nāga* is a symbol, snakes are real and deadly. By worshipping and placating the *nāgas* in the temple, a measure of protection from real snakes in the forests and fields is obtained.

The symbolic values of snake and tree have undergone changes of cult context through the millennia, but essentially they exert the same psychological power as they have always done. In southern India, women desiring children set up snake-stones (*nāga-kals*), for the snake is a penis symbol and is also associated with prolific offspring and with the fertility of the earth, being termed *kshetra-devatā*, deity of the fields. These stones, engraved with intertwined snakes, are erected in clusters beneath sacred trees. The cult of Manasā, Goddess of Snakes, probably originated in Bengal and is still largely confined to eastern India. She is, by association, a goddess of fertility, and may be prevailed upon to cure snakebite. The Hindu god Shiva is regarded as a healer of venomous infection, being called – among his many other epithets – Vishāpaharana, 'Remover of Poison'.

ANIMALS AND BIRDS

Warm-blooded creatures upon the land and in the air are the companions and allies of man. Very few temple sculptures represent the sacrifice or slaughter of animals. The few exceptions are significant: they are mostly symbolic slayings performed by the gods, not sacrifices made by man as offerings to them. Although such ritual killing does take place in certain tribal and Hindu cults, it has never been officially sanctioned by the brahmanical orthodoxy unless the animals concerned have already been intended for slaughter as food to sustain the community. In such societies, this mass blood-letting – usually in honour of The Goddess – takes place once a year in front of the main temple, and the method of killing is almost invariably decapitation.

Animals in India were closely studied, cherished and regarded symbolically as part of the great pattern of life. The fact that they were also hunted or sacrificed does not contradict this love of animals: it was noticed that certain creatures were natural prey, as part of the scheme of things. Deer, for example, were observed to be created only to die, being hunted by most predatory animals, and so were termed *mriga*, meaning literally 'death-goers' (**27**). It was also noticed that some creatures flocked together for protection and so goats, for example, were called *aja*, meaning a drove or herd animal. Of all creatures, it was probably the horse which was most loved and respected, particularly by the ruling military aristocracy, for it was the swiftness of a warrior's mount or the manoeuvrability of his chariot team which largely decided his prowess in battle; and upon that depended the survival of his clan. When a horse was sacrificed, therefore, it was a solemn and momentous occasion; one sacrifices that which one most loves only in times of greatest need for the good of the community, putting aside personal affection.

Man's study of animal behaviour led to the association of the main characteristics of a particular creature's habits with human strengths and weaknesses. Human personalities were given to animals in the stories of the previous lives of the Buddha (*Jātakas*) and in moral tales, corresponding in many ways to those of Aesop, collected (often for the instruction of princes in outwitting their enemies) in such Sanskrit anthologies as the *Panchatantra* and *Hitopadesha*. By the 6th century AD such stories were already spreading across the Middle East in the Pahlavi translation; new versions in Syriac and Arabic then reached Europe and were translated into Spanish, German and French, and many of the famous *Fables* of La Fontaine were based directly upon them. Indian narrative sculptures and foliate reliefs often depict animals acting out these human roles in vignettes (**25**) which must have afforded devotees at the temples much amusement and entertainment.

Animals are associated with particular deities; they also come spontaneously to the aid of divine incarnations. In the Hindu epic, the *Rāmāyana*, the wife of Rāma, one of the incarnations of Vishnu, is abducted in the forest by the demon-king Rāvana; but only after a savage battle with Rāma's ally, the mighty bird Jatāyu, son of Garuda, the eagle. An entire army of monkeys also allied themselves with Rāma under the rule of their king Sugrīva and the command of their general Hanumān. The latter played a vital role in the destruction of Rāvana, spying upon the demon's capital city,

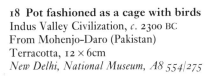

18 Pot fashioned as a cage with birds
Indus Valley Civilization, *c.* 2300 BC
From Mohenjo-Daro (Pakistan)
Terracotta, 12 × 6cm
New Delhi, National Museum, A8 554/275

19 Bird
Maurya period, 3rd century BC
From Sarnath (Uttar Pradesh)
Polished sandstone, 16 × 14 × 15cm
Sarnath, Archaeological Museum, 370

20 Monkey
Indus Valley Civilization, *c.* 2300 BC
From Mohenjo-Daro (Pakistan)
Terracotta, 5 × 6 × 6cm
New Delhi, National Museum, 11625/216

21 Bird *(not illustrated)*
Indus Valley Civilization, *c.* 2300 BC
From Mohenjo-Daro (Pakistan)
Terracotta, 6 × 6 × 12cm
New Delhi, National Museum, 10581389

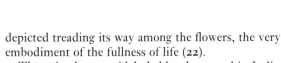

23

Lanka, which he reached by leaping across the sea in a single bound, and which he subsequently burnt down (see pp. 204–6). Such myths exemplify the ideally conceived partnership between man and animals in relation to the divine as opposed to the demonic forces which attempt to subvert the natural order.

This animal imagery – whether dramatic, literary or graphic – always contains a strong element of reality; this stems from man's close observation of animal life as part of the natural order, which he sought to establish and formulate in order to understand his own earthly existence. The closeness and precision of such observation is evident in works of art dating from the Maurya period to today. In the damaged sculpture of the 3rd century BC (**19**) the legs, toes and plumage of a bird walking on the water's edge are almost perfectly reproduced, while in the undulations of the endless lotus stalk, another of the best loved Indian animals, the elephant, is sportively depicted treading its way among the flowers, the very embodiment of the fullness of life (**22**).

The animal most widely held to be sacred in India is the cow. This has been so since Vedic times, when the herds represented the communal wealth of the early tribes; much of the warfare between the early Aryan settlers in India consisted basically of cattle raids. Like the cornucopia or the magical tree, the milch-cow became legendary in Indian lore as the *kāma-dhenu*, the wish-granting cow. More specifically, it was with the widely adored young Krishna, incarnation of Vishnu, that the cow became most strongly associated, as he was himself a cowherd in his youth (**24**). In fact, Gopāla, 'Cow herd', became one of his epithets and a popular name for male children – as it still is today, especially in the double form Gopāl-Krishna. The same preoccupation with the depiction of animals as an essential part of everyday life can be seen in Indian painting, from Mughal times to the present.

22

24

22 Elephants with riders and dancing girls
Shunga period, 2nd century BC
From Barhut (Madhya Pradesh)
Red sandstone, 28 × 264 × 9cm
New Delhi, National Museum, 68.168
This courtly scene within an undulating
lotus stalk formed the coping stone around a
Buddhist *stūpa*.

23 Elephant
c. 3rd century AD
From Amaravati? (Andhra Pradesh)
Bronze, 17 × 22cm
Private collection

24 Cow and calf with Krishna
Chauhan style, 10th century
From Agroha (Punjab)
Sandstone, 17 × 30cm
*London, Victoria and Albert Museum,
IM309–1921*

25

27

25 Goose and hare
Eastern Ganga period, 13th century
From Konarak (Orissa)
Khondalite, 28 × 28 × 29cm
Konarak, Archaeological Museum

26 Elephant *(not illustrated)*
Maurya period, 3rd century BC
From Patna (Bihar)
Ivory, 4cm high
Patna, Sri Gopi Krishna Kanoria Collection

27 Deer
18th century
From Mathurapur (Bengal)
Terracotta, 20 × 16 × 6cm
Calcutta, Gurusaday Bengal Folk Art Museum

CREATURES OF THE IMAGINATION

As if discontented even with the vast plurality of living things to be found in the natural world, artists populated the realm of *māyā* with creatures of their imaginations, creatures generated by the very complexity of nature. Sea- or river-dwelling beasts (*makara*) (**32**) were combined with land animals, such as the tiger, and with vegetal growths, to produce anomalous beings. Through these invented beasts, artists sought to combine and transgress the categories of nature as they observed and analysed them, as composite symbols of the aquatic and the serpentine, the warm-blooded and the cold-blooded, the four-footed and the earth-rooted. Once the natural world was seen in symbolic as well as realistic terms, any and every form of creature became thinkable and believable. These were not cult images made for worship – although equally strange multiple representations did indeed arise as icons – but rather attempted condensations of the living world. They were regarded as powerful presences of nature, concentrated and emblematic living symbols of the ubiquitous, self-perpetuating powers of the created world. As part of the iconographic scheme of a temple, they are benign and sanctifying, as are most representations of the natural world, whether realistic or formalized.

There is, however, another class of such creatures. These are generally termed *vyāla* (when used adjectivally, it means 'wicked' and 'vicious'). Most often depicted in tiger-like or leonine form (they are specifically named *shārdūla*, meaning tiger rather than lion), these creatures dwarf the figures of men who are shown either opposing or riding them. They too, like the composite beasts of the imagination, represent the force of nature, but here the element of fantasy is virtually eliminated, for the mighty attacking spring of the tiger is sufficiently well-known, respected and feared as to require no supernatural symbolism. Only its size is exaggerated in order to convey the gigantic power of the natural world, which is here objectified by man who sees himself small and alone before it.

For it is not only his proliferating natural environment, but also the wild – the uncontrolled passions and appetites rampant in every man – which are the *vyāla-shārdūla*. Unless this power is subdued, as a man alone in the forest must subdue panic, or tamed as a wild horse must be broken, the ideal of self-control cannot be said to have been achieved. Man must face this inner and outer riot of nature, combat it and bring it under his control, if he is to gain the state of self-possession, which is yet in harmony with nature, and know that inner peace without which he has not the discipline or knowledge through which to approach his god. In terms of architectural temple symbolism, the warrior of the spirit fights the *shārdūla* with the sword of knowledge and the shield of dispassion at the approach, and upon the platform itself before the entrance is depicted triumphantly riding the beast of his own nature (**30**, **31**). Beyond lies the heart of the temple and the presence of the divine.

28

28 Winged beast
Shunga period, 1st century BC
From Sanchi (Madhya Pradesh)
Stone, 68 × 61 × 30cm
New Delhi, National Museum, 67.614

29

29 Mythical beast
Kushāna period, 2nd century AD
From Mathura (Uttar Pradesh)
Sandstone, 89 × 107cm
London, Victoria and Albert Museum,
IS 712–1883

30 *Vyāla* **and rider** *(see also p. 60)*
Gupta period, 5th century
From Sarnath (Uttar Pradesh)
Sandstone, 93 × 56 × 14cm
New Delhi, National Museum, 49.115

31 Shārdūla
Gupta period, 6th century
From Sarnath (Uttar Pradesh)
Yellow sandstone, 89 × 33 × 24cm
New Delhi, National Museum, M.68

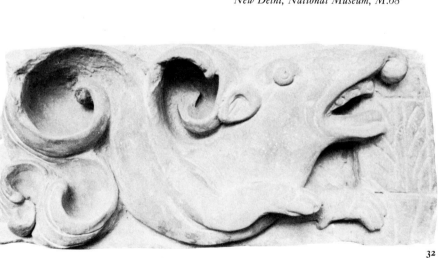

32 Aquatic beast, *makara*
Gupta period, 5th century
From Mathura? (Uttar Pradesh)
Terracotta, 20 × 42 × 13cm
Oxford, Ashmolean Museum, 1971.13

33 *Vyāla*
Eastern Ganga period, 13th century
From Konarak (Orissa)
Khondalite, 163 × 82 × 59cm
Konarak, Archaeological Museum, 854
Carved almost in the round, this rearing
beast was positioned high up in the wall of
the Sūrya Temple, peering down on the
devotee.

34 A mythical monster *(not illustrated)*
From the *Bhayanka Rasa* manuscript
Rājput school, late 18th century
From Bundi, 24 × 29cm
New Delhi, National Museum, 51.72/99

NATURE OBSERVED

The Ajanta painter rendered the lotus in many ways but always emphasized its organic structure and the natural principles of its growth, whereas the painters of later Jain manuscripts often used floral arrangements decoratively, creating designs from conventionalized blossoms (**35**).

When the Mughals arrived in India, they commissioned the first scientific nature studies. Bābur, the founder of the dynasty, devoted a long section of his memoirs to discussing the flora and fauna of his new country; his curiosity created a new tradition since these memoirs, illustrated four times in Akbar's reign, were the first artistic studies clearly distinguishing the major Indian plant and animal species.

Jahāngīr was also an ardent amateur naturalist, commissioning his artists to depict animals he encountered during the frequent periods when he was hunting or travelling. (His diary contains excited descriptions of animal behaviour as well as unusual species he saw.) For example, in 1607, when he was hunting near Kabul, Afghans presented him with a Himalayan *markhur* ('serpent-eating goat') they had killed. Astonished by its strangeness as well as its size, Jahāngīr immediately ordered his artists to paint it. Three versions of the work exist today; this one (**37**) is by the artist 'Ināyat, whose surviving *oeuvre* is small. At the beginning of his reign, Jahāngīr appears to have requested many artists to record the natural history he was so interested in. Gradually, however, his attention focused on the painter Mansūr whom he described as the best artist of such subjects. Mansūr confined himself almost exclusively to nature studies carrying out extensive commissions such as the recording of one hundred floral species. From his early work on the *Bābur Nāma* manuscripts, one can observe a growing mastery in his style. In the miniature of the *chear* pheasant (**48**), he has succeeded in recording precisely the complex patterns of the bird's feathers. The Himalayan region, including Kashmir, was an area the Mughals often visited, and so there are many records of mountain species seen there. The inspiration for these pictures came not only from northern Renaissance prints of all types but probably also from illustrated scientific works brought to India. It was probably Mansūr who depicted the *nīlgai* blue bull (**38**) a common Indian animal shot by hunters in great numbers; the artist has shown his sensitivity by dealing with a familiar subject without producing a dry cliché, capturing its lithe form as well as the softness of its hair and eyes.

The studies made for Jahāngīr, though remarkable, transmitted only certain aspects of animal life. The *nīlgai* or *markhur*, for example, are both seen as static subjects with little reference to environmental settings. Hindu painters, even when trained in the imperial atelier, often had a more intuitive, less studied approach to depicting animals. In 1596, for example, the artist Shankar did an illustration for the well-known group of fables, the *Anwār ī Suhailī*. (The *Anwār* stories were Islamic versions of tales that had originated in India and been transmitted to other lands, forming the core of *Aesop's Fables* and eventually returning with the Mughals to the country of their creation.) The story imaginatively depicted here by Shankar shows a monkey who has volunteered to lead the enemy group of bears into the burning desert by falsely acting as an ally despite the fact that the journey will also mean his own death. Here he sits astride

35 Page with foliage, geese and dancing figures *(detail)*
From the *Devasānlapādā Kalpasūtra* manuscript
Jain school, *c.* 1475
From western India
Patna, Sri Gopi Krishna Kanoria Collection

36 Cow with calf
Rajasthan school, *c.* 1800
From Devgarh
Hyderabad, Jagdish and Kamla Mittal Museum of Indian Art, 76.681

37 Himalayan *markhur* (goat)
Artist: ´Ināyat
Mughal school, *c.* 1615
24 × 20cm
London, Victoria and Albert Museum, IM 138–1921

37

36

38

38 *Nīlgai (detail)*
Attributed artist: Mansūr
Mughal school, *c.* 1610–15
29 × 23cm
Cambridge, Fitzwilliam Museum, P.D.78–1948
(There is a similar *nīlgai*, signed by Mansūr, in the Metropolitan
Museum of Art, New York)

one of the bears as they begin to feel the heat of the desert sun (**39**).

Though the Mughals set fashions in many ways at the Rājput courts, their brand of naturalism became blended with the Hindu sympathetic understanding of animals as its influence percolated through India; this rich aspect of Indian culture is exemplified in a humorous drawing of a cow and calf that captures all the warmth of the relationship with a few very simple lines (**36**). The portrait of Bijay Singh of Marwar (**42**) follows Mughal compositions and also owes much to the detailed observation of Mughal painters. Further south, the Deccani artists also borrowed Mughal models but transformed them; here a painting of a man in a meadow (probably the most common subject in Mughal painting) has been turned into a lyrical composition by a Deccani artist who, with an imagination characteristic of the region, has enlarged the flowers and butterflies into dream-like subjects (**41**).

Intuitive and objective cultural strains could also be said to have been blended during the British period when patrons attempted to familiarize Indian painters with the perspective and shading common to European watercolour. Surprisingly, their efforts did not crush the individuality of the Indian artists but inspired dynamic compositions. Some were accurate botanical studies while others were abstract essays on shape and colour employing Indian perceptions of nature in a new way (**46** and see **245**).

44

39 The bears in the burning desert *(see p. 81)*
From an *Anwārī Suhailī* manuscript
Artist: Shankar
Mughal school, 1596
Varanasi, Bharat Kala Bhavan Museum, 9069/18

40 Horse and groom *(see p. 44)*
Rajasthan school, *c.* 1660
From Ajmer (Sawar), 29 × 42cm
Private collection
This picture with the horse's name inscribed on the reverse is one of a series of portraits of the Sawar ruler's favourite beasts.

41 Prince with rose *(see p. 74)*
Deccan school, late 17th century
From Golconda, 31 × 20cm
New Delhi, National Museum 58.39/5

42 Rāja Bijay Singh of Marwar with his decoy buck *(see p. 75)*
Rājput school, *c.* 1720
From Marwar, 44 × 24cm
Bombay, Prince of Wales Museum

43 Lion and buffalo fighting
(not illustrated)
Provincial Mughal school, *c.* 1760
From Lucknow, 33 × 48cm (whole page),
17 × 27cm
London, Victoria and Albert Museum, IS 234–1952
The European derived landscape of this miniature exemplifies the knowledge of European prints.

44 Tiger attacking gazelle
From a *Madhu Malati* manuscript
Artist: Bhāgwān
Pahari school, 1799
From Kulu, 12.4 × 16cm
Hyderabad, Jagdish and Kamla Mittal Museum of Indian Art, 76.254
The tiger here kills the gazelle which pierces his shoulder with its horn.

45 Female elk (*sāmbar*) *(not illustrated)*
Attributed artist: Shaykh Zayn al-Din
East India Company school, *c.* 1780
From Calcutta, 41 × 54cm
Private collection
The signature has been trimmed apparently to pass the picture off as a European composition. It is actually part of the well known series of flora and fauna commissioned by Mary Impey, wife of the Chief Justice in Bengal and can be attributed to Zayn al-Din, one of her three artists.

46 Coffee arabica
East India Company school, *c.* 1827
From Calcutta, 67 × 42cm
*London, India Office Library and Records,
NHD 58/2*

47 Wild ginger
East India Company school, *c.* 1790–1800
From Calcutta, 67 × 42cm
*London, India Office Library and Records,
NHD 60/1*

46

47

48

48 Himalayan *chear* pheasant
From the Wantage Album
Artist: Mansūr
Mughal school, *c.* 1620
38 × 26cm
*London, Victoria and Albert Museum,
IM 136–1921*

49 Carnation
Deccan school, *c.* 1630
20 × 12cm
Private collection

49

जीवसमृद्धि

2

THE ABUNDANCE OF LIFE

Going alone into the dark forests, the Indian ancestral seers experienced, understood and so reclaimed man's natural inheritance; generations of sculptors and painters re-created this hallowed world of nature. Man has also to struggle to transcend the animal within himself, but this struggle rarely takes the form of a pitched battle between good and evil. The struggle is to be likened rather to the ascent of a ladder, each stage overlapping that below it. So did the ancestors climb the sacrificial stake to grasp the chariot wheel at its summit, imitating in ritual the ascent from the earth to the sun, from mortality to immortality. In those ancient times man built his ladder to eternity upon the sum of his actions, and if this was firm and true he merged with the eternal spirit beyond the sun at his death.

Nature has not changed, nor the elements of which it is composed. Rather than fight, man uses these elements as the rungs of the ladder to which he attaches his meditations in an unbroken ascending sequence from the dense to the rarefied, from the tight knot of his selfish fears to the infinite freedom of the divine. Of these, the earth, mother and tomb of man's mortal self, is the dense, the dark, the heavy; man labours upon her for his crops, his herds feed upon her, and for that he gives thanks. But the earth is also the birthplace of *māyā*, in which man may live out his hundred summers in peace. She is made fertile by water, from the great sacred rivers, and from the mighty purple clouds where Indra rages. Water mixes with earth to produce clay; with this the potter shapes the earth. It is thus more subtle than earth, yet more gross than fire which, as the raging and sacred one-who-goes-before (*purohita*) – as man names his priests – burned down the forests for the ancestors; which, tamed, bakes the pots and figurines made by the potter until they are hard and durable; which, as the ritual fire, devours the sacrificial offerings to convey them upward to the gods. It is by air and through air that fire burns, rushes through the forest, rises to heaven. Air is more subtle than fire, all life depends upon it, and in man's meditation, control over it as the breath-of-life (*prāna*) is exercised to alter levels of consciousness, to confirm awareness of man's grasp on life and, as air is everywhere, man's unity with all that lives. But at this level, too, man is involved in *māyā*. What is there, then, that transcends these four: earth, water, fire and air? It is the most subtle, called *ākāsha*, which is the highest, which transcends the four of which *māyā* is composed, and stands at their head as the sun stands at the zenith above all creation. This is the axis upon which the grosser four depend, the sacred fifth element, the centre and summit of all extensions of space. It is not seen in the manifestations of the natural world, for it is beyond and above them utterly; but it is known, and the ascent, controlled by the mind – which is made of the four elements – drives the spirit towards this highest, invisible goal.

It is often said that the golden number is four, as it represents perfect balance. Thus each cycle of time is divided into four ages (*yugas*) and the whole cycle is likened to a quadruped which loses one of its legs as each age passes; the cycle thus becomes increasingly unstable – for the four legs are the four parts of *dharma*, the natural law which all men must follow. It stands firmly upon all your feet only in the first age; in the last age, the *Kalī-yuga* (which man now inhabits), *dharma* stands on one leg only, and the minds of men are darkened by ignorance. This ignorance and instability leads to collapse; all life is destroyed in apocalyptic fire and dissolves back into the ocean of potential creation (*pralaya*) before the new world condenses and arises once again. By virtue of the fact that life thus perpetually renews itself, man knows that there must be a continuum not subject to change and deterioration. This is the fifth element, around which all that is known through the mind and the senses revolves. Five is the supreme number, and it is to the supreme fifth that man affiliates his spirit, for the innermost and eternal centre of man is of its essence.

But man works towards this centre by way of the four decaying elements in natural sequence. Here is encountered every manifestation of *māyā*, which must be honoured yet transcended. And in every manifestation of these four there are glimmerings of that which is beyond, the eternal axial fifth, which is reality. This man depicts in his religious imagery. So these images of clay and stone celebrate the abundance of life, but are conceived as stages in man's quest for the universal heart of which they are the outward signs. Here man seeks glimpses of the eternal among the temporal, as footholds in his ascent.

50

50 Lakshmī
7th–8th century
Sandstone, 67 × 54 × 18cm
New Delhi, National Museum, 68.100
As Goddess of Plenty, Lakshmī sits holding a lotus, with a lotus throne
and footstool. Flanking figures holding bulging pots are themselves
seated upon lotus blossoms. Above, supported upon yet more lotuses,
two elephants hold similar pots in their trunks with which they
lustrate the goddess. She is Nature, the elephants are the massive
blue-black rainclouds which fertilize her.

51

51 Garlands, pots with lotus flowers (*pūrnaghata*),
auspicious emblems and lions
Ikshvāku period, 4th century
From Nagarjunakonda (Andhra Pradesh)
Limestone, 98 × 83 × 18cm
New Delhi, National Museum, 50.19
Here, garlands, flowers, plant-like emblems and lion-like beasts are
combined to express the fertility and protection associated with
the Buddhist *stūpa*.

MOTHER GODDESSES

Innumerable clay images of the mother goddess are made
throughout India today as they were 4,000 years ago. The
terracotta tradition is a continuous one, having its origins in a
remote past long before stone sculpture was known on
anything but a miniature scale. It was in the Indus Valley
Civilization, with its widespread provincial culture, that
probably the first such cult – no doubt the amalgamation of
many – can be said to have been established. The small images
were produced in their thousands, the clay quickly twisted and
pinched to delineate limbs and features, the eyes, lips and
indispensable ornaments merely rolled and applied. In this
and most successive cultures, no matter what degree of
sophistication was being attained in the artistic working of
other media, this crudity of manufacture remained almost a
constant. There can be little doubt that it was, and is,
deliberate.

The earth-mother is most characteristically depicted as a
roughly shaped piece of the earth itself. Unlike the detailed
and often massive stone sculptures of the deities of the hieratic
pantheon, these images are temporary, disposable, abbreviated
symbols. At certain recurring festivals today, goddess images
are made for the occasion, then submerged in the river and
dissolved when the rites are finished: earth and water mixed,
shaped, and then returned to their original elements, the first
two in the ascent towards the immortal and eternal, the fifth
element. The body ornaments and the special insistence upon
tall headdresses of flowers and plants are, of course, symbols of
the vegetal fertility of the earth. Style and the degree of detail
an artist was prepared to put into such images varied
according to period and place, but the essential concept of a
lump of the earth fashioned into a female form as
personification of the fundamental first element has been
unaltered for thousands of years.

Occasionally the concept has been translated into stone – as
in the powerful image of the *nagna-kabandha*, simply meaning
'naked (headless) torso' (**55**), where the female generative
organs and breasts are prominently displayed, the head
completely replaced by a lotus. The latter feature is probably
derived, as is the entire sculpture, from terracottas: many early
clay figurines are backed by a stalk which blossoms into a lotus
flower on top of the head. Most frequently, when a fertility
goddess appears as an image in a temple, she is seen as a
serene and attractive figure, lacking the elemental force of the
earth images from which she derives. The religious importance
of these tiny figurines is immeasurable in all indigenous Indian
cults.

52 Mother Goddess
Sātavāhana period,
3rd century AD
From Ter (Maharashtra)
Terracotta, 5 × 6cm
*London, Trustees of the
British Museum, 1958.10–17.2*

52

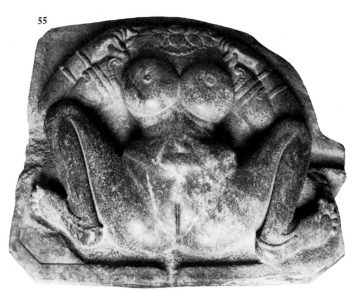

53 Mother Goddess
Shunga period, 1st century BC
From Sar-Dehri (Pakistan)
Terracotta, 25cm high
London, Victoria and Albert Museum,
IM 29–1939

54 Brahmānī
Maitraka period, *c.* 6th century
From Shamalagi (Gujarat)
Schist (greenish), 54 × 39 × 18cm
Baroda, Museum and Picture Gallery, 5130

55 Lotus-headed female figure
(*nagna-kabandha*)
Early Chālukya period, *c.* 8th century
From Sangameshvara (Andhra Pradesh)
Basalt, 91 × 104 × 13cm
Alampur, Archaeological Museum, 52
This image was laid horizontally and served
as an object of devotion. The libations
poured on the body were carried away by a
channel and spout.

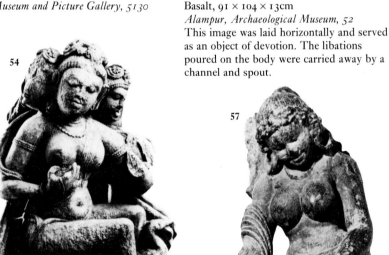

56 Ambikā, the Mother
Early Chālukya period, 7th century
From Aihole (Karnataka)
Sandstone, 160 × 110 × 42cm
Aihole, Archaeological Museum
A popular domestic deity of the Jains, Ambikā is sometimes
considered the consort of Nemināṭha, the twenty-second
Tīrthankara (see **343**). Ambikā rides a lion, and often
holds a child. Here, she is surrounded by attendant females,
behind are *shāla* trees, emblems of fertility.

57 Lady in a bending pose
Maitraka period, 6th century
From Shamalagi (Gujarat)
Schist, 60 × 21 × 20cm
New Delhi, National Museum, 69.137

58 Mother Goddess (*not illustrated*)
Maurya period, 3rd–2nd century BC
From Taxila (Pakistan)
Terracotta, 12cm high
London, Victoria and Albert Museum,
IS 23–1951

59 Mother Goddess (*see p. 50*)
Shunga period, 2nd century BC
From Mathura (Uttar Pradesh)
Terracotta, 26 × 9cm
Mathura, Government Museum, 66.2

60 Two rings (*murtajiganj*) (*not*
illustrated)
3rd century AD
Stone, 5 × 5 × 2cm and 6 × 6 × 2cm
Patna, Directorate of Archaeology and
Museums, Bihar

YAKSHĪS

The proliferation of vegetal life that springs from earth and water, the first two elements of nature, is most powerfully and majestically represented by the tree, and the spirit and personality of the tree is personified and defined by two classes of female figure: the *yakshī* and the *shālabhanjikā*. Archaic male earth-spirits of giant size and power were called *yakshas*. Their female counterparts are the *yakshīs*, the sinuous and seductive in-dwelling genii of trees, their bodies expressive of curved and burgeoning arborescence. A *yakshī* is of the nature of the tree in itself, not as a symbol, for both *yakshas* and *yakshīs* were regarded as inhabiting the sacred tree of a village, which it was necessary to hang with garlands and to which offerings of food and flowers were made.

Yakshas and *yakshīs* were local divinities believed to influence a particular community or village. Their relationship with the inhabitants was therefore immediate and intimate: they would protect, but only if properly propitiated; if ignored or disrespectfully treated, they were capable of terrible acts of destruction – what we would see as natural catastrophes or the results of human negligence. When the first stone images of them were made, they were represented as giants with massive physiques of implacable and ominous stillness. This quiet, threatening power can be felt still in the head of a *yakshī* (**63**), despite the attempts at beautification – the intricate headdress with pendant flower, the full and rounded contours of the face. The sexual grace and power with which the standing figures are charged is in part a representation of fertility; but it is also a complimentary disguise designed to assure these powerful forces that they are thought to be beautiful and are suitably admired. Flattery, whether verbal or visual, is a part of the propitiation process.

A frequently recurring motif is that of a woman beneath the

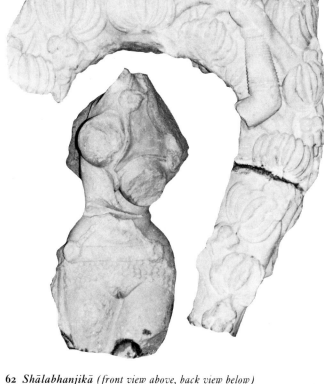

62 *Shālabhanjikā (front view above, back view below)*
Shunga period, 1st century BC. From Sanchi (Madhya Pradesh)
Sandstone, 73 × 31cm (figure), 94 × 84cm (with frame)
Sanchi, Archaeological Museum, 2794/2867
This figure, from the great *stūpa* at Sanchi, clutches a *shāla* branch.

61 *Yakshī*
Shunga period, 1st century BC
From Taxila (Pakistan)
Terracotta, 15cm high
London, Victoria and Albert Museum,
IS 18–1951

63 *Yakshī*
Shunga period, 2nd century BC
From Bharhut (Madhya Pradesh)
Red sandstone, 25 × 11 × 11cm
New Delhi, National Museum, 75.428

64 **Dancing** *yakshī*
Shunga period, 2nd century BC
From Mathura (Uttar Pradesh)
Red sandstone, 196 × 35 × 27cm
Mathura, Government Museum, J.2

65 *Yakshī (not illustrated)*
Shunga period, 2nd century BC
From Bharhut (Madhya Pradesh)
Sandstone, 57 × 57 × 7cm
Ramvan, Tulsi Sangrahalaya

66 *Yakshī*
Kushāna period, *c.* 3rd century AD
From Jaisingapore, near Mathura (Uttar
Pradesh)
Red sandstone, 89 × 18 × 18cm
Mathura, Government Museum, J.12

67 *Shālabhanjikā (see p. 53)*
Kushāna period, *c.* 1st–2nd century AD
From Sonkh, near Mathura (Uttar Pradesh)
Red sandstone, 77 × 25 × 7cm
Mathura, Government Museum, SO–IV.27

68 *Shālabhanjikā*
Kushāna period, 2nd century AD
From Mathura (Uttar Pradesh)
Red sandstone, 66 × 18 × 16cm
New Delhi, National Museum, J.55

69 **Girl playing with balls** *(see p. 57)*
Solankī period, 11th century
From Nagda (Rajasthan)
White marble, 101 × 33 × 22cm
New Delhi, National Museum, 71.L/5
This image and **71** both served as inclined
brackets sheltered beneath the eaves of the
temple porch, or located within the
columned hall. Typical is the cutting
through of the stone to permit an almost
three-dimensional modelling.

70 Dancing girl
Kākatīya period, 12th century
From Telasang (Karnataka)
Green schist, 138 × 40 × 20cm
Bangalore, Government Museum and Venkatappa Art Gallery, 179

71 Girl
Chandella period, 11th century
From Khajuraho (Madhya Pradesh)
Sandstone, 62 × 18 × 25cm
Khajuraho, Archaeological Museum, 1316

foliage of a tree. Some of these figures may represent *yakshīs*, but by no means all: some portray Queen Māyā giving birth to her son Siddhārtha who was to become the Buddha, while others depict mother goddesses of the Hindu or Jain pantheon. The classic figure upon which these images are based is that of a beautiful young woman raising one hand to grasp a branch of the tree while standing on one foot, bending the supporting leg so that the other foot touches the trunk, or even twining her other leg around it. In this image, the tree represents the dormant male principle and the girl the quickening power of nature. The sculptures derive from a game, possibly an ancient spring ritual, played by young girls which virtually amounted to flirting with certain trees such as the *ashoka* and the *shāla*. In reaching up to break off twigs from the trees, the girl's feet would strike the trunk, and this, it was believed, would waken a deciduous tree from its dormant state and cause it to blossom. The game became so popular and applicable in such a wide range of religious connotations that the sculpting of it became stereotyped and the image was given the generic name of *shālabhanjikā*, meaning 'she who breaks [a branch of] the *shāla* tree'.

Many sculptures of women and young girls in seductive postures appear to have been copied from real life, though often idealized. Nor are they all depicted as partners in the numerous combinations and permutations of sexual activity described in the *Kāmasūtra* and tantric manuals. Hundreds of beautiful women may be represented, standing or sitting, self-absorbed or exhibiting their spectacular charms, each quite alone, on a single temple. They are to be seen talking to a pet bird, writing, dressing (**71**), applying make-up with the aid of a mirror, or frankly flirting with the observer. The models upon which these sculptures were based were undoubtedly ladies of high birth, and they can be generally categorized as types drawn from the heroines of famous Sanskrit plays and epics known to all the worshippers approaching the temple. The brave heroine pining for her warrior-lover who is away fighting is a typical and popular example; she is often interpreted as the human spirit longing for union with God, her own sexual attraction drawing the attention of the devotee first to her figure, then to her plight, and so to his own mortal condition. Others are symbolic lures, representing in sexual terms the spiritual rewards of a pure life. Simple, idle pastimes, such as playing with a ball (**69**), could be turned to triple advantage by the sculptor to display sexuality, poetic eroticism and religious allegory. This sculpture is unquestionably a minor masterpiece. The activity of the sport turns the woman's body at the waist through a full ninety degrees, with no suggestion of unnaturalness, in an overstated but wholly credible display of supple sexuality, thus turning the game into an erotic act. As the sculptor must have known, one of India's greatest poets and dramatists, Kālidāsa, had composed a verse some five or six centuries earlier in which the ball is made the vehicle of a lover's desire:

> *Hit by the hand, soft as a lotus, of my mistress,*
> *   You drop, and drop, and rise again –*
> *Little ball, I know your heart,*
> *   It is as if you fail each time to kiss her lip.*

In fact, the posture of the girl is precisely that of a *shālabhanjikā*. In her playfulness, this girl is an essential part of nature, of *māyā*, her unwitting wantonness the very power of *prakriti*, the inherent dynamism of the wild.

72 Yamunā
Gurjara-Pratihāra period, 8th–10th century
Stone, 64 × 46 × 18cm
New Delhi, National Museum, 68.53

73 Gaṅgā
Gurjara-Pratihāra period, 8th–10th century
Stone, 66 × 41 × 28cm
New Delhi, National Museum, 238

RIVER GODDESSES

The two most sacred rivers of northern India are personified as goddesses who take their names from the rivers, the Gaṅgā (Ganges) and Yamunā (Jumna). The territory between the two rivers – the *dōāb* as it is known in Urdu, meaning literally '[the land between] the two waters' – up to their confluence at Allahabad, was considered the holy heartland of Sanskritik culture. After their union, the river is called the Gaṅgā and flows on to the Bay of Bengal. The territory on either side of this river system, from coast to coast, became known as Āryāvarta, the aryan homeland.

The divinity of this most holy river, Gaṅgā, is depicted as a beautiful young woman standing upon an aquatic creature. In early sculpture, this appears quite clearly in the shape of the river alligator with long thin jaws; still the river's most deadly carnivore, it attacks cattle and man as well as smaller prey. Soon, however, the sculptors transformed it into a mythical beast, the *makara*. Often the goddess Gaṅgā holds a lotus in one hand, the most beautiful – and symbolically charged – of the water flowers. She thus demonstrates her dominance over all animal and vegetal life in the river. Her other principal attribute is a waterpot. This objectifies the water itself as distinct from the river, and represents the small quantities taken from the river at sacred bathing places – for example Varanasi (Benares) – by pilgrims who live far from its banks. In domestic shrines, phials or pots of this water are kept near the household gods; it is regarded as the most holy and

purifying element, for the waters descend from the sacred Himalaya itself, the snow-covered mountain home of the gods.

Small images of the river goddesses, especially of Gaṅgā, were integrated with sculptures and bronzes of other major deities such as Shiva in the role of 'Upholder of the Gaṅgā'. The river is said to have originated in the sky (as the Mandākinī, a celestial current known to the West as the Milky Way), and the impact of its descent on to the earth to have been broken by the long hair of the god, which is often compared to the ranges of the Himalayas, in which the goddess Gaṅgā therefore sometimes appears. Images of the two main river goddesses, Gaṅgā and Yamunā (the latter being depicted standing upon a turtle), flank the entrances to many Hindu temples. The devotee therefore passes between the two rivers on the approach to his deity in the sanctuary, so setting himself symbolically in the holy land of the *dōāb*, wherever the temple may in reality be situated.

Temporary clay images of Gaṅgā are made at festival times, as they are of the earth-mother; at the end of the ceremonies these are immersed in the river she symbolizes to dissolve and merge with her own element, the second in the spiritual ascent.

Originally also a river goddess, Sarasvatī came to be identified with the Vedic goddess Vāch, the personification of speech. Though sometimes associated with the Hindu god Brahmā, both as his daughter and as his consort, Sarasvatī is worshipped as the patroness of speech, song and wisdom. Accordingly she carries a manuscript and the *vīṇā* (stringed musical instrument).

74

76

76 Lakshmī
Late Gupta period, 6th–7th century
From northern India
Copper seal, 7 × 6cm
London, Victoria and Albert Museum, IM 496, A–1924

74 Gangā
Gurjara-Pratihāra period, 8th–10th century
From central India
Sandstone, 40 × 34cm
London, Trustees of the British Museum, 1967.2–15.1

75

GODDESS OF PLENTY

Just as the tree reaches from the ground toward heaven, the lotus plant (one of the words for which is *pankaja*, literally 'born from the mud') grows from darkness in the bed of a river or pool to blossom in the light and air on the surface of the water. In this sense, the lotus is a transition symbol but, unlike the *nāgas*, it is not dangerous and is inherently beautiful. The sight of a lotus is always auspicious, and it is incorporated in temple sculpture as part of the profusion of the sacred, primeval forest. It is also represented as the throne of gods and goddesses, whose haloes often assume the shape of the lotus blossom, and is held by several deities of the Jain, Buddhist and Hindu pantheons. Real lotuses are among the principal offerings made to images of these deities; lotus petals may be strewn upon magical and meditational diagrams (*yantras* or *mandalas*), which are drawn in accordance with a pattern based upon the shape of a lotus. It is ubiquitous in Indian art, both as a living expression of the beauty of nature and as a literary or visual metaphor, expressing the radiance of a beautiful woman or the spiritual ascendancy of a god.

The most frequently used Sanskrit word for a lotus is *padma*. Its feminine form, Padmā, is another name of the goddess Lakshmī, known throughout India as the embodiment of good fortune and victory. Also known as Shrī, meaning 'The Radiant', 'The Glorious', 'Good Fortune', Lakshmī is best known in the Hindu pantheon as the chief wife of the god Vishnu, among whose hand-held attributes is the lotus.

75 Sarasvatī
Pāla period, 10th century
From Nalanda (Bihar)
Bronze, 15 × 9 × 7cm
New Delhi, National Museum

77 Lakshmī
Kushāna period, 2nd century AD
From Mathura (Uttar Pradesh)
Sandstone, 123 × 28 × 25cm
New Delhi, National Museum, B.89

78 Gods praying to Lakshmī *(not illustrated)*
From a *Santa Rasa* manuscript
Pahari school, *c.* 1775
From Kangra, 27 × 35cm
New Delhi, National Museum, 58.18/1

79 Jyeshthā
Pallava period, 8th century
From Tamil Nadu
Granite, 141 × 100 × 35cm
New Delhi, National Museum, 59.153/357

Although Shrī-Lakshmī has no hierarchical cult of her own, she is, like the lotus motif, ubiquitous in Indian sacred architectural relief. In early Buddhist sculpture she frequently appears standing upon a lotus, bathed with water from two pitchers held in the trunks of a pair of flanking elephants; she is, of course, intimately associated with water, the element connected with knowledge and mental power.

Lakshmī is known at the popular level as an idea or influence, not unlike the gambler's 'Lady Luck', and she could influence a game of dice in which a whole kingdom might be at stake, for gambling was taken very seriously among the aristocracy. Her influence was also felt in agriculture, for she could affect the crops, being associated with water, and so with fertility and the seasonal rainfall which might inundate the fields or leave them parched; here, her power approached that of fate. She often appears on doors and lintels of Hindu and Jain temples to ward off the influence of her dark sister, Alakshmī, the bringer of misfortune.

Jyeshthā, the goddess of sloth, is often thought of as the equivalent of Alakshmī. Her name in Sanskrit means the eldest, or chief wife, and she has the least attraction but the greatest authority in a royal household. Her chief emblem is a broomstick, which is seen rising behind her left arm (**79**); her animal cognizances are the ass and the crow, the bird of death. Today in eastern India she is virtually identical with Sītalā, goddess of smallpox, the associate of Yama, the god who rules the dead. Fat, ugly and indolent, she is affiliated to none of the major Hindu cults, but exerts her influence through her age and sheer malignancy. Propitiated, rather than worshipped, in order to avert the spell which she may cast, Jyeshthā personifies the fear of those who have lost the vitality of nature and cling merely to the power of age over youth.

80

FLYING FIGURES

Suparna, meaning 'fair-winged', was originally a term used in the *Rig Veda* to describe Garuda, the giant eagle of the sun. The *suparna* later became a class of aerial beings which were depicted with human torsos, bearing offerings of lotus blossoms to honour the symbols of the Buddha. Buddhist texts often refer to imaginary creatures of the sky, such as the *suparnas* and *gandharvas*, materializing to listen to the Buddha's discourses, as did the gods of the *Veda*, who are termed *devas*. A square enclosure was erected on top of Buddhist monuments which served as a place for the gods to alight when they descended to be near the great teacher. From its centre arose a pole with several parasols upon it; these were a mark of respect, for in real life only kings or nobility were shaded by such luxuries. This concern with aerial beings in Buddhism is notable: in relief sculptures they are shown flying to the highest point of a religious monument as if recognizing that air is the most subtle element, closest to transcendence of the material world; and the Buddha himself, imitating the practices of the ancestral seers of the forest, employed yogic techniques, which included control of air within the body, in his search for enlightenment.

Titanic battles in the air are also described in Hindu mythology, and it is no mean achievement of the Indian sculptors that they could depict with realism the cumbrous mounts of the warring gods – the elephant of Indra, the humped bull of Shiva – riding through the sky with weightless grace. Even the bodies of the protagonists, locked in aerial combat, were curved and streamlined as if they had themselves taken on the quality of the air in turmoil. The classic anatomy of the gods in sculpture is not muscular. They express life – or, rather, immortality – through a supple fullness of contour, for they appear in human form so that men may perceive them. But they are not physical beings; they assume a corporeal shape which is moulded from within and from without by the element of air – the first element they encounter in their descent from heaven, and the last with which man identifies himself in his spiritual ascent to their presence.

80 Winged being (*suparna* or *gandharva*)
Kushāna period, 1st century AD
From Mathura (Uttar Pradesh)
Red sandstone, 45 × 58cm
Lucknow, State Museum, J.106

81 Flying couple (Vidyādhara)
Maitraka period, 6th–7th century
From Sondani, near Mandasor (Madhya Pradesh)
Sandstone, 133 × 86 × 30cm
New Delhi, National Museum, 51.94

81

82 Flying female warriors *(section)*
Solankī period, 11th–12th century
From western India
Yellow sandstone, 32 × 129 × 21cm
London, Victoria and Albert Museum, IM 54–1916/55–1916
This lobed arch, carved in one piece, was originally suspended over a doorway leading to the columned hall of a temple.

83 Flying female warriors *(see p. 55)*
Chandella period, 11th century
From Khajuraho (Madhya Pradesh)
Sandstone, 33 × 31 × 22cm
Khajuraho, Archaeological Museum, 1821

82

84

84 Purūravas (or Vikrama) and Ūrvashī
Gupta period, 5th–6th century
From Ahicchatra (Uttar Pradesh)
Terracotta, 67 × 67 × 14cm
New Delhi, National Museum, 62.239

85

85 *Mithuna* (couple)
Chandella period, late 10th century
From central India
Red sandstone, 58cm high
London, Trustees of the British Museum, 1964.4–13.1

86 *Mithuna* (couple) *(see p. 54)*
Chandella period, 11th century
From Khajuraho (Madhya Pradesh)
Sandstone, 46 × 24 × 22cm
Khajuraho, Archaeological Museum, 1342

THE CELESTIAL COUPLE

Couples engaged in love-making (*mithunas*) are as recurrent a theme in later Indian temple sculpture as vegetation motifs. Humanity displays its own sexual promiscuity, as vital and prolific as the riot of reproduction seen in the animal and vegetal environment: humanity consists in being a part of the pattern. Here man and woman see themselves equally capable of enjoyment and tenderness and the transcendence of self through union with each other. Most such sculptures rarely appear in isolation; most often, they are integrated in friezes which run around a temple wall on three sides. The visual rhythms generated by the varied postures and modes of love-making reflect the passionate driving force of nature. Some of these relief carvings undoubtedly represent tantric initiation rituals, but the overwhelming majority of them are simply reflections and projections of human desires; the ritual element lies in the act of love itself.

A different kind of erotic self-transcendence is suggested by the terracotta plaque (**84**) which represents an aristocratic young man out hunting, carrying a bow and mounted on his horse. He encounters a mysterious female figure with serpent-like hoods above her head who rises from behind a lotus with her right hand raised in the gesture of reassurance with which images of divinities frequently greet their worshippers. He is, apparently, human, while she is clearly one of the spirits that inhabit the lake or river along the bank of which he rides. One of the most famous of such encounters between a mortal and a spirit is that recounted in the myth concerning Purūravas and Ūrvashī. A *gandharva*, or, in other versions, an *apsaras* (a sky-dwelling nymph who frequently descends to visit lakes) assumed a human form with the name Ūrvashī and married a mortal man called Purūravas, who was infatuated with her beauty. She set out certain conditions, which he accepted, before their union was consummated; but Purūravas was tricked into breaking one of these conditions, whereupon she vanished leaving him alone and heartbroken. The fact that he knew she was pregnant added to his distress. He roamed about the countryside searching for her, and one day found himself on the banks of a lake full of lotuses and geese. One of the geese was Ūrvashī, who had changed her form yet again. She recognized him and, rising before him in her beautiful human form, warned him of the danger of living with a mortal woman. She refused to return to him in such a form, but did agree to meet him at the same place after the birth of their child. The other *gandharvas* offered to grant him one wish; on the advice of Ūrvashī, he asked to be transformed into a *gandharva* himself so that he might always be with the nymph he loved. By means of a protracted magical fire ritual his wish was fulfilled, and the lovers were finally united.

Numerous interpretations have been placed upon this ancient story, but it remains clear that the only connection between the female spirit and the man was love, of a very human kind, and their child, a son; it is also notable that it is the man who represents struggling, sweating, passionate humanity, while the cool, transcendent state is embodied by female beauty. In general terms, it might be said that all the alluring female figures that pose erotically upon the temple walls are in the role of Ūrvashī the nymph, while the footsore devotee walking around the shrine and gazing up at them re-enacts the toils of Purūravas in the hope of self-transcendence.

87

87 Mother and child (Birth of Krishna?)
Kalachuri period, *c.* 10th century
From Gurgi (Madhya Pradesh)
Sandstone, 32 × 47 × 10cm
Bhopal, State Museum, 797

88

88 Pūrneshvarī
Pāla period, late 12th century
From Jaynagar (Bihar)
Black basalt, 82 × 37cm
London, Victoria and Albert Museum,
IS 71–1880

89 Indrānī *(not illustrated)*
Gupta period, 5th century
From Shahabad (Bihar)
Stone, 53 × 31 × 10cm
Varanasi, Bharat Kala Bhavan Museum,
26.362

MOTHER AND CHILD

Woman as mother is represented, in secular and deified forms, in the sculpture of all the religions of India. Despite the deification of womanhood in this role, however, it is a male child that is desired. The protagonist of conventional Indian legend and epic is masculine, although the faithful wife – beautiful, modest, self-effacing but strong-willed – is his necessary counterpart. The power of women is usually exercised behind the scenes, except in the literature and imagery of those *shākta* and tantric cults which have deliberately elevated the female principle above that of the male. It was the fortitude and devotion to the convention of an ideal wife – who called her husband *pati*, lord – that drove her to become a *satī*, a good and true wife, by entering her husband's funeral pyre to burn alive with his corpse rather than continue living the wretched life of a widow. Commemorative *satī*-stones were often set up to such exemplary suicides. To be barren, to bear only female children, to have no husband, to exist as a widow: these were the main fears of Indian women. The goddesses of abundance, such as Pūrneshvarī, were depicted clasping, suckling, surrounded by sturdy baby boys; these were the ideals which were worshipped.

Women in India were thus subjected to enormous and sometimes tormenting social pressures, and these in turn grew from society's perception of nature. This is represented in all its fundamental power in the threshold slab (**90**). On the left is the wild proliferation of *prakriti*, and next to it one of those creations of the human imagination, part leonine and part vegetal, which express the ferocity of nature both in man and in his environment. On the right, flanked by two women, sits a goddess surrounded by flowers and children, making the gesture of wish-fulfilment (*varada-mudrā*) with her right hand. She is offering all this abundance to her devotee, who desires to be like her – an expression of, and a channel for, the creative energies of the world of *māyā*.

90

90 Mother and child, monster mask and tree *(detail)*
Solankī period, 11th century
From western India
Yellow sandstone, 27 × 88cm
London, Victoria and Albert Museum, IM 84–1916
This carved stone once served as a threshold for a doorway to a temple sanctuary.

92

92 Couples, monster masks and entwined *nāgas*
Gurjura-Pratihāra period, 8th century
From Abaneri (Rajasthan)
Grey sandstone, 29 × 156 × 39cm
New Delhi, National Museum, 69.133
This fragment was once the lintel over the entrance of a temple sanctuary, which explains the crowded juxtaposition of many decorative, and protective, motifs.

91 Kubera
Kushāna period, 2nd century AD
From Ahicchatra (Uttar Pradesh)
Sandstone, 96 × 45 × 35cm
New Delhi, National Museum, 59.530/2

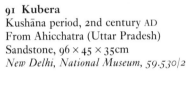

PROTECTORS OF EARTHLY TREASURE

Kubera is a very ancient, indigenous Indian god of chthonic character, regarded as chief of the *yakshas*, and guardian of the precious metals and gemstones found under the earth. He later became the god of wealth. Something of his mysterious and potentially dangerous *yaksha* nature still adheres to him, however. According to legend, he was a half-brother of Rāvana, the demon-king of Lanka who fought Rāma, the incarnation of Vishnu; when Rāvana conquered his territories, Kubera sided with Rāma, and so was admitted to the company of the Hindu gods. Partly due to his archaic origins, and partly because he embodies the idea of wealth, he is depicted as very fat, often seated like a stunted ogre under a tree, beneath which treasure was thought to be hidden. Being essentially an earth-god, he is associated with the fertility of the soil as well as with the mineral wealth which lies under it.

In the later art of Buddhism and Hinduism, Kubera becomes the guardian of the northern quarter of the universe (see p. 122). He is also connected with Ganesha (see p. 223), and the Buddhist god of wealth, Jambhala, both of whom share with Kubera the characteristic pot-belly. In turn, both Kubera and Ganesha are related to the impish pot-bellied dwarfs, the *ganas*, usually attendant on Shiva (see p. 223). But the *ganas* have a life of their own independent from the great cult god; they are celebrated for their sense of humour, sometimes bordering on the obscene, and their love of music and dance (see **472**).

91

मनुष्यस्य विश्वजगत्स्थानम्

3

MAN IN THE COSMOS

This section deals with man's orientation in the universe. In Indian thought, religious imagery and ritual, the two questions, 'Where am I?' and 'Who am I?' are answered at two levels. Man is where the forces that sustain the universe place him. But by personifying them, he can to a degree control them, and so locate himself at the point at which he needs to be in specific circumstances. If the forces of the universe are personified in the forms of gods, demons and other supernatural beings, they can be manipulated in various ways. For example, they can be turned into the *dramatis personae* of mythological cycles in which cosmic conditions favourable to man prevail. As images, these forces may be selectively placated by worship, in order to manoeuvre the worshipper into a position where certain forces predominate. The place or location desired by an individual is not, of course, a geographical one. The 'where' of this question ranges from caste position to a spiritual condition harmonious with the whole universe. Thus entire communities may upgrade their social status by exchanging one set of gods for another, with a corresponding alteration in their mores and ritual practices. Or an individual in a temple, wishing to be in the most advantageous 'position' from which to approach his chief deity in the sanctum, is secure in the knowledge that various minor gods are properly arranged in a coordinated series around the outer walls of the temple, which is thereby temporarily and in ritual terms the centre of the universe.

The identity of man, the 'who?' of the two major questions, is answered at the social and the psychological levels. In social terms, man belongs to a certain caste (*varna*) within a complex and self-sustaining system of social orders forming in aggregate – and ideally – a hierarchy at the temporal level which is the perfect reflex of the forces at work within, and which shapes the greater organization of the universe. A balance between human society and cosmic order is vital to every kind of stability which permits existence to continue, which is why caste mobility is such a delicate and ritually dangerous human endeavour. At the other end of the identity spectrum, everything devolves upon the individual viewed dispassionately as a psycho-physical entity. The potential of the individual in spiritual terms is unlimited. He can surpass the gods, using them as mere stepping stones to a transcendent state which is permanent, whereas the gods are, ultimately, perishable, although they are known as the immortals (*amānushya*). More, the potential within man is coextensive with the universe, and this vastness of the self can be cultivated and realized through yogic techniques which use the body and intellect and will as instruments to total liberation from all temporal conditioning, known as *moksha*.

All phenomena apprehensible by the five senses belong to the seeming world of reality, to *māyā*, which is composed of the basic range of elements. These may be differently disposed, however, in different individuals and objects. A perfect balance is desirable, and this man can achieve through his own efforts, as a springboard from which to launch himself out of the conditioned world into eternity. But it is not he who emerges. In treating the body as an instrument, the real self within it is separated, and it is that which finds liberation.

The personification of the elements as gods, as man in his fullest nature, as symmetrical balances of forces, is therefore essential to the purpose of mankind in the universal scheme. The ways in which the elements as orientation points in the religious quest for liberation are presented and used will be clarified in this section of the exhibition.

THE GUARDIANS OF SPACE

Just as figural representations of the forces of nature expressed the vital powers of the earth and its treasures, so the actual elements that constitute the natural world – air, fire, water, earth, light etc. – were themselves personified. Indian mythological texts conceived these elements in the form of particular deities, frequently grouped together as the eight regents of the directions of space (*dikpālas*). The personified elements are identified with the divinities invoked in the *Rig Veda*. Although their symbolic functions have altered through the millennia, they preserve their essential Vedic character, so strong is Indian conservatism.

Varuna was the god of waters (in the sense of oceans, rivers and rainfall); he also gazed down like the sun upon the whole pattern of nature and man's behaviour as part of it, alert to any transgression of its proper balance, and forever ready to seize with a noose the perpetrator of any imbalance in the world. The noose was used as a symbol with which Yama (the ruler of the dead) plucked wrongdoers from the world of the living into his death-kingdom. In this example (**97**), Varuna is seated upon a *makara*, the imaginary composite aquatic creature, the noose raised behind his right shoulder, against a background of rainclouds, as if flying with the storm; he is accompanied by his consort, Gaurī (though she may also represent the rivers Ganges and Jumna). A pedestal in the form of a lotus completes the aquatic symbolism.

This image of Varuna would not have been worshipped as the principal deity in a temple, but set into the western wall, for this god had been transformed into the guardian of the west, one of the eight guardians of the directions of space (the *dikpālas*). Such directional deities orientated the temple correctly in symbolic terms: thus the waters, representing the primeval state before creation and personified by Varuna, should be at the back of the temple structure which in itself was intended to imitate the cosmos, and the back of most temples is the west wall, as most entrances face the dawn. In this way, the personified elements were employed to set man in an environment which artificially conformed to the patterns governing the universe. With the loss through the ages of the visionary experiences of the ancestral seers in the forest, among the elements in their natural condition, the temple became necessary as a three-dimensional reconstruction of their understanding. And water, second in the elemental hierarchy, first in the cosmogenetic process, was an essential part of their knowledge and was symbolically rebuilt in stone, just as the forest itself was imitated in the sculptured foliage across the temple façades.

In the Vedic age, Indra was the war-leader of the gods, who was also connected with rainfall and hence with the thunderstorm – he wields the *vajra*, a weapon symbolizing the thunderbolt. As a leader, he was in later times placed in the east, at the head of the guardians of space, also known as the guardians of the directions, or guardians of the quarters.

Also associated with forward or eastward movement was Agni, the fire god. In the sacrificial arena the fire-pits were always in front of the priests, who made offerings into them to be carried upward to the gods. As a directional deity, therefore, Agni was placed on Indra's right, in the south-east quarter. More subtle than water, and said to rise from it as the sun arises from the eastern sea, fire is the element which mediates between man and the gods. Figures of the fire god frequently represent him holding the sacrificial ladles with which oblations were offered into the flames, as if he were himself a priest – as indeed he is described in the opening verse of the *Rig Veda* – and accompanied by a goat or ram, the animal most often sacrificed.

It is a following wind which propels ships across the sea or down the rivers, which moves the water and the forest, which strengthens the fire and drives it forward, which brings the rainclouds. So Vāyu, Vedic god of air and the wind, came to be stationed to the right of Varuna, in the north-west. Unlike fire, air is limitless, effortlessly crossing the boundaries which contain land and sea, earth and water. Invisible, it pervades all that lives and without it all would die; it pervades all space, crossing the oceans and continents, and is higher than the reach of fire, the flight paths of migrating birds or the clouds. Air is the breath of life (*prāna*), through the control of which man attains a state of consciousness which is at one with the empyrean.

93

93 Yama
Maitraka period, 8th century
From Rajasthan
Stone, 97 × 48 × 19cm
New Delhi, National Museum, 31

94   95   96

94 Agni
Eastern Ganga period,
11th century
From Bhubaneshwar (Orissa)
Chlorite, 63 × 37 × 26cm
*Bhubaneshwar, Orissa State
Museum, AY–195*

95 Indra
Eastern Ganga period,
11th century
From Bhubaneshwar (Orissa)
Chlorite, 63 × 39 × 26cm
*Bhubaneshwar, Orissa State
Museum, AY–196*

96 Vāyu
Eastern Ganga period,
11th century
From Bhubaneshwar (Orissa)
Chlorite, 57 × 32 × 22cm
*Bhubaneshwar, Orissa State
Museum, AY–193*

97 Varuna and consort
(not illustrated)
Rāshtrakūta period, 8th century
From Karnataka
Trap rock, 84 × 56cm
*Bombay, Prince of Wales
Museum, 75*

98 Agni *(not illustrated)*
Stone, 81 × 47 × 29cm
Madras, Government Museum

99 Vāyu *(not illustrated)*
Stone, 82 × 44 × 27cm
Madras, Government Museum

100 Varuna *(not illustrated)*
Chandella period, 11th century
From Ajayagardha
(Uttar Pradesh)
Stone, 65 × 30 × 16cm
*Varanasi, Bharat Kala Bhavan
Museum, 20.768*

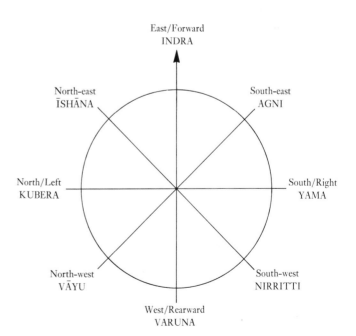

Above: The Guardians of Space include three of the personified
elements: water (Varuna), fire (Agni), air (Vāyu); the remaining two
are earth (Bhū, the circle of the horizon) and the transcendent fifth,
ākāsha (the vertical axis through the centre point).

PLANETS AND THE ZODIAC

The clearest indication that man made himself the object controlled by his own symbolic world lies in the astrological figures which are found in most Indian temples: the devotee consults, as a frame of reference which he allows to govern his life, a set of celestial bodies including the sun and the eclipser of the sun, all of them personified in human shape. The *navagrahas*, as the nine planets are called, are rarely the focus of cult worship, rather they serve as protectors of the natural world, and by extension, the whole universe. In these roles they are placated by those desiring peace and prosperity, ample rains for crops, nourishment and long life.

The most important of the planets is the sun (Sūrya). The idea of the god riding in a chariot drawn by seven horses was already well formulated in the earliest Vedic texts, and from the later Epics it is clear that a solar cult flourished in early India. At that time the sun was regarded as a symbol of the supreme soul, the creator of the universe, the source of all light, warmth, life and knowledge. First represented by emblems such as a chariot wheel, later the sun appears in human form riding in a chariot, images closely conforming to ancient Vedic invocations. In the early centuries of the Christian era, however, the cult of Sūrya was strongly influenced by the Zoroastrian mode of sun and fire worship and Sūrya was depicted clothed in foreign garments, such as a long tunic, girdle and high boots.

Sūrya's attendants include the legless charioteer Aruna, symbolizing the dawn, and his two wives, variously known as Ushas, 'Dawn', and Pratyūsha, 'Twilight'. Images of Sūrya show him standing erect, holding lotus blossoms in his two hands. In an example from eastern India (**104**), a diminutive Aruna appears beneath Sūrya to guide the seven horses that speed the god through the heavens – the flying tassels of Sūrya's crown conveying the rapid movement; on either side is a consort.

The other planets include the moon (Chandra), Mars, Mercury, Jupiter, Venus, Saturn and two other deities related to the nodes of the moon – Rāhu, the cause of eclipses, and Ketu, the comet. Rāhu is shown with a fierce disposition holding crescent-shaped objects, the moon and the sun; these he devours, causing eclipses (**106**). Ketu is shown with the body of a serpent and holding aloft a tall sword (**107**). Although free-standing sculptures of the lesser planets are rare, figures of them are often incorporated into architectural pieces such as lintels – for example, those at Konarak – where they are evidently intended to bring benefit to both worshipper and temple.

The signs of the Zodiac, imported from the Middle East and Europe are also associated with the planets. The twelve signs (**105**) accord with those of astronomy in the West and are recognized by similar emblems.

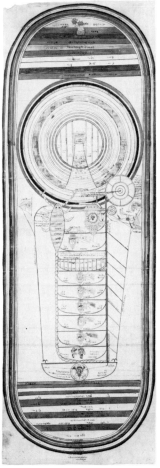

101

101 Diagram of the path of the planets
c. 1750
From eastern Deccan or Tamil Nadu, 160 × 48cm
London, Victoria and Albert Museum, IS 09329
Stripes at the end are the outer limits of the universe; the figure at the top is the *deva* in charge of the cosmos; next are the paths of planets including the sun, then zones showing the zodiac. Two registers also showing the path of the sun are below and further down on either side are two small chariots representing the eclipse cycle.

102 The concentric island – continents of Jain cosmology
From a *Sangrahanī Sūtra* manuscript, folios 16, 17, 18 *(18 not illustrated)*
Jain school, mid-18th century
From western India, each 25 × 12cm
London, Victoria and Albert Museum, IS 35–1971

102

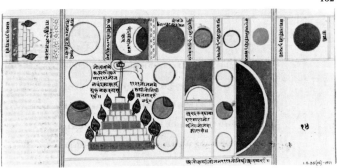

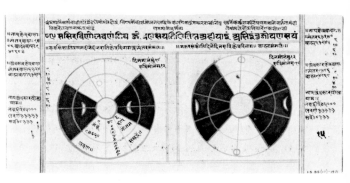

103

104

105

103 The nine planets
From Bihar
Stone, 10 × 17 × 72cm
New Delhi, National Museum, 59.368

104 Sūrya
Pāla period, 12th century
From eastern India
Basalt, 168 × 83cm
London, Victoria and Albert Museum, IS 929

105 Lotus with signs of the Zodiac
Kākatīya or late Chālukya period, 12th century
From Pattancheruvu (Andhra Pradesh)
Granite, 54cm diameter, 24cm high
Hyderabad, State Museum

106

107

106 Rāhu
Eastern Ganga period, 13th century
From Konarak (Orissa)
Basalt, 97 × 51cm
London, Trustees of the British Museum, 1951.7–20–2

107 Ketu
Eastern Ganga period, 13th century
From Konarak (Orissa)
Basalt, 97 × 51cm
London, Trustees of the British Museum, 1951.7–20.3

MAN AS A COSMIC SYMBOL

Man perceived his environment as a whole within which he stood as an essential part. But he also saw it in terms of symbolic values by means of which he might transcend nature, including his own human nature, by establishing a hierarchy among the elements. This meant that he was simultaneously the perceiver and the perceived, the subject and the object, potential god and actual man. This distinction does not correspond to 'the divided self' of modern psychology, for the psyche is not shown to be at war with itself, but rather composed of two facets, one of which is blind or dark while the other perceives the whole problem of the human condition clearly. Beyond these two moieties within man stands the *brahman* which is the constant, undecaying reality behind the world of appearances. The bright, perceptive half of the self, the *ātman* (meaning 'the breath', 'the life principle'), is of the same nature as the *brahman*; a man can therefore merge the two – his individual soul with the universal spirit – and so achieve immortality.

In the profuse world of nature, of *māyā*, the animal man is an expression of *prakriti*, the ever self-reproducing force of nature; here, man is the object of the workings of nature. He perceives as any animal perceives, with his five senses, motivated by instinct which is *prakriti*, not his independent self, in action.

But he can perceive, too, the fact that this world of nature is a painted screen upon which a likeness of himself appears as part of the pattern of *māyā*, hiding the ultimate source of *prakriti* and of himself. Such a perception cannot stem from blind instinct. It is, therefore, a higher awareness, and exercising it makes man the subject who perceives not only his environment, but his lower self as well, as object.

Through the operation of this duality, man is his own witness. This interiorization of responsibility for one's actions is an advance over the old Vedic teachings according to which it was a separate god, Varuna, who was the constant witness and judge of human behaviour. By contrast the *Upanishads* teach that the critical act of human perception is that to be made by one's animal self: it must recognize that sense with which a man observes himself, the sense which does not participate in the animal pursuits of the self, but is independent of them.

Having recognized the higher self as the subject, and the lower self as the object, the higher self – the *ātman* – is free to operate and identify with the eternal *brahman*. This self-identification is transcendent reality, where the duality of self, and its loneliness, are abandoned. The state of union with the *brahman* can be achieved in life – through meditation – and is not confined to the moment of death. Those who have attained such a state are the *brahma-vidah*, the knowers of the *brahman*.

So man was both subject and object at various levels of perception. The most significant consequence of this was that man, having attributed symbolic values to certain aspects of his environment, now saw their importance as signs of the higher self's perceptions and projected himself into their midst. Man himself became a symbol.

Hindu images of cosmic man, in the guise of one or other of the gods in human shape, were projections of man as symbol into the existing world of symbols. Many Indian paintings show a man with the centres in his body which are activated in the course of meditation leading to self-transcendence, shown as lotuses or other symbolic shapes: man as a psycho-physical entity is seen as the channel through which the mortal condition is used as a means of transcending itself.

108 Cosmic man
Jain school, late 17th century
287 × 217cm
Jean Claude Ciancimino collection

109 Figure of a cosmic man showing nine subtle centres (*chakra*) of the body (*not illustrated*)
From a *Siddh Siddhānt Paddhati* manuscript, leaf no. 4
Rajasthan school, (VS 1881), *c.* 1824
From Jodhpur, 119 × 45cm
Jodhpur, Maharaja Museum, Umaid Bhavan Palace

110 Figure of the cosmic man supported by the primordial tortoise showing the location of the various worlds (*loka*) comprising the universe (*not illustrated*)
From a *Siddh Siddhānt Paddhati* manuscript, leaf no. 6
Rajasthan school, (VS 1881), *c.* 1824
From Jodhpur, 117 × 43cm
Jodhpur, Maharaja Museum, Umaid Bhavan Palace

108

4

THE FOUR GOALS OF LIFE

How did man integrate his religious view of himself with his place in society? Since Vedic times, the cohesion of the group – whether a family, clan, tribe, alliance or empire – had been a primary concern. In fact, the perpetuation of social identity and religious attainment amounted almost to an obsession. One of the reasons for the importance attributed to the birth of a male descendant was the ritual relationship between the dead – the ancestors in the kingdom of Yama – and the living: only a son could perform the ancestral rites, without which the dead became lost souls who could malign and haunt the world of the living. The son who neglected these rites disgraced his lineage.

It was around the religious aspirations of man that social activities were organized, divided in principle into four phases or aspects of life. These were designed to regulate activity as an internal control, leading the individual morally and spiritually unscathed through his physical dealings with others, so that his religious development might not be impeded. The primary phase was an understanding of *dharma* in its secular sense as duty to class and kin, and the exercise of justice, morality and virtuous and unselfish conduct. This was to regulate the pursuit of the next two goals, which were material gain (*artha*) and sensual enjoyment (*kāma*). The man or woman who was not wholly dedicated to the pursuit of religious ideals – and such people of course constituted the great majority – could then turn to their spiritual concerns (*dharma* in its higher sense) without remorse or any other hindrance resulting from contravention of the moral code (in other words, without having acquired the stain of *karma*). The aim of spiritual pursuit was *moksha*, the fourth phase, meaning escape or liberation from the cycle of rebirth in this world. (*Paintings and small sculptures illustrating dharma, artha and kāma are grouped together under 'Life at Court', and those illustrating moksha and its Buddhist and Jain equivalent, nirvāna, are shown under 'Enlightenment'.*)

DHARMA: SACRED LAW

Dharma has several levels of meaning and its significance varies according to its cult context. As applied to the social order generally, however, it is regarded as a code of conduct pertaining to man simultaneously as a member of one of the four main classes, called *varnas* (priests, warriors, merchants and menials), and as involved in one of the four stages of life, called *āshramas* (as religious student, householder, religious recluse, and, finally, as an old man, a pilgrim without home or destination). This idealized classification and categorization of an individual's lifetime is referred to as the *varnāshrama-dharma*, the 'code of class and stage of life'. The system of *varnas* or classes cannot be applied to the monastic orders of Buddhism or Jainism, which deny caste hierarchies in principle, but it remains a fundamental principle of Hindu society. On the other hand, the ideal of a wandering holy life, if this be an individual's personal *dharma*, is encouraged by Buddhism, Jainism and Hinduism; thus a casteless monk may instruct a prince or a king of the ruling warrior class in matters of warfare and diplomacy.

The two codes of *varna* and *āshrama* are each fourfold; the number four is symbolic of stability, and it was for the sake of social stability that this secular system was devised. In numerological symbolism, however, it is the central fifth element which is most sacred, being the axis upon which all else depends. It was around the religious aspirations of man that these social divisions were organized; in cases of conflict between two loyalties within this system, therefore, it required divine revelation to resolve the problem. This was recognized and made the pivotal point of one of the great epics of India, the *Mahābhārata*. In one of its sections – the *Bhagavad Gītā*, which is probably the most famous of the Hindu scriptures – Prince Arjuna is seen in his war chariot between two armies about to engage in battle. On the opposing side, he recognizes his own kinsmen whom his familial duty forbids him to harm; yet his social status of warrior compels him to fight. As a man he is quite unable to resolve this inner conflict and lays down his bow in an agony of indecision. It is at this point that the fifth element, the divine axis of existence, manifests itself; for Arjuna is a man of principle, obedient to the concept of *dharma*, which appears to have placed him in an impossible situation. His charioteer, Krishna, reveals that he is God incarnate and allows the Prince to see his true divine form, which towers above the battlefield in a blaze of light, consuming those very warriors whom Arjuna feels he cannot fight: it is already accomplished, the slaughter is pre-ordained, and as a member of the warrior class the Prince must fight. His class *dharma* is higher than his concern for his kind. The social structure is more important than individual concerns. Arjuna fights, society is not threatened. The social fabric, with its hierarchies and priorities, is woven around divine principle, and action in accordance with it fulfils the divine destiny of man, however painful this may seem to the individual.

ARTHA: POLITY

Artha can be interpreted in several ways; it may mean an aim or cause, a thing or object, and hence substance and wealth. Among the four goals of life, therefore, it refers to material pursuits and the acquisition of wealth, advantage and power in the temporal sense. Of the four stages of life, it would be in the second, that of responsible householder (*grihastha*) building a reputation and raising children, that *artha* would be the primary pursuit. All classes of men, of course, would pursue it, from the priests (who mostly enjoyed a fairly comfortable life, receiving gifts either in kind or in money for their ministrations) to the mercantile and servile classes.

The class that epitomized the goal of material prestige, however, was the ruling military aristocracy of the warrior class. In fact, there exists a remarkable text called the *Artha Shāstra*, attributed to Kautilya, the minister of the ruler, Chandragupta Maurya; more probably the text in its present form dates from the Gupta period in the 4th or 5th century. The title of the work means 'Treatise on Polity', but its contents may be described more realistically as 'The Science of Material Advantage Through Politics'. It is a textbook for royalty in matters of government, making obsolete much of the former priestly power behind the throne, and dealing quite cynically with matters ranging from politics within a kingdom to urban government, from taxation to spies, from methods of winning in war to prostitution and gambling. Aimed at holding a kingdom together, the *Artha Shāstra* is a prescription for holding on to imperial power. The sculptures illustrated here are mostly demonstrations of this temporal power and its material advantages.

111

114

114 Courtiers, elephants and imps
Ikshvāku period, 3rd–4th century
From Nagarjunakonda (Andhra Pradesh)
Limestone, 36 × 56cm
Nagarjunakonda, Archaeological Museum, 129

115 Royal effigy, possibly of Chashtana, the Kushāna governor (*right*)
Kushāna period, 1st–2nd century AD
From Sarnath (Uttar Pradesh)
Red sandstone, 138 × 62cm
Mathura, Government Museum, 12.212
Excavated from the Kushāna dynastic shrine outside Mathura, this effigy has been attributed to both Huvishka (ruled AD130 and to Chashtana (ruled 1st century AD)

111 King Narasimha and his spiritual preceptor
Eastern Ganga period, 13th century
From Konarak (Orissa)
Carboniferous shale, 79 × 39cm
London, Victoria and Albert Museum, IS 938

112 Vessantara Jātaka (*not illustrated*)
Calcutta, Indian Museum

113 Bali's gift (*not illustrated*)
Stone, 62 × 31 × 13cm
New Delhi, National Museum, 80.1314

116 Horse and warrior
Nāyaka period, 17th century
From southern India
Wood, 87 × 42cm
London, British Museum, 1964.6–18.1

116

117

117 Hunting scene *(both sides of capital illustrated)*
Shunga period, 2nd century BC
From Sarnath (Uttar Pradesh)
Sandstone, 33 × 60cm
Sarnath, Archaeological Museum, 537

117

115

119

119 Hunting scene
Chandella period, 11th century
From Khajuraho (Madhya Pradesh)
Sandstone, 27 × 200 × 34cm
Khajuraho, Archaeological Museum, 1318

118 The intoxicated courtesan, possibly a scene from 'The Little
Clay Cart' (*Mriccha-katikā*)
Kushāna period, 2nd century AD
From Mathura (Uttar Pradesh)
Sandstone, 101 × 82 × 39cm
New Delhi, National Museum, 2800
This scene is sometimes also interpreted as a depiction of drunken
yakshīs, supported by *yaksha* revellers. Here there is a reference to the
liquid essence of fertility, carried in cups. Carved on both sides (*see p.
52*), this slab probably served as a support for a stone drinking bowl.

118

KĀMA: PLEASURE

The third goal of a balanced life, *kāma,* is in the West often
thought to be sexual pleasure; but this is only a part of the
urbane and cultured outlook, only one of the enjoyments of an
educated man. Pleasures which come under the heading of
kāma include, in addition to sexuality, cool and fragrant
surroundings at home, gambling, drama, music, dance,
painting, and all of these together in a religious setting when
festivals were held in the temples for the entertainment of the
gods; in a word – relaxation.

The cultivation of an aesthetic sensibility – whether through
love-making, literary subtleties (in which Sanskrit works
abound), the grace of acting or dancing, or in the colour
schemes of paintings – was considered good and necessary
exercise, helping to attune the mind and senses to the later
spiritual phase of life. The man dedicated to a spiritual search
since his boyhood in the forests, out of touch with urban
civilization, would of course have no training in matters such
as these. It should not be forgotten, however, that the two
greatest men in the tradition of the forest-seers – Siddhārtha
who became the Buddha, and Majāvīra the Jain hero – were
approaching their thirties when they set out for the forests,
having already been trained in *artha* and *kāma,* and having
lived as married men. Abandoning their opulent lives in the
palatial surroundings of the court, both these men searched
within themselves for the spiritual experiences that they later
taught to city dwellers whose life styles were similar to those
led by Siddhārtha and Mahāvīra before they had renounced
the twin pursuits of *artha* and *kāma.*

120

**120 King Narasimha on
a swing**
(*see also p. 58*)
Eastern Ganga period, 13th
century
From Konarak (Orissa)
Chlorite, 87 × 49 × 28cm
*New Delhi, National Museum,
50.185*
Sitting the ruler on a swing
was part of an elaborate
courtly ritual in which the
king gave audience. (Images
of deities, too, are sometimes
brought out of the temple
sanctuary and publicly
displayed in swings.)

121 Female courtiers
Kushāna period, *c.* 2nd century
AD
From Gurgaon (Uttar Pradesh)
Red sandstone, 105 × 29cm
*Mathura, Government Museum,
12.186*

122 Toilet bearer *(not
illustrated)*
Kushāna period, 2nd century AD
From Mathura (Uttar Pradesh)
Stone, 18 × 11 × 16cm
*Varanasi, Bharat Kala Bhavan
Museum, 695*

121

124

124 Head of the Buddha
Gupta period, 5th century
From Mathura (Uttar Pradesh)
Red sandstone, 53cm high
Private collection

123

123 Female courtiers
Kākatīya period, 13th century
From Warangal (Andhra Pradesh)
Basalt, 75 × 58 × 30cm
Hyderabad, State Museum, 3340/A

MOKSHA: LIBERATION

Moksha, the fourth goal, means release, escape, liberation.
What, it was reasoned, can result from worldly activity after
death if not the just rewards or punishments for that activity,
in the same worldly terms? Escape, therefore, from the endless
wheel of birth, death and rebirth became the core of all
salvation doctrines taught by Hinduism, Buddhism and
Jainism alike. The aim of all religious endeavour became
liberation from life itself as experienced through one's untrained
senses. Flight from a reality that was seen as illusory assumed
the aspect of a quest for immortality; this was the only
legitimate goal for one committed to spiritual progress. The
verb from which the noun *moksha* derives is used also to
describe the act of an archer releasing or letting fly an arrow.
If the archer represents the mortal body, the bow is the will,
and the arrow the spirit finally released to home on the target
of eternity.

Despite the differences in technique, doctrine, symbolism
and organization, Hinduism, Buddhism and Jainism basically
offer a key to this final release; or, to put it another way, it is
only those religions that offered this release that have survived
and expanded. It is clear that the concept of *duhkha* – misery
or suffering caused by the human condition – was considered
the essential nature of worldly existence driven by fear. The
methods employed by man to escape from this trap of life on
earth pushed him to the extremes of endurance, as evidenced
in the life of the Buddha, and led him to experience the
fullness of his potential.

राजसभाचार

5

LIFE AT COURT

The collapse of the Gupta Dynasty meant not only the loss of a central governmental power for almost a millennium but also loss of a strong urban influence on Indian culture. The urban culture which had exported much to Rome was shaken by the break-up of western Classical civilization as well as by internal stresses. India returned to being an agricultural economy with the villages as its most important units. During the period from 500–1200, power lay in the caste system itself, distributed authority between priests and *kshatriyas* (the warrior aristrocracy) but not centered in a single political force.

The medieval Rājput chieftain inherited ancient precepts on *artha*, or government, which prevented any one clan from acquiring political dominance. For example, the convention that the ruler was supposed to consider his immediate neighbours hostile to his interests led to long, exaggerated and sometimes ludicrous quarrels that stalemated cooperative initiatives between territories.

The positions of the Rājputs began to change with the establishment of the Muslim Sultanate kingdoms. The pre-Mughal Islamic period was a bewildering one of shifting boundaries, but culturally it was a time of significant revolution. The refugees from Mongol destruction from all parts of Asia, the *sūfi* mystics, and ambitious political leaders all poured into India bringing ideas from their native lands. The Islamic rulers did not hold positions determined by any philosophy comparable to *dharma* which accorded rights at birth; many were slaves who rose despite precedents of social order. Various Islamic peoples helped to revive city life and broaden the sciences, and the energy shown by newcomers was matched by native achievements in developing a written language and literature.

As the idea of a unified India re-emerged, the physical structure needed to support a strong central government was created; for example, just prior to Akbar's time, the Afghan Sher Shāh began to build the Grand Trunk Road (a vital link between points in northern India) and started to standardize the system of land taxation. When Akbar came to power, the times were propitious for centralized rule and a regularized bureaucracy. Muslim orthodoxy demanded an active role in this government, but Akbar worked hard to prevent such influence, abolishing the cruelly restrictive poll tax on Hindus

and so forth. Thus the spirit of government was secular and distinct from any before it.

For more than one hundred years of Mughal rule, the imperial court was shifted from place to place by rulers whose ancestors had been accustomed to a nomadic life. For example, Akbar built the city of Fatehpur Sikri as a residence and then abandoned it for Lahore, and until the end of Shāh Jahān's reign, the court regularly moved between Delhi, Agra and Kashmir.

While village life remained basically unaltered, the Rājputs became a part of the Mughal bureaucracy; many travelled more and had greater responsibilities. Most based the design of their courts on those of the Mughals in some way, with similar halls, decoration, and gardens. During most of the Mughal period, admiration mixed with tension resulted in conflicting feelings of loyalty to the throne, while the Mughals often betrayed the interests of their Rājput allies, deliberately causing dissension in order to subordinate Rājput power.

THE PALACE

Palaces vary greatly in India, from small attractive villas for hill capitals to great rambling complexes of halls, courtyards, terraces and gardens. It is important to visualize these labyrinthine palaces in order to comprehend the relative distribution of power between the Mughals, important Rājputs and minor Rājputs. Shāh Jahān's white marble buildings in the Red Fort at Agra which form backdrops for many different paintings probably give the most vivid impression of the Mughal way of life. Here it is possible to sense the way in which the emperor's sanctity and remoteness was ensured by the plan of the architecture so as to preserve his safety in an environment rife with intrigue. Characteristic was the hierarchical regulation of audience chambers – from the pavilion in which all nobles were required to register their loyalty daily, to select halls where the privileged met in closer proximity to the revered imperial presence. Even more cloistered were the tiny mosques, the zenana, the baths and other parts of the emperor's private domain.

The Rājput palaces in Rajasthan are even more complex, bewildering and claustrophobic. Passages wind throughout the buildings, sometimes terminating mysteriously. Closed doors and secluded rooms give a sense of constant intrigue, overheard conversations and betrayed schemes. The Rājput buildings of the early Mughal period are somewhat sombre with strong beautiful ornamentation. However, these cannot be really indentified as settings for paintings. Most romantic scenes for example, seem to take place in small decorative pavilions invented by the artist's imagination. 18th-century palace decorations in Rajasthan have an air of frivolity with coloured windows, tiles, mosaics and wall paintings. In Udaipur, especially, this type of decoration was copied in miniatures with much detail. Though the map-like projections are somewhat confusing, buildings can be precisely identified. Rāja Ari Singh (ruled 1761–73) relaxes in his 17th-century lake palace, the Jag Mandir, in an imaginative scene that is nevertheless detailed and naturalistic according to its conventions (128). The same is true of the bird's-eye view of the Amar Vilās pavilion (126), looking as it does today.

Among the most splendid paintings juxtaposing white marble buildings, gardens and water are the scenes painted by artists from Kishangarh who depicted the palaces of that small state with unparalleled panache (125). Many such palaces were set in small domains but the artists managed to convey magnetism and power beyond that which was actually commanded by the raja.

129

127

THE RULER

The Mughal emperors were under the will of 'Allāh alone; they were unrestricted by any man-made laws and even the religious leaders voiced any words of censure at their own peril. Because there was no absolute right of primogeniture, it became almost accepted that princes were destroyed in contests for this absolute power. Prime ministers could be very strong advisers, but they kept the exact extent of their influence discreetly veiled from the ruler himself. Courtiers could not approach the emperor except on rare occasions when they might be honoured for some service or for exceptional bravery, but in general they stood behind railings at the daily *durbār* or assembly. Imperial subjects could catch a daily glimpse of the emperor, however, in the early morning when he presented himself at a small window high up in the outer wall of his palace to prove his continuing health and receive adulation.

All honour merely contributed to isolation and unrelenting watchfulness. Dishes of food were formally sealed and stamped in the imperial kitchens by the persons responsible for preparation before being conveyed to the emperor, and food tasters were employed to ensure safety. Even the ruler's children approached him only with permission and were required to stand at prescribed distances from his person. As Jahāngīr noted with anguish upon the revolt of his oldest son, no one was related to a king. Even the vast array of priceless possessions became cloying and isolating; on prescribed occasions the *mansabdārs* (high ranking court officials) were obliged to give presents that represented a monetary value appropriate to their official rank, a gesture that was inevitably impersonal. Ironically, the emperor was thought to convey a blessing on the donor if he deigned to accept even a small part of the offered present. If twenty jewels were given and one accepted, this would indicate that the emperor looked indulgently upon his official.

The rulers with character developed personal interests that helped them to endure the isolation of their position. Shāh Jahān had a passion for constructing perfect buildings, and Jahāngīr was absorbed in his natural history studies. Akbar was fascinated by the threads of truth in the many conflicting religious ideologies around him, and spent evenings listening to debates between religious leaders. He and Jahāngīr recognized that the persons most likely to be impartial as well as genuine acquaintances were those who had forsaken materialistic aims. Jahāngīr regularly sought out ascetics such as the Hindu Jadrup who lived in a cave; the emperor's diary indicates that he did this apparently for psychological reasons, in order to speak with a person of intelligence who had no interest in the court.

The Rājput rulers might quarrel with brothers who challenged their powers, but a typical resolution of this situation was the formation of a smaller state by the younger brother. The extended family had formidable loyalties that regulated the Rājput in an entirely different way from his Mughal counterpart. Though the Rājput might be a head of his clan, he was more likely to be dominated by family ties than isolated from the family by his office. Because he had a rural background associated with a particular locality, his approach to life was different from that of the Mughal ruler. The retainers around him had probably served his family for

131

131 The ruler watching the making of *pān*
Ni'māt Nāma manuscript
(Folios 103 and 111)
Sultanate school, *c.* 1500
From Mandu, each 27 × 19cm
London, India Office and Records, 86 (Folio 111 not illustrated)
In Folio 103 he is being offered *pān* and Folio 111 servants are perfuming water.

132 Ibrāhīm 'Ādil Shāh II (*not illustrated*)
Deccan school, *c.* 1610
From Bijapur, 21 × 12cm
London, Trustees of the British Museum, 1937.4–10.02

133

133 Ruler and son with small boys
Pahari school, *c.* 1730–40
From Chamba
Hyderabad, Jagdish and Kamla Mittal Museum of Indian Art, 76.800

138

140

several generations, so that the two parties were accustomed to one another and to their relative responsibilities.

Under the patronage of the Mughal emperors royal portraiture was greatly developed, and subsequently imitated at provincial Hindu and Muslim courts. There had, however, been earlier precedents: the Sultanate ruler of Mandu, for example, was represented in a generalized fashion sampling various foods in the many illustrations of his cookbook, the *Ni'mat Nāma* in about 1500 (131). The naturalistic portrait was at first resisted, probably because it was thought to have magical or life-imitating powers. The artistic means for achieving such an image were provided by contacts with Europeans. Painters under Akbar and Jahāngīr were fascinated by European art, and Jahāngīr delighted in having his artists copy Renaissance and Baroque paintings.

One of the clearest indications of Mughal influence on art at the courts of Rājput India was the development of portraiture. Previously in Hindu society, painting was primarily at the service of religion; however, for the Muslims it was a sign of a cultivated ruler. Thus, during the Mughal period the Hindu rulers, in imitation, adopted miniature paintings, especially portraiture, as a kind of court hobby and status symbol. Among the Rajasthani rulers, those of Mewar were among the last to yield to the delightful vanity of being depicted by their artists; but by about 1700, having succumbed to this type of flattery, they allowed themselves to be painted in every aspect of life – hunting, watching festivals, or being entertained in the zenana. The rulers of Bundi, Kotah and Jodhpur had surrendered earlier to the pleasant recreation of posing for court artists, as had the Rājputs of the Pahari courts (195, 198). In both Rajasthani and Pahari depictions, it is interesting to observe that the ruler is often shown as larger than those around him; the consorts, attendants, and even the heir apparent are portrayed as of very minor importance in comparison (137). An equestrian portrait of Rāja Dhīraj Singh of Ragogarh shows his figure roughly twenty times larger than those of his two attendants (136).

Though rudimentary portraiture was well developed in the Muslim kingdoms of the Deccan before contact with the Mughal court, at the end of the 16th century the artists of these kingdoms were significantly affected by the Mughal style. Ibrāhīm 'Ādil Shāh II of Bijapur (ruled 1580–1625) was one of the most influential patrons of painting and music, and was portrayed numerous times in different styles. This portrait of him (132) shows the influence of Mughal and European derived attitudes towards figure modelling; it is more subtle, less purely intellectual, and more sensual than Mughal examples.

One of the most interesting associations between the Mughal and Deccani courts occurred during Jahāngīr's reign. The emperor was concerned about his inability to subdue the Deccan and wished to gain a psychological insight into the character of his adversaries. One particular artist, Hāshim, was apparently commissioned to take on the task of portraying the Deccani leaders and about five examples of his work remain. It is doubtful that the artist himself ever visited the Deccan, but it is known that portraits were being exchanged between the regions. Remarkably, it seems that Hāshim composed precise portraits of rulers he had never seen from less exact originals. His achievement may be judged from Hāshim's dignified and naturalistic portrait of Muhammad Qutb Shāh of Golconda (ruled 1611–26) (134).

134 Muhammad Qutb Shāh of Golconda *(see p. 41)*
From the Minto Album
Artist: Hāshim
Mughal school, *c.* 1620
37 × 26cm
London, Victoria and Albert Museum, IM 22–1925

135 Shāh Jahān with Mewar ruler *(not illustrated)*
Rajasthan school, 1640
From Mewar, 27 × 30cm
New Delhi, National Museum, 50.14/23

136 Rāja Dhīraj Singh on a rearing horse *(not illustrated)*
Central Indian school, *c.* 1700
From Ragogarh, 56 × 35cm
Private collection
289 is another painting of this ruler by a different artist.

137 Rāja Sundar Dās and sons *(not illustrated)*
Rajasthan school, *c.* 1710
From Sawar, 39 × 30cm
Patna, Sri Gopi Krishna Kanoria Collection

138 Rāja Pratāp Singh examining a horse
Rajasthan school, *c.* 1740
From Nagaur, 27 × 33cm
Private collection

139 Ari Singh in his palace *(not illustrated)*
Rajasthan school, *c.* 1765
From Mewar, 30 × 48cm
New Delhi, National Museum, 58.25/26

140 Rāja Rām Singh II and servants
Artist: Govind Rām
Rajasthan school, *c.* 1840
From Jaipur, 31 × 37cm
Hyderabad, Jagdish and Kamla Mittal Museum of India Art, 76.163

141 Lady painter in the zenana
Mughal school, *c.* 1635–40
Varanasi, Bharat Kala Bhavan Museum, 683

THE ZENANA

The painting of a woman working on a portrait in the zenana, or women's quarters (**141**), is important evidence of a practice that was suspected but not previously documented. The few existing signed miniatures by women are not feminine genre scenes but copies of older literary subjects and as yet there is no adequate evidence to prove that male artists were allowed to paint women from direct observation. Women were commonly depicted simply as beauties and were not sketched in the same exacting fashion as men.

The frequency with which upper-class women were seen and how much freedom they enjoyed depended to some extent on the individuals. Jahāngīr's consort, Nūr Jahān, is the legendary example of the strong-willed woman who was not confined to the zenana and exerted considerable political influence. Many rulers spent time daily resolving problems that had been brought to the attention of their women, or consulting them about state affairs that the women had

observed whilst hidden behind grilles; in general, however, zenana women led lives of inactivity and enforced seclusion.

The main duty of all women was to bear and nurture children, particularly males: marriage took place with this aim in mind. Birth, although status-giving, was surrounded by endless taboos that made the mother's role difficult and more dangerous. The Mughal scene showing the birth of a prince (**142**) gives an idea of the varied ceremonies that were held for a male child. Surprisingly, this miniature of the closed female quarters contains revealing and vivid detail; most important are the astrologers in the middle of the painting whose prognostications outlined the destinies of Indian children from all classes; the carrying of a crib, the playing of music and the decorating of roofs with leaf garlands are other frequently shown activities. In the zenana, young male children were surrounded by women and often cared for by wet nurses as well as by a prince's blood relations. The atmosphere was highly competitive as a prince's mother's welfare and even survival might depend on the success of her son. Boys were separated from their mothers in both Hindu and Muslim

147

147 Prince receiving a lady
Mughal school, *c.* 1720
27 × 39cm
New Delhi, National Museum, 79.195

148

142 The birth of Prince Murād in 1570
From an *Akbar Nāma* manuscript
Outline and colouring by Bhūrah, portraits
by Basawan. Mughal school, *c.* 1570,
38 × 25cm
*London, Victoria and Albert Museum,
IS 2–1896 80/117*

143 A raja with a favourite
Pahari school, *c.* 1730–40
From Kulu, 17 × 17cm
*London, Trustees of the British Museum,
1966.7–25 07*

144 Woman with spinning wheel
(not illustrated)
Pahari school, *c.* 1680–90
From Bilaspur, 21 × 15cm
*London, Trustees of the British Museum,
1965 6–12 02*

145 A raja with women in landscape
(not illustrated)
Rajasthan school, *c.* 1770
From Kishangarh, 35 × 21cm
*Patna, Sri Gopi Krishna Kanoria Collection,
P80/BH/601*

146 Lovers *(not illustrated)*
Rajasthan school, 1662
From Bundi, 25 × 20cm
New Delhi, National Museum, 56.36/33

148 Arup Singh receiving *pān*
Attributed artist: Bakhtā
Rajasthan school, *c.* 1770
From Devgarh, 12.6 × 9.2cm
*Chandigarh, Government Museum
and Art Gallery, 2500*

149 Rāja Amar Singh with women *(not
illustrated)*
Rajasthan school, *c.* 1700
From Mewar, 22 × 40cm
*Bombay, Prince of Wales Museum of Western
India, 56.32*

150 A raja approaching the zenana *(see p. 45)*
Rajasthan school, *c.* 1760
From Kishangarh, 22 × 15cm
*London, Trustees of the British Museum,
1959.4–11 01*

151 Parvīz and women *(not illustrated)*
Artist: Govardhan
From the Minto album ms 7a.2
Mughal school, *c.* 1615–20, 22 × 13cm
*Dublin, The Chester Beatty Library and
Gallery of Oriental Art*

upper-classes homes at an early age, as education and conditioning demanded (while girls remained in seclusion), though maternal influence often continued in adult life.

Village women probably led fuller lives than women of the upper classes as illustrated in depictions of Yasodā, Krishna's foster-mother, who is often shown caring for the children, churning butter and doing other household tasks. Certain village occupations were divided in ways that might differ in other societies; for example, it was men who regularly did weaving though the women spun on wheels whose graceful design continued unchanged through centuries of usage. An idealized depiction of this activity was one of the subjects of a Pahari *Rāgamāla* series (**144**).

The ruler's zenana was the residence of older women, such as his mother and his aunts, as well as his numerous wives and concubines and all their attendants. Reflecting his importance and temperament, a ruler's zenana could be a large, expensive and troublesome establishment. How it was run depended very much on his personality; Akbar, for instance, honoured the many Rājputs who acceded to him by taking their daughters

or sisters into his court, so cementing his conquests with these marital hostages, while the Rājputs, in turn, hoped to win the emperor's notice through the wisdom or child-bearing abilities of these women. By contrast, Jahāngīr, in his younger days, frequently became infatuated with a new beauty, and pleaded to add her to his household.

While his whims were always gratified, the circumstances of a ruler's life prevented the development of his private feelings. Thus Amar Singh and his consort sit on a terrace surrounded by other harem women (**149**), and an idealized Bundi raja leads a woman accompanied by two attendants towards a bed (**146**). The necessity of begetting sons underlay the atmosphere of sensual flirtation, and could become a grim anxiety – as it almost did in the case of Akbar, who did not have healthy sons for some years.

The epitome of a desirable consort was the shy woman ushered forward reticently by her companions (**147**). Another ideal woman, a much rarer type, was the delicate but sultry beauty whose ripeness seems to be echoed by the mango and banana plants in the Kishangarh miniature (**150**).

152 Lovers on their wedding night
Shunga period, 1st century BC–1st century
AD
From Kaushambi (Uttar Pradesh)
Terracotta, 12 × 9 × 2cm
New Delhi, National Museum, 0.67

153 Lovers *(not illustrated)*
16th century
From Orissa
Ivory, 10cm high
*London, Trustees of the British Museum,
1972.12–13.2*

154 Lovers
13th century
From Orissa
Ivory, 9.5cm high
*London, Trustees of the British Museum,
1972.12–13.1*

152

154

IDEAL LOVERS

In early Indian sculpture the subject of the loving couple,
handled with tender expressiveness, appears countless times.
The entwined lovers almost always radiate warmth and
serenity, smiling down from the ceilings of Buddhist cave
temples or from the inner doorways of Hindu temples.
Blessing the world through the fruition of their own
relationship, the couple inspires a feeling of gentleness and of
kinship with all mankind. Even in small terracotta plaques and
ivory carvings (**152**, **153** and **154**), great profundity is often
achieved in the portrayal of lovers. In later sculpture, as more
emphasis was placed on eroticism or mere physical adroitness,
the feeling of spontaneity was lost.

In paintings of the Mughal period the relationships of lovers
are depicted very differently: love is rarely shown in soft or
beneficial aspects; instead it often seems to have a harsh
quality, as if representing a temporary truce between
opposites. It is interesting to note that the romantic literature
underlying much of Indian painting, especially that associated
with Krishna, tended to foster transience or anxiety in love
rather than an eternal or resolved relationship. For example, in
seven charming successive scenes of Rādhā and Krishna in the
forest, the happy Rādhā is entertained by Krishna as they

move through an idyllic wood; in the final frame, however, he
has disappeared and left her alone (**159**).

A large proportion of Indian miniatures seem to have been
created for the eyes of women to relieve the boredom of their
isolation as well as to keep their attention focused on an elusive
male ideal. This hero can generally be visualized as Krishna
who represents romance, aspiration and the fulfilment of
dreams as well as a consummately satisfying lover. A
significant point regarding the eroticism that forms part of this
tradition is that although miniatures may be explicitly
descriptive, strong desire is more likely to be revealed through
expressionism (**156**). The explosions of colour, pattern and
shape in romantic paintings convey the power of sensual
allurement far more than does the depiction of action.

Surprisingly, since Krishna is domineering and capriciously
neglectful, woman is generally the central actress in the love
drama. It is her emotions and conflicting passions that the
painters and poets survey more than Krishna. In a painting
from Mewar, the handsome Krishna bends over Rādhā, who is
depicted as a sort of emotional abstraction of fluid hair,
jewellery and textile patterns (**157**). In a painting from the
thikana of Devgarh by the intelligent and witty painter
Chokhā, Krishna is only a voyeuristic head in the forest, slyly
acknowledged by the opulently beautiful Rādhā who is being
bathed by her attendants (**155**).

155

158

156

155 Rādhā being prepared for Krishna
Artist: Chokhā
Rajasthan school, *c.* 1810
From Devgarh, 14 × 10cm
Hyderabad, Jagdish and Kamla Mittal Museum of Indian Art, 76.181

156 Krishna making love to Rādhā
Rajasthan school, *c.* 1740
From Kotah, 27 × 20cm
New Delhi, National Museum, 56.49/12

157 Rādhā and Krishna in a bower *(see p.85)*
Rajasthan school, *c.* 1700
From Mewar, 16 × 22cm
Bombay, Prince of Wales Museum of Western India, 52.18

158 Rati and Kāmadeva in a landscape
Rajasthan school, *c.* 1620
From Bikaner, 15 × 20cm
Baron and Baroness Bachofen von Echt collection
Kāmadeva, the equivalent of Cupid, stands with his flowery bow beside Rati (Pleasure) while Krishna, the ideal lover, and Shiva's family are on either side of the background.

159 Rādhā and Krishna in the forest
(not illustrated)
From *Bhāgavata Purāna* manuscript, No.38
Rajasthan school, *c.* 1770
From Jodhpur, 65 × 41cm
Jodhpur, Maharaja Museum, Umaid Bhavan Palace

160 Krishna and Rādhā lost in admiration *(see p. 88)*
Attributed artist: Chokhā
Rajasthan school, *c.* 1810
From Devgarh, 22 × 16cm
Private collection

161 Rādhā and Krishna in a game *(not illustrated)*
Rajasthan school, *c.* 1825
From Mewar, 27 × 22cm
New Delhi, National Museum, 56.52/1

THE DESPERATE HEROINE

In Hindu tradition, noble and faithful wives, such as Sītā (see pp. 204–6), are upheld as feminine ideals; but in the Muslim era, the woman who stands out is the one who challenges the structures of the social order; this is the desperate heroine who braves the storm and goes out into the night to find her lover. Though she went against all customs of feminine seclusion and family solidarity, she held a prominent place in the annals of this period apparently because a certain sympathy underlay the overtly restrictive code; in addition, according to Vaishnavite symbolism, a woman who truly yearned for her lover as the soul yearns for god could break free of encumbrances in the pursuit of her happiness.

This kind of heroine, however, led a difficult life; the obstacles to her happiness were enormous, and lay not only in challenging society but in gaining the full attention of her lover. Occasionally she won loyalty and loving recognition; Rūpmatī of Mandu, Banī Thanī of Kishangarh and Nokhu of Kangra all became legendary for their succeess in winning the hearts of influential men who reconciled love with conflicting social obligations. In most cases, the heroine in literature who restlessly seeks love already belongs to another man and can enjoy only a few hours of secret happiness.

Waiting plays a large part in the life of a typical Indian literary heroine, and innumerable of her situations mirror the actual conditions of the period. Confined to a passive role, a woman always faced the possibility that her man might be occupied not only in hunting, war or commerce but in dallying with other women. Often the woman's situation is portrayed as erotically stimulating: in one painting the waiting heroine's ardour is being cooled by attendants pouring water over her (168). But Indian poets also recognized that the neglected woman's passion could endanger her, and they recount the stages of her disappointment and her disillusionment that culminate in her insanity and, finally, death.

The desperate heroine is one driven by passion on the one hand and frustration or anxiety to seize the initiative on the other. She must take action not only against an oppressive home or social environment, but also against her lover's thoughtlessness. For example, a painting from Kotah (164) depicts a heroine who goes into the forest to make a bed of petals and wait for her lover who is late and may have abandoned her. Rather than being truly passive, the woman is called upon to exert herself through competition: in a strange theme (165) that appears to relate to fertility, the heroine Deshākh exercises on a *linga*-like pole so that she will become supple and sexually attractive to her lover, thereby winning a position over her co-wives. Perhaps the boldest and strongest heroine of all is Āsāvarī who pulls or charms snakes from sandalwood trees in order to assuage her passion by embracing the cool tree trunks (163).

Female ascetics portrayed in miniatures are very often shown practising austerities which, even if depicted in a religious context, are endured in order to achieve power in love. The lady with the *vīnā* (musical instrument) over her shoulder in this miniature (162) is typical of a large group of pictures of women who are shown disciplining themselves in solitude for the sake of love. Ardent asceticism has always been a recognized means of gaining power whether for good or evil.

162

162 *Yoginī* with *vīnā*
Deccan school, *c.* 1620
From Bijapur, 15 × 9cm
Hyderabad, Jagdish and Kamla Mittal Museum of Indian Art,
76.404

163 Āsāvarī in the wilderness
(see p.45)
From the *Āsāvarī rāginī c.* 1640
From central India, Malwa
Varanasi, Bharat Kala Bhavan Museum, 7475

163

164

165

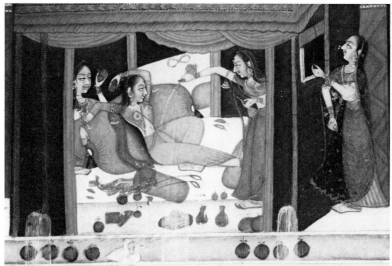

168

164 Kāmod *Rāginī*
Rajasthan school, *c.* 1660
From Kotah, 21 × 11 cm
Hyderabad, Jagdish and Kamla Mittal
Museum of Indian Art, 76.126
Kāmod, torn by anxiety, awaits her lover in
the forest. This *rāginī* Kāmod has been
mislabelled Purabi. The same composition,
called Kāmod, is known from several other
Bundi and Kotah versions.

165 Deshākh *Rāginī*
Rajasthan school, *c.* 1720–40
From Bundi, 24 × 18 cm
Bombay, J. P. Goenka Collection
Deshākh does acrobatics on a linga-like pole
to gain sexual superiority over her co-wives.

166 Madhu Madhavi *Rāginī* (*not*
illustrated)
Rajasthan school, 1628
From Mewar, 25 × 18 cm
New Delhi, National Museum, 63.1622
The heroine is aroused by the fructification
caused by the approaching rain.

167 Waiting heroine (*see p. 48*)
From a *Rasamanjarī* manuscript
Pahari school, *c.* 1720
From Nurpur, 17 × 28 cm
New Delhi, National Museum, 48.58

168 Heroine in a pavilion (*detail, see also p. 84*)
Rajasthan school, *c.* 1770
From Bundi
Varanasi, Bharat Kala Bhavan Museum,
8872

IDEAL BEAUTY

An ideal of courtly beauty has been present in Indian art since the earliest carvings. Shunga period ivories, for example, are miniature expressions of this ideal, closely related to the *yakshī* type. Even in later paintings, the connection between courtly beauty and the personification of the forces of nature is never lost. This continuity is illustrated in a miniature from Bundi in which a woman reaches up to clutch a branch in the familiar *shālabhanjikā* posture (**170**).

It is clear, however, that there was no generally accepted formula in Indian painting for depicting the ideal woman. In the early Mewar miniature (**169**) the woman seated, surprisingly, on a chair (a European custom thought to have been adopted later in Rajasthan), is one of the heroines in a Rājput poetic manuscript that was often illustrated. In the poetry the women are presented according to their relative experience of love, as artless, youthful or mature – a common conceit in India. The aim of such literary work was to describe the reactions of each type of woman in a specified situation. The tone of the poetry is generally lyrical in describing the

inexperienced heroines, and humorous in discussing the courtesans. Such classifications delighted Indians at an early period and grew ever more complex with time.

In painting, the ideal woman was not always a fertility symbol with large breasts and hips. Among the most consciously developed of female images is that found in Guler and Kangra paintings, where the main quality of the woman was her tender grace (**175**). The long, curved rhythms of these styles emphasize the woman's delicate hand gestures, her lightness in walking, and her youthful but poised demeanour. While the female type in Kangra paintings was based on balance and moderation, artists in other areas had different poetic and religious ideals which governed their conceptions of women. The artists of Kishangarh and Basohli, for example, were intent on transforming women from the commonplace, and rendering their emotions symbolically. The women they created were strictly conventionalized to show that their appeal transcended human experience (**174**). By contrast, the Mughals almost totally ignored female beauty until the early 18th century, and even then their artists merely created pretty women (**173**), and never attempted to depict the subtleties of female emotion understood in Hindu philosophy.

169

169 Heroine seated on a chair
From a *Rasamanjarī* manuscript
Rajasthan school, *c.* 1620
From Mewar, 25 × 19cm
New Delhi, National Museum, 55 50/9
Forty-two folios of this early Rajasthani set with mixed stylistic characteristics are in the National Museum while others are scattered in Indian, European and American collections.

170 *Shālabanjikā*
Rajasthan school, *c.* 1680
From Bundi, 24 × 19cm
London, Victoria and Albert Museum, IS 34–1971

17

174

175

174 Andhryārī *Rāginī*
Pahari school, *c.* 1690
From Basohli, 17 × 12cm
Baron and Baroness Bachofen von Echt
collection

175 Woman, child and letter
Pahari school, *c.* 1810
From Kangra
Varanasi, Bharat Kala Bhavan Museum

171 Ladies bathing *(not*
illustrated)
Late Shāh Jahān period album
Mughal school, *c.* 1650
23 × 16cm
Dublin, The Chester Beatty
Library and Gallery of Oriental Art

172 Woman bathing
Rajasthan school, *c.* 1725
From Sirohi, 23 × 13cm
Hyderabad, Jagdish and Kamla
Mittal Museum of Indian Art,
76.204

172

173 Princess with attendants
in the garden
Provincial Mughal school,
c. 1760
From Lucknow, 23 × 16cm
Bombay, J. P. Goenka Collection

173

MUSIC, DRAMA AND DANCE

As the savant warned the dilettante in an early Hindu treatise, before one can learn about painting, one must learn about dance and the other arts. Such an inter-relationship is crucial since the feeling of movement in Indian painting or sculpture comes mainly from dance, while themes are often borrowed from literature. Like larger temple sculptures, small terracottas (177, 180) demonstrate that performing musicians and dancers had been popular subjects in the visual arts throughout India's cultural history.

The painted wooden book cover from the Pāla period apparently illustrates the drama *Shakuntalā*, concerning a prince who falls in love with a beauty in the forest. The cover was painted centuries after the death of the author, the great classical poet Kālidāsa, yet it still embodies remnants of his idealized Gupta descriptions. The heroine, Shakuntalā, is shown in a dance-like posture, her sinuous curves reminiscent of forest creepers and her features conforming to ideals analogous to nature (eyes like lotus buds, etc.). Later Rājput painting continues this extremely close relationship with literature and its metaphorical symbols.

Actual music, drama and dance performances provided the subjects on which numerous miniature paintings were based. Dancers of the early Mughal period are commonly shown as ladies of the court wearing the tall *chāghatai* hats of the Mughal's Turkic ancestors (183). The depictions of *nautches* (performances of dancing girls), usually dating from the 18th or 19th century, show the dancers before a ruler and select audience (184). *Nautches* were such popular Indian entertainments that the British, at first delighted by them, came to dread their frequency. Another popular entertainment was the melodrama, typically performed by an all male cast (189). Both these examples are from mid-18th-century provincial cities whose urban dandies were great patrons of such entertainments.

Singers and musicians are depicted so frequently with idealized princes or court ladies that their presence is almost a stereotype. Yet the numerous scenes in which they appear probably reflect accurately the role of musicians in the Mughal, Rājput and Deccani courts (184). These performers were so important that they were sometimes depicted alone (185), an unusual honour for commoners. Other musicians are to be found in the middle of army charges, at weddings, playing from a palace tower to mark certain hours of the day, or at rural amusements.

Rulers appreciative of music or dancing were also likely to be inclined toward painting, combining their artistic interests by having themselves portrayed at concerts. One such patron was Govardhan Chand of Guler (ruled 1741–73) who contributed much to forming the revolutionary Guler style of painting (188). Another cultured patron was the princely Balwānt Singh of Jammu (1724–63), a devoted patron of music and painting who is depicted engaged in correspondence (190). The long relationship between Balwant and his artist, Nainsukh, exemplifies a sympathetic agreement about pictures and a deep personal communication unique in the field of miniature painting.

The most common musical theme illustrated in painting is the *Rāgamāla*, or 'Garland of Melodies'. Each modal series of notes (*rāga*) used as the basis for musical improvisation was considered to possess its individual mood, and poems describing these in personified form were collected into treatises (*rāgamālas*) and illustrated by painters. One of the most popular ways of organizing the *rāgas* within a *rāgamāla* was to arrange them in six groups of six, each comprising a personified male (*rāga*) with six wives (*rāginīs*) (see 163, 164 and 165). Most *rāgas* and *rāginīs* have recognizable motifs repeated over many years by artists; *Shrī*, meaning 'Lord', emphasizes the masculinity of the *rāga*, and a lord listening to two musicians is generally shown. His group consists of melodies appropriate to winter and early spring as well as to the afternoons. Although the *Rāgamāla* was originally a musical concept, the paintings are expressively illustrative in their own right. Highly charged with emotion, these compositions can evoke powerful impressions of amorous passions, the heat of spring or the driving force of the monsoon.

176

176 Musician
From Sannati (Karnataka)
Terracotta, 7 × 5 × 2cm
Mysore, Directorate of Archaeology and Museums

177 Musicians
Gupta period, 4th–6th century
From Varanasi (Uttar Pradesh)
Terracotta, 9 × 5 × 5cm each
Varanasi, Bharat Kala Bhavan Museum,
6–1389, 7–4752

178 Flute player
Kushāna period,
2nd-3rd century AD
From Mathura? (Uttar
Pradesh)
Sandstone, 51 × 25cm
London, Trustees of the
British Museum, 1965 2.26.1

178

181

179 Balarāma dancing with dagger and
trumpet
17th century
From Madras
Ivory, 19cm high
Edinburgh Royal Scottish Museum, 1887.152

180 Dancing girl *(not illustrated)*
Maurya period, 3rd century BC
From Sonpur (Bihar)
Terracotta, 24 × 11 × 9cm
Patna, Directorate of Archaeology and Museums,
Bihar

181 Krishna and Balarāma with
musicians *(see p. 48)*
From *Bhāgavata Purāna* manuscript
Pahari school, *c.* 1710
From Mankot
Bombay, J. P. Goenka Collection

182 Jester leading the prince of Shakuntalā
Pāla school, 12th century
Painted wooden book cover for a palm-leaf
manuscript, 5 × 20cm
Calcutta, Suresh Neotia Collection

182

183 A ruler entertained by *Chāghatai* dancers
Mughal school, *c.* 1565–70
26 × 19cm
University of Oxford, Bodleian Library, Douce Or. Bl Fol.12B

183

184 Ruler at a *nautch*
Provincial Mughal school, *c.* 1760
From Oudh
Varanasi, Bharat Kala Bhavan Museum

184

185

185 Five musicians of Sangram Singh II
Rajasthan school, 1730
From Mewar, 20 × 28cm
New Delhi, National Museum, 56.116/20
These same musicians appear in a large
picture of Sangram Singh II now in the
Udaipur Palace.

186 Prince and consort with musicians:
Shrī Rāga *(not illustrated)*
Rajasthan school, *c.* 1640
Possibly from Ajmer
Bombay, J. P. Goenka Collection
Classified here as Ajmer, the style is a
puzzling mixture of Rajasthani and popular
Mughal features.

187 Prince with musicians
Deccan school, *c.* 1660
26 × 35cm
New Delhi, National Museum,
50.14/29

188 Govardhan Chand with
dancer and musicians
Pahari school, *c.* 1745
From Guler
Varanasi, Bharat Kala Bhavan
Museum, 93

187

188

190

189

189 Actors and musicians giving a drama
Attributed artist: Mir Kalan Khān
Provincial Mughal school, *c.* 1760
From Lucknow, 35 × 22cm
University of Oxford, Bodleian Library, Douce
Or. B3 Fol. 20

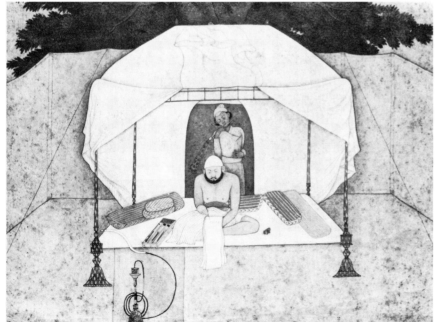

190 Balwānt Singh writing
Pahari school, *c.* 1750
From Jammu, 21 × 28cm
Bombay, Prince of Wales Museum of Western
India, 33.108

191 Death of 'Ināyat Khān
Mughal school, 1618–19
20 × 25cm
University of Oxford, Bodleian Library, Ouseley 171/2, Fol. 4v

192 Rāo Bhārah and Jassah Jām
From the Wantage Album
Artist: Bishndās
Mughal school, *c.* 1620
38 × 26cm
London, Victoria and Albert Museum, IM 124–1921

191

192

COURTIERS AND PAINTERS

Both Hindu and Muslim courts had complex chains of command; the Mughal imperial hierarchy was staffed by officers who took posts in all parts of the empire. Many had civil positions, yet because the state was defined in military terms, they were unsuitably called *mansabdars*, a term referring originally to military rank and unfortunately minimizing the incentives for peacetime accomplishments. In order to ensure that power factions did not build up against the central government, officers were often shifted from one part of the empire to the other.

The emperor himself travelled a great deal; in Gujarat, for instance, the local rulers Rāo Bhārah and Jassa Jām came to pay their respects to Jahāngīr during his tour of western India in 1617–18. Here (**192**) they are shown together in a composition, apparently compiled from separate sketches made several years earlier, by Bishndās, the artist whom the emperor called his best portraitist. Bishndās spent many years at the Persian court on Jahāngīr's orders sketching the monarch there so that Jahāngīr could have an adequate idea of his rival's personality. The fact that the artist is known to have remained in Persia until 1619, and that Jahāngīr seems to have seen Rao Bharah and Jassa Jām at different times, indicates a typical delay in the process of composition. The two figures have, however, been very successfully amalgamated into a single design so that their personalities, as fully expressed as if the painter had been working directly from observation, are made distinct but harmonious. The two give a memorable

impression of the quiet nobility and dignity of the Gujarati upper class which would have been novel to the Mughals.

Among the courtiers surrounding Jahāngīr were many who had been with him since his days as an irresponsible prince. A major difficulty of the Mughal hierarchy was that the emperor was absolute and above any criticism. Courtiers believed that their destinies hung on constant flattery and gift-giving. This was demoralizing not only to them but also to the emperor himself, who was aware that he rarely heard the truth. One of the courtiers who was in Jahāngīr's service for a long time, the young and handsome 'Ināyat Khān, had been depicted as a popular favourite wearing an unusually elegant costume. When, only a few years later in 1618–19, he asked for permission to leave court on account of illness caused by opium and alcohol, he was brought before the emperor who was shocked at his emaciated state and immediately called for his artists. The painting as well as the drawing of this subject show the influence of European art at its height, and also reveal the atmosphere of the court. The emperor, generally kept aloof from human contact by his position, reveals himself in his diary as extremely vulnerable at times. He was clearly moved by this experience and mentions that even the bones of 'Ināyat Khān seemed to have dissolved; but his objective curiosity shows in the complex mixture of pity and self-concern which affected him since the situation had sobering relevance to his own heavy addictions as well as to the fates of many in his dissolute court. While Jahāngīr lamented the deaths of courtiers and faithful servants, the atmosphere of the court was generally indifferent towards individual lives.

The situation in the Rājput courts was probably more stable

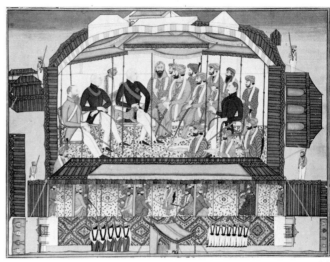

193 Sa'idullāh Khān dispensing justice
Mughal school, *c.* 1655
41 × 29cm
University of Oxford, Bodleian Library, Douce Or. B3. Fol. 21

194 Durbār to ratify the second treaty of Lahore
Sikh school, *c.* 1846
From Lahore, 40 × 54cm
London, Trustees of the British Museum, 1948 10–9.0109

because they were based on clan associations and hereditary rights. However, the Rājputs were gravely affected by internecine feuding as well as by alterations in Mughal policy. Excellent depictions of the Rājput courts show the ruler surrounded by his many classes of hereditary retainers. In the example from the small *thikana* (fiefdom) of Ghanerao (**197**) the artist has taken pains to communicate the manliness and pride of these various groups.

Daily assemblies before the Mughal ruler were extremely formal; nobles of different ranks stood at prescribed distances from the throne. The same priorities are clearly evident in a scene of Shāh Jahān's prime minister dispensing justice (**193**). In addition, the military nature underlying the empire is revealed by the swords and shields worn for this civil function.

Europeans also often appeared at court gatherings. Portuguese Jesuits had been present in Akbar's court for long periods, and a few English travellers had visited briefly. In Jahāngīr's era, the English ambassador, Sir Thomas Roe, remained in residence near the emperor for over three years. The Mughal emperors, however, were not highly motivated toward diplomatic or trading relations with other nations, though Akbar and Jahāngīr were very curious about foreign novelties. Mercantilism had no relevence to the etiquette of courtly life. British negotiations with the provincial rulers, or nawabs, of the imperial court came after they had established themselves in positions of strength, in the mid-18th century. The newly influential foreigners were increasingly portrayed in the late 18th and 19th centuries: a scene painted in 1846 (**194**) shows stiff British officers including Sir Henry Lawrence, who a few years later was to die a hero of the Mutiny, seated on

chairs concluding a treaty with a group of formidably bearded Sikhs from Jammu and Kashmir in their camp at Lahore.

Artists who were employed by the Mughals were in a strange position since they were commoners who were required to understand all the nuances of courtly life. Group portrait commissions required judgement of the relative power of officials, of the ways in which the emperor could be flattered and of the procedure that lay behind complex ceremonies. A number of such miniatures also contain a self-portrait of the painter with a tablet under his arm. Though he might sign his name with a properly abasing epithet and place the signature symbolically under the emperor's feet, the inscriptions themselves testify to a certain amount of self-respect as well as official recognition.

Since artists could be called upon at any hour to sketch a scene, in some ways their position was similar to that of the court newswriters, who were present on all occasions to write down the emperor's words and describe events. Though not of the same status as a calligrapher or educated literary man, the best painters were considered to be above the level of mere servants and were treated as extraordinarily gifted people who could be singled out for unusual rewards or praise.

The first generation of Mughal painters (including many Hindus) were trained by two Persian artists. In this first generation, rapid assimilation was required as a new style was created. The artists had to keep pace with changes or they were relegated to less interesting manuscript assignments. It is noticeable that the artists who could psychologically adjust to the court were better able to cope with the demands put upon them whereas many who had to struggle with provincial

195

197 Padam Singh in court (*not illustrated*)
Artist: Chhaju
Rajasthan school, 1725
From Ghanerao, 34 × 27cm
Bombay, Prince of Wales Museum of Western India, 55.32

198 Jaswant Singh in court (*unfinished work*)
Rajasthan school, *c.* 1660
From Jodhpur, 15 × 22cm
London, Trustees of the British Museum, 1948 10–9 0125

198

195 Six nobles of Jaswant Singh's court
Rajasthan school, 1640–50
From Jodhpur, 11 × 18cm
London, Trustees of the British Museum, 1924 12.28.03

196 Muhammad Shāh with courtiers (*see p. 42*)
Mughal school, *c.* 1740
35 × 50cm
*University of Oxford, Bodleian Library, Douce Or. A3.
Fol. 14*

training and were apparently in great awe of their new surroundings produced very tight paintings.

It was quite likely that the court painters of the 17th century might be 'palace-born', meaning that their fathers had been in imperial service. Such artists grew up in the court milieu and absorbed some of its social conventions. Their relatives acted as their painting teachers, so that family traditions of service and even style were gradually accumulated. Whether artists resided within the court precincts is uncertain; they did, however, work together in a body producing manuscripts during Akbar's period, and during Jahāngīr's era some probably stayed within the court at least part of the year.

During Akbar's period, the tasks of drawing and colouring a composition were often divided between two people; if a painter was to do colouring, he set to work with his squirrel hair brushes, and his colours in shells that had been prepared by an assistant. Colouring was the most arduous part of his work because the rapidly drying paint had to be meticulously applied in thin, even layers. Shading (done in almost any colour) was often painted like a veil over a base tone, but pigments were not blended freely when wet.

Artists could radically alter their styles to suit different situations; among those discharged from Mughal courts were painters who went to Rājput courts where their work combined popular local conventions and Mughal traditions. The Rājput artists generally held positions as retainers of particular rajas, but they might sometimes be free to move between courts. The artist Bakhta, for example, went from the service of the Udaipur *rāna* to the small *thikana* of Devgarh where his style became more mannered and colourful. Artist families might spread out over a fairly wide area, and pass on sketches for use by other branches of the family. Rājput artists, who worked in home studios and submitted paintings for approval, were often maintained by grants of property in which they were allowed to live without paying tax. If the family continued to produce acceptable work, these grants from the local ruler were renewed from generation to generation.

The portrayal of the position of the Rājput ruler was not artificially controlled by his painters as it was to a degree at the Mughal court. Since the imperial Mughal dynasty had risen from nothing, the Mughal painter, despite his common background, had some power to sway public opinion by his elegant and formal compositions. Although the Rājput ruler was worshipped almost as a god, his status was not created by hierachical isolation and painters thus created warmer, less remote compositions of Rājput courts.

199

199 Battle with Sishupāla and Jarāsandha, figures who opposed Krishna
Rajasthan school, *c.* 1750
From Kotah
Varanasi, Bharat Kala Bhavan Museum, 570

200 Muhammad Dāud Khān
Rajasthan school, *c.* 1690
From Bikaner, 24 × 15cm
New Delhi, National Museum, 63.1729

200

WAR

Wars on the Indian subcontinent were generally confined to small areas; often they were violent feuds rather than real wars. Though groups such as the Buddhists and Jains promoted non-violence, the very fact that one of the four Hindu castes was the *kshatriya* (warrior aristocracy) was an acknowledgment that war was an accepted part of earthly life. Because the Rājputs fought passionately for their own glory and that of their clans, their battles were fierce but were governed more by emotional fervour than by cool organization. One of the notorious traits of their bravery was the *jauhar*, the immolation of women and children, when a struggle was deemed hopeless, and the warriors had themselves vowed to fight to the death.

Despite their tradition of holy war, Muslims mostly fought for territorial and other gains. Just as life in India's fortified citadels resembled that of the European Middle Ages, so did their arms and armour. The helmets and armour of the pre-Mughal period are well represented in a miniature of the early 16th century Sultanate school (**202**). Both chain mail and leather armour were used; horses and elephants often wore armour made of large pieces of toughened hide overlapped like

201

201 Seated officers
Attributed artist: Payog
Mughal school, *c*. 1650
17 × 23cm
*Dublin, The Chester Beatty
Library and Gallery of Oriental
Art*

202 Lāur in armour
(see p. 72)
From a *Lāur Chandā*
manuscript
Pre-Mughal school, *c*. 1520
21 × 15cm
*Bombay, Prince of Wales
Museum of Western India*

203

203 A hero at war *(see also p. 79)*
From a *rāgamāla, Nat Rāginī*
Central Indian school, *c*. 1730–40
From Malwa, 21 × 15cm
New Delhi, National Museum, 63.1696
Nat Rāginī personifies the passions that are expressed in love as the
hero at war.

scales (**203**). The Muslims were the first to use the cannon and
gun in India; although firearms were known at least by the
early 16th century, when they appear in a dated Hindu
manuscript, Bābur's conquest in 1526 is usually considered the
first efficient employment of firearms. Akbar, ambitious to rule
all India, won his battles largely through the successful use of
surprise tactics – fast marches, unexpected agility of combat
forces and mobility of firepower – which won the admiration
of the Rājputs and often, as a result, their capitulation. While
one battle painting shows war as a rather overwhelming free-
for-all (**199**), there also existed a well-regulated military
organization, a prototype that included cavalry, heavily
armoured elephants, foot soldiers and musicians. But the
ponderously conventionalized order of such troops spelled
defeat in wars with guerilla forces or Europeans. The most
frustrating campaign for the Mughals was the long indecisive
attempt to gain control in the Deccan, which seemed to be
won only to begin again in some other form, eventually
developing into a guerilla war. Many officers from all parts of
India were involved in this long Mughal campaign – among
them were Rājputs from Bikaner who appropriated many
Deccani miniatures as part of the spoils of war. Judging from
details of the belt and background figures, this Bikaner portrait
of a proud, rather austere looking warrior riding near an army
procession was probably inspired by a 17th-century Deccani
painting (**200**).

HUNTING AND SPORT

The early Buddhist illustrations of *Jātaka* tales at Bharhut, Sanchi and Ajanta bring out the conflict which was already a significant one between those who hunted and those with non-violent attitudes. The Jains carried this struggle on into the Mughal period, pleading with Akbar and Jahāngīr, sometimes successfully to ban both hunting and meat eating on certain days. However, as in other countries, hunting was considered a practice for war, a test of virility and a rightful class privilege. Neither the Mughals nor the Rājputs could abandon this activity which for many was a total way of life. If an emperor or noble inherited his position with little interest or ability, he often gave hunting priority for weeks or even months on end at incredible expense to the ordinary population. Both Mughals and Rājputs believed they were entitled by birth to kill without restraint and thus slaughtered huge numbers of animals – sometimes more than a thousand in a day. The belief that the emperor had a noble prerogative over life and death meant that he was entitled to be careless of human as well as animal life; this attitude is often unconsciously reflected in miniatures such as the scene of Aurangzīb balancing his rifle on a huntsman's shoulders to shoot *nīlgai*; the loud report of the gun, its kick and the danger of misfire were probably all taken as a matter of course by the attendant.

Though hunts were artistic subjects from the period of the earliest narrative relief carving, naturalistic depictions of the chase were occasioned by Akbar's desire to record historical events in paint. By this time, both Mughals and Rājputs had developed many methods of hunting. Because of its vast systematic organization, the hunt most akin to a war-game was the chase created by beaters; over a period of weeks, hundreds of beaters would drive animals into a confined area to be killed by the emperor or noble at his leisure. The latter usually hunted alone or with a few selected intimates since he was acting out a role of hierarchial authority. The miniature of Akbar hunting tigers is an exception to the rule that the emperor as a figurehead was usually never in danger though he was made to appear a hero (**204**). The ferocity of this encounter is typical of Akbar's own headstrong courage which won the admiration as well as the political support of the masculine Rājputs. Hunting lions or tigers was the epitome of royal privilege – the despatch of such animals was usually reserved for royalty.

A further type of hunting involved waiting for the quarry in a hunt tower or behind camouflage, often with a decoy animal. The shooting of *nīlgai*, the big blue bulls who still run so gracefully across much of India's grassy terrain was very common. The picture of Aurangzīb with camouflaged huntsmen shows a bridled decoy animal who has lured male and female *nīlgai* (**212**).

Other kinds of hunting included the equestrian chase, pursuit by cheetahs and falconry which was a much practiced sport, even involving women (**226**). Though women's activities were severely curtailed, they did go hunting. In one miniature (**211**), they appear as part of the family unit casually accompanying the man.

Not surprisingly, it is often noticeable that the type of hunting which involved waiting, as opposed to the quick mobile kind of hunting such as boar-spearing, was recorded with far more detailed observation by artists, who were

204 Akbar hunting tigers near Gwalior
Double page with outlines by Basawan, colouring by Tara Kalan, Sarwan
From the *Akbar Nāma* manuscript
Mughal school, *c.* 1590
38 × 25cm
London, Victoria and Albert Museum, IS 2-1896 17 and 18/117 (17/177 not illustrated)

205 Elephants with riders
(not illustrated)
Sātavāhana period, 2nd century AD
From Brahmapuri (Maharashtra)
Bronze, 6.4 × 5.1cm
Kolhapur, Kolhapur Museum, BRN–31

206 Hunting procession
18th century
From Bengal
Terracotta, 18 × 18cm each
Calcutta, Gurusaday Museum of Bengal Folk Art

207

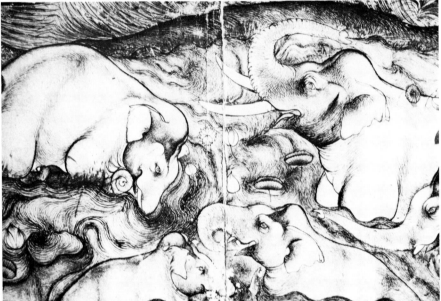

208

207 A royal hunting party
Rajasthan school, *c.* 1670
From Bikaner, 38 × 106cm
Private collection

208 Capturing wild elephants *(detail)*
Rajasthan school, *c.* 1745
From Kotah, 45 × 51cm
Dublin, The Chester Beatty Library and Gallery of Oriental Art

209 Two elephants running out of a tent
(see p. 76)
Rajasthan school, *c.* 1720
From Kotah, 24 × 49cm
Bombay, Prince of Wales Museum of Western India, 55.96

probably actually sitting in the jungle. Rājput artists were sometimes sent ahead of large hunting parties to whitewash the walls of hunting lodges; later, when the raja arrived, they sketched the action. The most stylistically developed Rājput scenes presently known are from the states of Kotah and Mewar. In both areas, artists produced complex animal-filled landscapes closely resembling local terrain. However, even small *thikanas* seem to have isolated examples of hunts with a lively atmosphere and much individual character (**213**).

In Kotah, the hunt miniature has a very long tradition and indeed was the quintessential product of this original school. Several generations of patrons commissioned pictures that combine natural observation, Mughal refinement and Rājput expressionism. Many of the best artists concentrated on elephants which appear in all kinds of poses ranging from the humorous to the furious. The painters seem to sketch not only from observation but also from a sympathetic imagination which is part of Hindu tradition. Though the two painters of elephants represented here are anonymous, their drawings are distinctive enough to be easily identifiable. Scenes of elephant capture contrast the struggles between these beasts and man (**208**).

Some of the brutality in hunting also carried over into sports which, like the chase, related to war; and animal fights of all kinds were popular spectator activities. Cock fights (**210**), antelope fights and elephant fights were all the subjects of wagers. Elephants, tigers and other large exotic animals could be matched only by the emperor or Hindu rajas, but ordinary city dwellers organized gaming between the smaller animals. Elephants could be roused to extraordinary wildness and fury often energetically portrayed in miniatures (**209**).

Many of the Mughal emperors had menageries; Jāhangīr, the amateur naturalist, had menageries that were lavishly staffed departments which existed not only for sport but also for his own curiosity about animal behaviour. The Rājputs followed this practice of keeping animals, most commonly the types of antelope which could be trained as hunting decoys.

Indians were either the inventors or enthusiastic players of many familiar games. Polo and chess were considered excellent preparations for battle manoeuvres; blindman's buff and kite-flying were well-loved, as were toys such as the yo-yo and the hoop (*see* **133**), all of which were frequently illustrated in miniatures of the Mughal period.

210

211

212

213

210 Cock fight
Deccan school, *c.* 1590
From Ahmednagar, 29 × 19cm
Hyderabad, Jagdish and Kamla Mittal
Museum of Indian Art, 76.407

211 Prince hunting
Rajasthan school, *c.* 1700
From Ajmer, 27 × 35cm
New Delhi, National Museum, 69.24

212 Aurāngzīb hunting *nīlgai*
Mughal school, 1660
24 × 34cm
Dublin, The Chester Beatty Library and
Gallery of Oriental Art

213 Thakur Akshay Singh hunting *(see*
p. 77)
Attributed artist: Pemji
Rajasthan school, *c.* 1810
From Bednor, 23 × 44cm
Hyderabad, Jagdish and Kamla Mittal
Museum of Indian Art, 76.200

214 Ruler hunting with falcon *(see p. 78)*
Deccan school, *c.* 1725
29 × 12cm
Private collection

215 Sangram Singh II with wrestlers
(not illustrated)
Rajasthan school, *c.* 1720–30
From Mewar, 86 × 73cm
Udaipur, Zenana Museum

216 Sangram Singh II watching
elephant fights *(not illustrated)*
Rajasthan school, *c.* 1720–30
From Mewar, 83 × 65cm
Udaipur, Zenana Museum

THE VILLAGE AND THE LANDSCAPE

An excellent impression of peaceful Indian rural life is provided by Indian miniatures, for example the picture of a simple, orderly house with a minimum of furniture (218). No theme seems to emphasize the virtues of pastoral life as well as the Krishna story, though the *Rāmayāna* also contains scenes celebrating Rāma's unspoiled existence in the forest. Brindaban, where Krishna and Balarāma grew up, is synonymous in Indian thought with a rural idyll. The brothers and the cowherds are depicted playing in fertile landscapes that are revered as a part of the devotion of Krishna himself. The Kangra painters especially imparted religious meaning to the landscape by simplifying angles and rounding contours to achieve an atmosphere of tranquility (398).

Landscape backgrounds were an important element of many miniatures, but figures are almost always included in the scenes. Miniatures with no human presence are virtually unknown; thus, the Kangra painting here is a rare example of a landscape showing only animals and plants (223). Unlike Chinese art, there is no depiction of the awe-inspiring wilderness, which was indeed considered dangerous.

Early philosophy acknowledged humans as part of nature rather than as intellectual beings responding to the natural world. In painting this older, innocently subjective view of man and nature is represented mainly by the Jain miniaturists. The paintings at Ajanta have landscape elements such as rock escarpments, but they do not demonstrate an attempt to visualize whole environments. The Jain miniaturists tentatively begin to coordinate aspects of nature; rocks and trees spring up against their red backgrounds and gradually come together so that they can be understood as single images. In a *sūtra* recounting the conversions of monks and nuns, a woman who has retired to a cave to meditate, rebukes a would-be seducer, inspiring him by her truthful words to become a Jain monk (see 263). (Interestingly the artist has telescoped the story into a moment of time showing the man already as a righteous monk.) The landscape is not only charmingly symbolic but despite simplicity is painted with great feeling for the energies of nature. The fish-filled stream, shown as a diagonal stripe, has a few flowers on each side representing the vegetation of the area, while birds are symbolized by a peacock and animals by two bucks. Since it is always difficult to interpret space in this type of painting, one cannot judge whether the antelopes are dancing on the jagged mountain peaks that encircle the cave or whether they are on a plane behind.

By the Mughal period, man was viewing the universe more consciously from a non-subjective viewpoint. Curiosity about the physical appearance of things pervades both Mughal and Rājput miniatures despite freer imagination in the Rājput examples.

Although territory was largely divided into villages and feudal outposts in medieval times, tribal groups roamed in the unclaimed forest lands. The Bhils and Santals, for example, were among those entirely outside the Hindu caste system. The Bhils were regarded with curiosity by the Mughals, and repeatedly portrayed in their leaf or skin clothing. Viewed by the Mughals as 'noble savages' and generally treated as clichés in miniatures, the Bhils fully reveal the Mughals' own remoteness from nature; here (219) in one of the few sensitive

217

217 Tribal woman in palm leaf skirt
Nāyaka period, 17th century
From Tamil Nadu
Ivory, 19cm high
Edinburgh, Royal Scottish Museum, 1887.151

218 Empty bed
Mrigavat manuscript
Early Hindu school, *c.* 1520
Varanasi, Bharat Kala Bhavan Museum, 7974

218

219

219 Bhils hunting
Mughal school, *c.* 1635
22 × 14.7cm
New Delhi, National Museum, 50.14/13

220

220 Mountainous landscape
From a *Gajendra Moksha* manuscript
Rajasthan school, *c.* 1640
From Ajmer, 22 × 30cm
*Patna, Sri Gopi Krishna Kanoria
Collection*

**221 Rāja Jaswant Singh of Sawar in
a garden** *(not illustrated)*
Attributed artist: Pemji
Rajasthan school, *c.* 1815–20
From Sawar, 85 × 59cm
*Patna, Sri Gopi Krishna Kanoria
Collection*
Jaswant Singh (ruled 1812–55) is shown
here six times, mainly in conversation
with holy men on an unidentified
festival day. At bottom right he watches
a fight of black bucks.

**222 Mian Mukund Dev on a riding
picnic** *(not illustrated)*
Artist: Nainsukh
Pahari school, *c.* 1750
From Jammu, 31 × 46cm
*London, Victoria and Albert Museum
IS 7-1973*

portrayals of them they are shown in their camp, as
women prepare food before a hut and a couple in the
foreground attempt to kill elephants.

Rajasthani painters often rendered their native countryside
in partially abstract terms, perhaps because they attempted to
depict intangibles such as heat as well as features of the
terrain. One expressionistic picture from Ajmer (**220**) showing
pink rocks, triangular trees and fantastically coloured animals
comes from a text 'The Salvation of the Elephant' including a
description of seasons in different types of landscape; this
particular set of illustrations is unusual in consisting of
numerous scenes showing lakes and land formations. Another
Ajmer example (**221**) by Pemji is rare, not only because an
artist's name is recorded, but also because he is known to have
done several map-like landscapes of this type.

The landscape of the Deccan can be very rich; a scene
painted in Hyderabad (**225**) shows such realistic features as
palm trees growing in a long row, plentiful water birds on a
lake, and deep green vegetation. Artists from the Deccan were
considered to be poetic and dreamy, so the fact that he has
here blended elements of naturalism with fantasy or caprice is
not surprising. The first of three men, seen walking through a
landscape filled with animals, birds and snakes after a hunt,
has a cobra in his belt, while the last enigmatically extends his
hand to the tiger that follows them.

Though people in most of India are pictured spending
leisure time on garden terraces, in the cooler Pahari region
they could enjoy the natural landscape more freely. The artist
Nainsukh shows a party going out on a picnic accompanied by
musicians and riding horses that brush through wild flowers in
a lush meadow (**222**). A further Pahari miniature shows a
group of women on a hunt, dressed in male costume; their
beauty is probably deliberately romanticized by the artist
through the use of the landscape, with its lotus-covered water
and large wading birds (**226**). Despite its sophistication, this
miniature is a surprisingly early naturalistic landscape for this
region, whose painters had previously treated trees almost as
very large flowers.

223

223 Landscape with animals
Pahari school, *c.* 1800
From Kangra, 26 × 14cm
New Delhi, National Museum, 65.310

225

226

224 River scene *(not illustrated)*
Deccan school, 1750
26 × 36cm
New Delhi, National Museum, 54.61/11

225 Hunters in a landscape
Deccan school, *c.* 1750
From Hyderabad, 26 × 44cm
University of Oxford, Bodleian Library,
Douce Or. A3. Fol. 8

226 A lady hunting
Pahari school, *c.* 1750–60
From Guler, 17 × 26cm
New Delhi, National Museum, 51.207
This painting, once thought to have an
inscription with the queen's name, merely
says that a queen is hunting.

227

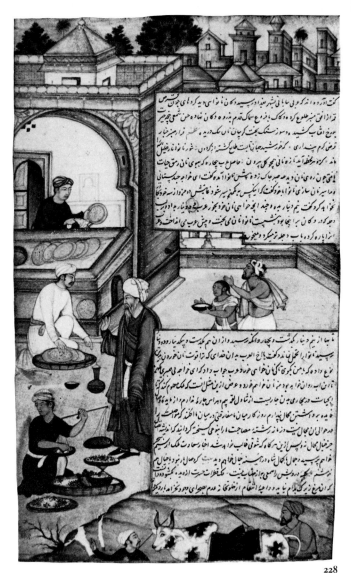

228

THE MARKET PLACE

The Mughal artists were renowned for lively genre paintings, which were far more naturalistic than those created by the Persian contemporaries whom they admired. Their depictions of butchers and cooks, for instance, in scenes of army encampments or feasts, seem to have been exaggerated for the delight of the patron as well as the artist. It was unusual, however, for such genre elements to be more than background vignettes, since miniatures were usually part of historical narrative sequences or official ceremonial depictions. Building construction, which occupied full pages in the illustrated histories because it was so significant in Akbar's reign, is one of the few exceptions. Scenes of this date (**230**) are often crowded with figures – supervisors with long batons, water-carriers with animal skin bags helping to mix mortar, workers with two-man saws cutting planks, and many others – all gesturing characteristically. A further genre scene from a group of fables illustrates the moral tale of the naïve baker ruined by the Arab who is offered as much bread as he can eat. The baker is making his flat loaves as the Arab comes toward him, and a peddlar kneels to weigh his merchandise for a customer (**228**). In general during the rest of the 17th century, because the Mughal patron was a ruler or a nobleman, the activities of common city dwellers and artisans were slighted.

One of the rare miniatures (**227**) from the Pahari area that focuses on the market-place is from Mankot, whose artists specialized in portraiture. The scene, which has no background to identify a particular environment, shows a woman, her face carefully detailed, holding out a bowl as a seller calculates the measure.

227 Woman measuring rice
Pahari school, *c.* 1720
From Mankot, 20 × 17cm
Bombay, Prince of Wales Museum, 64.5

228 The Arab and the baker
From the *Anwār ī Suhailī* manuscript
Attributed artist: Dharm Dās
Mughal school, *c.* 1590–5
20 × 13cm
Dublin, The Chester Beatty Library and Gallery of Oriental Art

229 Water carrier (*bhīstī*) (*not illustrated*)
Kalighat school, *c.* 1800
From Calcutta, 45 × 28cm
London, Victoria and Albert Museum, IS 1890–1955

231 Stall for sale of religious icons
Company school, *c.* 1860
From Patna, 20 × 34cm
London, Trustees of the British Museum, 1948
10–9 0

232 Seated official (*not illustrated*)
Company school, *c.* 1820
29 × 20cm
London, Trustees of the British Museum, 1949
2.21 01

233 Horse merchants (*see p. 43*)
Company school, *c.* 1830
From Delhi, 24 × 38cm
London, Trustees of the British Museum, 1966
10–10 08

230 Workmen erecting a palace
From the *Akbar Nāma* manuscript
Mughal school, *c.* 1605–07
27 × 14cm
London, Victoria and Albert Museum, IS95–1965

In the 18th century, wealthy merchants in northern Indian cities such as Lucknow were active patrons; because these men were interested in bettering their social positions, however, they selected idealized subjects popular among upper-class officials. There was much cultural pride among the city dwellers of the north who were enjoying new forms of music, drama and literature, but the urban man did not find equal expression of his lifestyle in miniature painting. It was the commercially-minded British patron, curious about aspects of Indian life that were similar to those at home, who commissioned pictures of trades and professions; thus artists of the East India Company school turned out whole sets of paintings showing bangle sellers, cloth sellers, and so on. The Company painting shown here (**233**), which portrays a row of shrewd horse merchants from Kabul, is executed in a style similar to that used by artists employed by the ambitious and cultivated mercenary Colonel James Skinner. Working with bright tones, but using European watercolour techniques, the painter shows the traders sitting in upright, self-contained positions that express the independence of their class. A more lively Company-style work from Patna (**231**) shows a potter by the stall of an icon seller who is seated among rows of figurines of Hanumān, Ganesha, Durgā and Krishna. A Company painting from the Deccan of a minor official (**232**) shows him seated in an exaggeratedly refined pose on a striped *dhurrie* and holding out a flower – a common touch in Deccani royal portraits. A 19th-century folk painting of the kind sold by generations of artisan families to pilgrims visiting the Kālī temple in Calcutta, shows a water-carrier similar to those in the building scene (**229**). It is one of the non-religious compositions that portray local genre, street vendors or folk heroes.

238

SYMBOLS OF THE OUTSIDE WORLD

People who came to India over the centuries brought with them their own religious and mythological symbols. While they enlarged the artist's vocabulary with new subjects, their contributions also penetrated to a deeper level and stimulated creative responses. The symbols themselves are of interest because of their extraordinary variety and because they show the significant exchange India has had with many other nations. The early contacts of the Near East with the Indus Valley, the Achaemenids with the Mauryas, the western Classical world and northern Asians with the Kushānas all resulted in an enrichment of artistic symbolism.

Following the establishment of the Muslim Sultanate kingdoms, the Turks, Afghans, Central Asians, Persians and others came to India, bringing with them their motifs and epics. The symbolic heroes and heroines of Persian literature were greatly appreciated at the new Sultanate courts, and made a lasting impression on Hindus. The tragic lovers Lailā and Majnūn, separated by adverse social conditions, always remained popular, easily identifiable symbolic figures. Among the literary subjects were such figures as Solomon, often utilizing his powers of intellect to converse with the birds or animals (**236**). Alexander the Great was the subject of a romance which included his journey to the island with a tree of talking heads, the *waq-waq*. The term *waq-waq* came to stand for symbols created by the playful amalgamation of smaller beings into some larger form, a conceit used by many Indian painters but especially those of the Deccan. Here (**239**) the artist has created a *waq-waq* elephant driven by a *mahout* while an attendant behind handles a wine cup and bottle.

The first big artistic project under young Akbar was the creation of the *Hamza Nāma*, consisting of approximately 1400 large paintings on cloth. The story concerns Hamza, the prophet's uncle, and his encounters with infidels. This insubstantial theme was not repeated, but its adventurous

spirit and magic symbols seem to have inspired the Hindu painters who did many illustrations for the tale (**235**). The giants and spotted demons of the *Hamza Nāma* became such potent symbols of the imagination that in many cases they were confined only with difficulty to the dimensions of the page. Turbulent storms, strange flying objects and terrible beasts were all enthusiastically portrayed by artists – an exercise which extended their stylistic talents. The creations of fantasy in such a powerful style seems to have enabled artists to paint historical and other scenes with great dynamism.

Contacts with European art came at the same time as the *Hamza Nāma* was being prepared. European symbols quickly became immensely popular. Figures of the Virgin (**237**), men in Portuguese costumes, buildings with Classical columns, were all included in miniature scenes. The more esoteric symbol of the angel and fish illustrated here (**234**) is an excellent example of the type of adaptation that occurred. The story comes from the Jewish *Apocrypha* and concerns a fish given by the angel Raphael to strengthen a young boy, Tobias. Not only was this motif used several times in the early Mughal era, but the style of such paintings was also partially westernized. The modelling is handled rather decoratively but its inspiration is European; in addition, the diminutive landscape with its scattered buildings is sensitively treated according to northern Renaissance conventions. At the beginning of Akbar's reign, Basāwan, who was to become the emperor's best artist, was the earliest to translate European stylistic conventions successfully. His concepts were imitated by others, including his own son Manchar.

An astonishing number of miniatures and wall paintings dating from about 1580 to 1620 show European influence. Some of the imperial palaces have lifesize depictions of Biblical figures on the walls, which aroused comment among orthodox Muslims who had a traditional horror of iconic representation. The Jesuits and the English Ambassador, Sir Thomas Roe, were among the chief sources of such motifs, and both Akbar and Jahāngīr were keenly acquisitive of European works though it was generally only prints which reached India.

234

236

234 Angel and fish
Mughal school, *c.* 1590
Varanasi, Bharat Kala Bhavan Museum, 9947
This painting may be by Kesu, an artist renowned for Christian subjects. Note the strange faces in the rock formation and the artist's misunderstanding of the angel's wings.

235 The prophet's uncle Hamza and the infidel, Zamurrad Shāh
(not illustrated)
From the *Hamza Nāma* manuscript
Mughal school, *c.* 1570
On cotton, 68 × 52cm
Cambridge, Fitzwilliam Museum, PD 204–1948

236 Solomon and the animals
Artist: Dhanu
From the *Anwār ī Suhailī* manuscript (folio 4.84)
Mughal school, *c.* 1590–5, 20 × 13cm
Dublin, The Chester Beatty Library and Gallery of Oriental Art

237 The Virgin *(not illustrated)*
Attributed artist: Manchar
Mughal school, *c.* 1595
6.3 × 4.5cm
Private collection

238 'Odalisque' on ivory
Company school, *c.* 1810
From Murshidabad, 7 × 15cm
Private collection

239 Man on *waq-waq* elephant
Deccan school, *c.* 1600
From Bijapur, 23 × 18cm
Dublin, Chester Beatty Library and Gallery of Oriental Art, MS.11A.37

239

भक्ति

6

DEVOTION

The Indian concept of devotion in its many forms finds a central expression in religious life, incorporating different forms of social behaviour. One of its facets is a strong element of diligent and tenacious application, an intensity of adherence to the recipient of the devotion. Western notions of loyalty and chivalrous conduct are rather engulfed in Indian devotional concepts such as *bhakti*, which carry overtones of passionate, clinging adoration and self-abasement.

Whether king or commoner, priest of layman, the devotee is expected to adopt a reverential attitude on entering a temple. Although the outward signs of this attitude may, through familiarity appear almost casual, the marks of respect are always honoured: the devotee removes his sandals before entering, bows or prostrates himself, and carries an offering of some kind, from money or food to some sticks of incense or a few stray blossoms, to place before the image or symbol of the deity in the sanctuary. But on holy days at famous temples, the fervour of pilgrims flocking to a shrine is evident in their demeanour, which ranges from sitting quietly or reciting the praises of the god, to feverish jostling in the crowd for a glimpse (*darshana*) of the sacred image. The ideal devotee will be meticulously clean, in a serious frame of mind, and bearing himself with dignified humility.

Devotees include the itinerant beggar, his long hair bound in the particular style favoured by the sect to which he belongs, naked but for a loincloth: here the idea of renunciation (*sannyāsa*) is held up as the mark of true commitment and devotion. More representative of this attitude is the image of a *sannyāsin*, the direct descendant of the forest seers of long ago, his hair and beard allowed to grow long, dressed in bark and such other materials as he can gather from the forest, often carrying a wooden stave, his eyes either closed in contemplation or staring fixedly at the inner object of his endless pilgrimage. Sometimes his devotion may carry him to self-mortification of the kind the Buddha rejected, such as seeking no alms but deliberately starving himself as a sign of his renunciation of the body and all its distracting appetites, until he is little more than a skeleton. Then, like the god Shiva, he may dance in the most repellent of places, such as cremation grounds, thus associating himself with the death of the body.

TEMPLE AND MOSQUE

Depictions of religious sites in miniature painting show that they attracted animated groups of people. Unlike buildings that open only for congregational worship, the Hindu or Jain temple is a place to visit more freely. A miniature of a Shiva temple outside the provincial city of Murshidabad (245) shows that such shrines have a communal and social significance as well as religious importance.

The usual constituents of temple worship, not identified with any particular sect, include the ringing of a bell to attract the god's attention and the offering of flowers and food. Early morning *pūja* (worship) is the most complex at both Shaivite and Vaishnavite temples. In a Vaishnavite temple where the god is very personalized, ceremonies connected with feeding, dressing or entertaining the image proceed throughout the day.

The rite of circumambulation around the temple exterior means that surprisingly little emphasis is given to the central shrine. The confined, often rather hidden, inner chamber is traditionally unornamented and can be awesome because of its simplicity in contrast to the detail outside. *Dvārapālas* (guardian figures) are positioned either at the entrance to the temple or at the sanctuary door and are usually dressed like the gods whose shrine they protect. They do not, however, represent the deity or receive devotion. The relaxed poses of the two Chola examples (241, 242) contrast with their fierce expressions.

Artists who were commissioned to paint religious complexes regularly treated them in map-like fashion. In the illustration of a Shiva temple in the Pahari region (247), the tall, narrow temple structure echoes the shape of the icy Himalayan peaks jutting behind it. Nandin is shown in front, along with subsidiary buildings and a smaller temple to the left. The shape of the tower *shikhara*, roofs and finial are typical of the Pahari area where northern non-Indian influences are amalgamated with Hinduism.

Often temples were clustered in groups so that sites like Bhubaneshwar or Osian were dotted with buildings. Though these structures might be comparatively small, they could make a town famous, attracting pilgrims from a wide area.

240 Temple column
Early Chālukya period, 8th century
From Alampur (Andhra Pradesh)
Sandstone, 136 × 37 × 37cm
Alampur, Archaeological Museum
On each side of the column shaft are illustrations of the mythic stories
associated with Shiva, Vishnu and The Goddess.

241 & 242 Door guardians
Chola period, *c.* 10th century
From Tamil Nadu
Granite, 178 × 61 × 37cm and 177 × 61 × 38cm
New Delhi, National Museum, 59.153/161 and 162
This pair of guardians flanked the entrance doorway to the temple
sanctuary. Though the poses are complementary, they are not
perfectly symmetrical.

Pushkar in Rajasthan is one of the best known religious sites
which has drawn visitors from great distances for almost two
millennia. Its notoriety is due to the lake at its centre,
supposed to have been created when a lotus dropped from the
hand of Brahmā. Many temples grew up on the terraces
around the lake for the comfort of the pilgrims, but they were
destroyed in the latter part of the 17th century by the
iconoclast, Aurangzīb. In the earlier part of the century,
however, they had been illustrated in a folk romance painted at
Aghatpura near Udaipur (**246**) from which no other miniatures
are presently known. Because Pushkar drew crowds from all
over Rajasthan, it is probable that these shrines were painted
from the artist's own recollection of a visit there, or if not,
from the description of a pilgrim from Pushkar.

Like the temple, the mosque also attracts people of the
community who sit around the shaded periphery of the walled
courtyard with its central tank intended for the purification of
the worshippers. The periodic calls to prayer made from the
minarets at the sides of the mosque draw the faithful. Inside
the columned prayer hall the *mihrāb*, or pointed niche,
indicates the direction for prayers towards Mecca. In contrast
to Hinduism, Islam has congregational worship, as shown in a
miniature (**248**) which commemorates a Near Eastern event,
though the artist has used Indian features.

243 Model of a columned hall showing Tirumalai Nāyak
Nāyaka period, 17th–18th century
From Madurai
Bronze, 32 × 36 × 13cm
London, Victoria and Albert Museum, 98.70
This model of part of the columned hall facing the great temple at
Madurai was probably cast after the hall had been completed as a
commemorative gift.

244

246

246 Worshippers at Pushkar
From a *Dhola Māru* manuscript
Rajasthan school, 1632
From Aghatpura, 13 × 29cm
New Delhi, National Museum, 51.52/36
This extensively illustrated manuscript is important because of the
unusual and controversially dated style.

244 Model of a Shaivite shrine
18th century
From central India
Sandstone, 122 × 46 × 46cm
London, Trustees of the British Museum,
1880–4081

247 Shaivite temple in the Himalayas
Pahari school, early 19th century
From Chamba
Chandigarh, Government Museum and Art
Gallery, 3955
While this temple has not been identified, it
is typical of those in Chamba State.

245

245 Shaivite shrine
Murshidabad, *c.* 1760
25 × 33cm
London, India Office Library and Records,
Add. Or 483

247

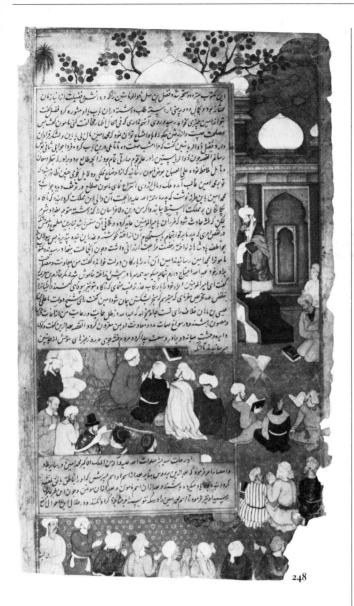

248

251

251 & 252 Ascetics
3rd–4th century
From Gandhara (Pakistan)
Grey schist, each 52 × 47cm
London, Spink & Son Ltd
These slightly curved panels coated the
circular drum of a model *stūpa*, probably
constructed of brick.

252

248 Mosque scene
From Akbar's *Tārikh-i-Alfī* manuscript
Mughal school, *c.* 1595
41 × 22cm
New Delhi, National Museum, 50.356

249 Door guardian (*not illustrated*)
17th century
From Kerala
Wood, 152 × 69 × 27cm
Bangalore, Government Museum and Venkatappa Art Gallery

250 Muslim tomb in a garden with water channels
(*not illustrated*)
Company school, *c.* 1810–20
From Rajasthan, 111 × 180cm
London, Royal Asiatic Society

ASCETICS AND SAINTS

Perhaps the most celebrated feature of religious life in India is the cult of the ascetic, dedicated to the pursuit of enlightenment, to the power of ultimate knowledge. The fame of India's ascetics spread to the Greek and Roman world; Alexander the Great was eager to meet India's holy men when he reached the Indus River in 327 BC.

Sculptures of holy ascetics are known from the earliest period of Indian art. In Gandhara reliefs, for example, they frequently appear in scenes illustrating the life of the Buddha; the naturalism of these early carvings can be seen in the carefully observed emaciated bodies, long matted hair, bearded faces, and simple clothing. Typically, ascetics bring their hands together in attitudes of reverence (**251** and **252**). They

253

254

255

255 Devotee offering his head
Chola period, 10th century
From Koyambedu (Tamil Nadu)
Granite, 80 × 39 × 21cm
Madras, Government Museum, 116/3940

254 Ascetics
Gupta period, *c.* 5th century
From Harwan (Kashmir)
Terracotta, 53 × 30cm
*London, Victoria and Albert Museum,
IS 9-1978*
This is one of many plaques that display
clear evidence of the use of moulds. These
plaques were used as facings on a wall or
platform around a courtyard in which there
was an apsidal temple.

253 Sage
Vijayanagara period, 15th–16th century
From Tadpatri (Tamil Nadu)
Granite, 88 × 32 × 18cm
Madras, Government Museum, 2546

crouch in huddled postures (**254**) or lean heavily on their
staffs. In Hindu art, ascetics are often associated with Shiva,
especially in his role as the terrible Bhairava. The most
extreme ascetic was one who offered his own head in an
ultimate gesture of self-surrender. Whether in terracotta or
granite, self-decapitation was the excuse for a type of sculpture
portraying complex postures, the body twisted around with the
arm thrown above the head (**255** and **256**).

There exists, however, another group of holy men that
actually attained the status of saints, and their images are often
installed in southern Indian temples. The saints were
individuals whose devotion to the Hindu gods Shiva or Vishnu
was so strong that they virtually identified with the divine
object of their worship. Twelve were devotees of Vishnu and
are termed *Ālvārs*; sixty-three were Shiva worshippers and
called *Nāyanārs*. The *Nāyanārs* composed a collection of
devotional verses in the Tamil language, entitled the
Tirumurai. This is divided into eleven books, one of which, the
Tiruvāchakam, was composed by Mānikkavāchakar (**259**).
Bharata, half-brother of the legendary hero Rāma, was another
saintly devotee. He refused to rule out of devotion to Rāma
and guarded the throne in Rāma's absence (**258**).

257

258

259

256

256 Ascetic offering his head
Gupta period, 5th century
From Mathura (Uttar Pradesh)
Terracotta, 32 × 12cm
Mathura, Government Museum, 38.39.2792

257 Tamil saint, Sundaramūrti
Chola period, 10th–11th century
From Kilaiyur (Tamil Nadu)
Bronze, 77 × 39 × 23cm
Thanjavur, Art Gallery, 99

258 Bharata, younger brother of Rāma, showing his devotion
Vijayanagara period, 14th–15th century
From Tamil Nadu
Bronze, 76 × 29 × 22cm
New Delhi, National Museum, 69.49

259 Tamil saint, Mānikkavāchakar
Late Chola period, *c.* 13th century
From Tamil Nadu
Bronze, 57 × 21 × 21cm
New Delhi, National Museum, 47.109/25

261 Female lamp holder (*not illustrated*)
Kākatīya period, 11th–12th century
From Andhra Pradesh
Bronze, 16 × 4 × 6cm
Hyderabad, State Museum

262 Worshipper (*see p. 59*)
Vijayanagara period, 15th–16th century
From Tadpatri (Tamil Nadu)
Granite, 46 × 31 × 29cm
Madras, Government Museum, 2544

263 Conversion of monks and nuns
(*not illustrated*)
From the *Uttaradhyāna Sūtra* manuscript
(folios 22v and 23r)
Jain school, *c.* 1460
From western India, 12 × 10cm
*London, Victoria and Albert Museum,
IS2–1972*
The first folio shows the birth of a future
saint on a boat, the execution of a criminal
and the saint's subsequent conversion to
non-violent Jainism symbolized by the
cutting of his hair; the second leaf shows a
nun who causes the conversion of a man by
rebuking him for his advances.

264

265

266

264 & 265 Two leaves of yogic positions
From a *Bahr al Hayāt* manuscript
Mughal school, *c.* 1600–5
22 × 13cm each
Dublin, The Chester Beatty Library and

Gallery of Oriental Art, Ms. 16, folios 23 and 24a
This unusual manuscript, probably done for Jahāngīr, as a prince, describes yogic exercises exactly.

266 Shaivite *yoginī*
Deccan school, *c.* 1620–25
From Bijapur, 20 × 11cm
Hyderabad, Jagdish and Kamla Mittal Museum of Indian Art, 76.406

YOGA: DISCIPLINE

A seal of the ancient Indus Valley civilization appears to depict the god Shiva in a yogic position: it establishes the ancient lineage of *yoga* through artistic evidence as well as showing that Shiva has always been worshipped as the great *yogī*. Several millennia later, a Deccani miniature painting shows a Shaivite ascetic (identified by his trident) practicing austerities, his hands reverently raised (**266**). He stands, on one leg, alone in simple deep green landscape. The exercise of balancing on one leg is the famous penance performed by Arjuna to win Shiva's recognition. A Basohli drawing shows a small boy poised easily on the toes of one foot as he fingers a rosary (**273**). Although he is in a forest filled with terrifying fire-breathing animals, he appears quite indifferent to them. Neither the demons throwing rocks or shooting arrows are making any impression, and their missiles appear to be deflected. The woman next to him is also accepting her peril very cooly.

While *yoga* was connected with the worship of Shiva, it was not confined to any particular devotional belief, but was simply one of the earliest methods accepted for attaining *moksha* or salvation. It was intended to go along with *jnāna* – salvation through philosophical knowledge. Krishna discusses these as

being important to Vishnu devotees in the *Bhāgavad Gītā* and blends them with the newer, less austere concept of salvation through personal worship.

A drawing attributed to Basāwan, Akbar's most perceptive artist, shows simple *yogīs* in loincloths being handed a flower by a shepherd (**274**); the ascetics are humorously drawn, and yet the artist handles his subjects with gentle tolerance rather than sarcasm or cynicism. Deprived of attention, their bodies have grown into strange shapes resembling tree stumps or roots which their spirits hardy seem to notice. Members of the Kanphat sect of *yogīs* are often portrayed in miniatures; they had their ears pierced and large bone earrings inserted as a pledge of their calling. The practices of these *yogīs* influenced *sūfi* mystics including the Qalandar dervishes who adopted their custom of wearing earrings and travelling with a pet animal. This particular ascetic (**267**) travels with a tiny sheep rather than the more usual dog.

While Indian society honoured the ascetic, it also recognized that physical austerities did not necessarily have any relevance to spirituality. Thus the ascetic who deprived himself for disreputable motives, such as notoriety, became a subject for 19th-century caricaturists. The man in the background of a drawing of Vaishnavite ascetics (**275**) is straining the intoxicating drink *bhang*, while his compatriots are in different states of confusion and debauchery.

267 Ascetic with pet sheep
Artist: Mukund
Mughal school, *c.* 1595
11.4 × 5.8cm
Private collection

267

268

269

268 *Yogī* and disciple
Artist: Nānhā
Mughal school, *c.* 1595
7 × 7cm
London, Victoria and Albert Museum,
IS229–1951

269 Princes visiting *yogīs*
Rajasthan school, *c.* 1690
From Bikaner, 27 × 17cm
Baron and Baroness Bachofen
von Echt collection

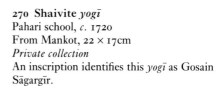

270 Shaivite *yogī*
Pahari school, *c.* 1720
From Mankot, 22 × 17cm
Private collection
An inscription identifies this *yogī* as Gosain
Sāgargīr.

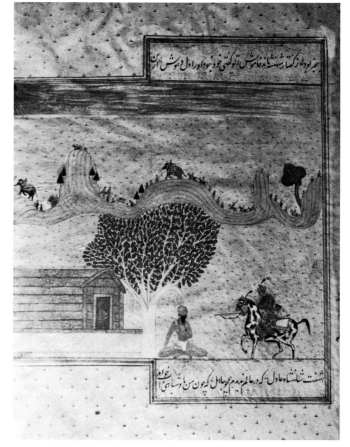

**271 Rāja Parīkshit offends the hermit
Angiras**
From a Persian translation of the *Bhāgavata
Purāna*
Deccan school, early 18th century
New Delhi, National Museum, 70.14

272 A stout *yogī*
Attributed artist: Nainsukh
Pahari school, *c.* 1759
From Jammu, 26 × 19cm
Private collection

273 Demons attacking boy *yogī*
Pahari school, *c.* 1710
From Basohli, 21 × 32cm
London, Trustees of the British Museum, 1966 7–25 05

273

274

274 Two ascetics offered a flower by a shepherd
Attributed artist: Basāwan
Mughal school, *c.* 1590
23 × 18cm
London, India Office Library and Records, J22.13

275 Caricature of Vaishnavite ascetics
Pahari school, early 19th century
From Chamba, 17 × 30cm
London, Trustees of the British Museum, 1949 10–8 021

276 Addicts *(not illustrated)*
Rajput school, 1825
From Jaipur, 36 × 26cm
New Delhi, National Museum, 51.218/28

275

SŪFISM: ECSTASY

The *sūfi* movement arose in Persia around the 9th century AD as a reaction to the hierarchical and intolerant nature of the state religion. The early *sūfis* recognized the need for greater personal awareness of god and sought to feel the deep ecstacy of his possession or control. They believed in acting from a personal rather than doctrinal point of view. The movement came to be regarded as heretical by orthodoxy and it was in order to avoid the resulting persecution that *sūfis* fled to India.

In the early 13th century, the Chishti order of *sūfis* was founded at Ajmer. Centuries later Akbar, a ruler who genuinely searched for universal truth and religious tolerance, acknowledged the enormous contribution made to India by the Muslim *sūfis*, especially by those of the Chishti order, and made frequent pilgrimages to Ajmer on foot to show his reverence for them (**277**).

The term *sūfi* is derived from the word *sūf* (wool), which referred to the garment sometimes worn by these ascetics. The Chishtis were the best known of the dervishes, 'poor men', who achieved a state of ectasy through song and dance. Under the influence of Islam, dancing *sūfis* became a usual theme in Indian painting; the group represented here (**278**) illustrate the Persian story of *Yūsuf u Zulaykhā*, the love between Joseph and Potiphar's wife which is apocryphal to the Jewish and Christian Old Testament.

The centuries between the arrival of the Chishtis and Akbar's death in 1605 measured a span of close communication and harmony between religious groups – of which the Chishti sect of *sūfis* and the Hindu *Rāma-bhaktis* were the most open and forward-looking. This atmosphere of tolerance culminated in Akbar's reign. Akbar proclaimed a new faith, the *Dīn-i-Ilāhī* 'Religion of God' which included elements of the creed of non-violence in Jainism, sun worship, *sūfi* tolerance and many other beliefs, but it never gained popularity outside Akbar's immediate circle and nor did the emperor appear to push its acceptance.

Akbar's son and grandson who succeeded him both had Rājput mothers but had comparatively little sympathy for the cultural aspects of Hinduism that Akbar had found satisfying. Shāh Jahān's oldest son Dārā, intended to be his successor, was interested in uniting Hinduism and *sūfism*. He was taught by both Hindu and Muslim *mullahs* and many pictures exist of Dārā seated before his well-known teachers Mīān Mīr and Mullah Shāh. A contemporary painting shows another upper-class young man also posed before a *mullah* preceptor (**279**), a subject made fashionable by Dārā's example. From the inscription and the flowing rhythm of style, the miniature seems to have been done in the hills though its painter was thoroughly trained in Mughal techniques. This anonymous artist has created a portrait of the Islamic religious type whose appearance can be universally understood and yet has been conditioned by a particular training and approach to life. The sunken body with the intelligent head thrust forward seems to signify that the victory of age has been gentle, serving only to accentuate the *mullah*'s compassion and breadth of religious experience.

When Dārā was killed in a struggle for the throne, the religious tolerance that had been promoted by Akbar was decisively snuffed out at court.

277

277 Akbar walking to Ajmer
From an *Akbar Nāma* manuscript
Outline by Basāwan, colouring by Nand Gwaliori, portraits by Nānhā
Mughal school, *c*. 1590
38 × 25cm
London, Victoria and Albert Museum, IS2–1896–77/117

282

278

279

278 Dancing *sūfīs*
From the *Yūsuf u Zulaykhā* manuscript
Attributed artist: Muhammad Nadir of Samarkand
1650
From Kashmir, 30 × 16cm
London, India Office Library and Records

279 Prince with *mullah*
Pahari school, *c.* 1700
From Bilaspur, 21 × 15cm
Hyderabad, Jagdish and Kamla Mittal Museum of Indian Art, 76.234

282

280 *Sūfī* around a Muslim shrine *(not illustrated)*
Deccan school, *c.* 1630–40
From Bijapur, 30 × 23cm
University of Oxford, Bodleian Library, Douce Or. B2. Fol.1

281 *Sūfīs* *(not illustrated)*
Mughal school, *c.* 1640
Shāh Jahān period
11.5 × 8.5cm
New Delhi, National Museum, 52.33

282 Shāh Rājū and his son Akbar Shāh *(two details)*
Deccan school, *c.* 1670
From Golconda, 19 × 25 and 17 × 22cm
Private collection
The *sūfī* Shāh Rājū moved to Golconda to teach the last king, Tānā
Shāh, the epicurean Prince of Taste.

175

283

283 Krishna *bhājan (worship)*
Rajasthan school, *c.* 1790
From Jaipur, 22 × 30cm
Chandigarh, Government Museum and Art Gallery, 3203

BHAKTI: LOVE

Bhakti, or devotion, is a concept connected with the worship
of Vishnu's two *avatāras* Rāma and Krishna. Shiva, the great
yogī, welcomes devotion in his followers through the sterner
path of asceticism, but Rāma and Krishna, *avatāras* of the
universal protector and saviour, are approachable through
personal love. The essence of *bhakti* was often expressed by an
analogy with the deep yearning in the heart of the lover for the
loved one, and indeed, reflects some of the strongest desires of
the Indian personality.

Rāma *bhakti* was culturally and politically influential in the
Sultanate period but its influence waned while that of Krishna
worship rose just prior to the arrival of the Mughals. The
predominance of Rāma, the elevated unselfish prince, seems to
have faded with increased Muslim influence, while the
cowherd Krishna, associated with India's strong rural
tradition, came to the fore to meet a need for religious re-
identification.

Bhakti as a movement appeared early (the concept is
implied in the Krishna texts of the *Bhāgavata Purāna* and
Bhāgavad Gītā) and went through several phases of evolution.
Each phase began as a spontaneous burst of popular emotion,
was articulated by poets and then by philosophers. Several
centuries of passionate hymn and poetry writing culminated in

a period of ardent devotion in Bengal, an area which produced
not only the poet Jayadeva, who wrote the *Gīta Govinda*, but
also other great *bhakti* figures. It was also the area in which the
bhājan, a communal singing that dramatized various aspects of
Krishna's relationship with Rādhā, developed. This kind of
religious singing became a significant part of *bhakti* and
survives in Krishna temples today. The absorption of the
musicians and the adoration, especially of the worshipper who
lies prone before the image of a Jaipur miniature (**283**), are
typical of the *bhakti* spirit.

The popular pre-Mughal *bhakti* movement was perhaps
most effectively redirected by the philosopher Vallabhāchārya.
He capitalized on the great fervency of popular devotion to
found a sect dedicated to a particular image of Krishna which
he titled Shrī (Lord) Nāthjī. Vallabhāchārya maintained that
this image which had been buried had revealed itself to him
together with directives for its worship. The doctrine of the
sect was *pushti-marg*, the enjoyment of plenty and beauty,
which included the commissioning of paintings as part of
religious devotion.

Shrī Nāthjī worship spread to other areas of India. Kotah
produced paintings connected with the cult; a large
composition shows several generations of devotees, the
youngest dressed as Krishna (**286**). Kishangarh also
celebrated this worship. One of the paintings from there shows
the interior of a roofless shrine with many priests attending the

284

284 Worship at a shrine of the Vallabhāchārya sect
Rajasthan school, *c.* 1780–90
From Kishangarh, 29 × 22cm
New Delhi, National Museum, 58.39/3

285

285 Rām Singh II worshipping Shrī Nāthjī
Rajasthan school, *c.* 1865
From Kotah, 27 × 20cm
Hyderabad, Jagdish and Kamla Mittal Museum of Indian Art, 76.150

286 Devotees of Shrī Nāthjī
Rajasthan school, *c.* 1800
From Kotah, 30 × 76cm
Hyderabad, Jagdish and Kamla Mittal Museum of Indian Art, 76.154

286

small images of Rādhā, Krishna and Garuda on a thronelike
dias (**284**). The deities are being fanned, while tiny offerings
are prepared for them. In front of the shrine, murals of
elephant riders, common on the sect's buildings, symbolize the
royal status of the divinity, while at the back of the interior,
murals of cows indicate Krishna's simple life as a cowherd.
The birds, which also appear in a few other paintings, seem to
be part of a festival which involves their feeding.

Among the other Vaishnavite images also included in the
sect's elaborate ritual is one which is pictured at Kotah (**285**),
where it was temporarily placed in the 19th century. The
image is being worshipped by Rām Singh II (ruled 1827–65)
during the eighth month (May–June). As the monsoon is
expected at this time, water very naturally is the focus of
attention: one small icon goes on a boat ride, another is rinsed
with showers of water and this four-armed image is
entertained by an elaborate display of toy boats, little islands
and lotus blossoms arranged in ankle-deep water.

During Aurangzīb's reign, Shrī Nāthjī was moved to a site
on the borders of Mewar, to save the image from
iconoclasm. The town, Nathadwara, which grew up around
the image to serve its needs, is full of shops selling all kinds of
devotional reminders to the pilgrims. The actual images are
worshipped and adored by the devotees as though they were
revered and beloved human beings; Shrī Nāthjī is attended by
priests who bathe, dress, feed and entertain him.

CEREMONIES OF BRĀHMANS AND RULERS

Though rulers had great influence over the religious beliefs of their peoples because they were so profoundly admired by their subjects, their religious functions were not defined by the Hindu caste system. It is the *brāhmans*, whose caste was specially designated to carry out religious ceremonies, who are at the heart of religious worship in India. A *brāhman* is born into the rights of his caste, but his investiture with a sacred thread is the act which confirms his life role. This viral ceremony takes play in boyhood, commonly in his eighth year and is an initiation into manhood, to brahmanical education and to the responsibilities of caste. The thread under ordinary circumstances is worn over the left shoulder and across the chest (**290**). The *brāhman*'s tasks are communal in the sense that he is understood to be a moral force upholding the rightness of things in the community. For example, if *brāhmans* fail to lead sufficiently pure lives – perhaps only inadvertently eating impure food – their lapse can rock the community through fear of the possible cosmic disasters that might result. Through their traditional rituals *brāhmans* are thought to ensure the continuity of nature – for instance, the pre-sunrise ceremony is believed to free the sun from darkness for its daily ascent – but personal salvation can nevertheless be attained through other disciplines; *yoga*, philosophical knowledge or devotion to a personal god are paths towards that salvation wholeheartedly followed by many people that a *brāhman* may or may not choose to pursue.

Unfortunately, since it was only the rulers who patronized artists, there are few pictures of *brāhmans* at their worship. The lives of the Rājput rulers, however, included worship, some of which had general similarities to that of the *brāhmans*. The miniatures illustrating these devotions show detailed arrays of graceful metal lamps, spoons and tiny metal dishes. One (**287**) portrays an unidentified raja, surrounded by offerings of flowers heaped on stands, with an image of Krishna playing the flute. Another miniature shows Rāja Dhiraj Singh with his hand inside a *gomukhi* (rosary bag) counting his 108 rosary beads in private, an action which he would repeat a certain number of times as a duty, possibly followed by additional prayers for merit or a boon (**289**).

Different attitudes could be accommodated in Hinduism. The devotions of the Pahari area have a flavour unlike those in other parts of India. The religious beliefs of the relatively remote area of Mandi were more akin to magic than to an intellectual brahmanical tradition, as two miniatures of Sidh Sen (ruled 1684–1727) clearly demonstrate. In one, Sidh Sen is depicted standing before Shiva and Pārvatī who have manifested themselves to him. This illustration, however, is not as surprising as a more refined painting by another artist showing Sidh Sen as an ascetic actually metamorphasized into a four-armed Shiva with drum, trident, discus and horn (**292**). Sidh Sen wears a long necklace of *rudrāksha* berries traditional for *sādhus* and his turban carries eyes of supernatural vision akin to those of Shiva.

Among the devotional subjects rare in miniature painting is the worship of a Jain Tīrthankara image by a ruler (**291**), and the worship of the Buddha figure by Vishnavite *brāhmans* (**288**). By the beginning of the 18th century the assimilation of Buddhism had long been accomplished by incorporating its founder into the Hindu pantheon as an incarnation of Vishnu.

287

287 A raja worshipping Krishna
Pahari school, *c*. 1700
From Bilaspur, 23 × 17cm
Hyderabad, Jagdish and Kamla Mittal Museum of Indian Art, 76.235
The purifying aspects of water are represented by ewers filled with water theoretically from India's holy rivers – in this case the Jumna.

288 *Brāhmans* worshipping the Buddha incarnation of Vishnu
From a Vishnu *avatāra* set
Pahari school, *c*. 1710
From Mankot, 19 × 27cm
Bombay, J. P. Goenka collection

288

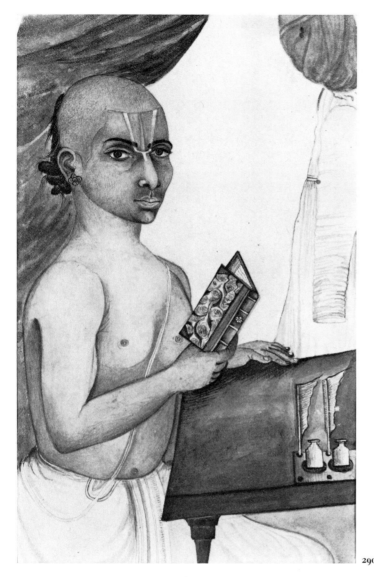

289

289 Rāja Dhīraj Singh worshipping
Central Indian school, *c.* 1700
From Ragogarh, 30 × 24cm
Private collection

290 *Brāhman* **with forehead marks
signifying devotion to Vishnu**
Deccan school, mid-19th century
From Maharashtra, 14 × 9cm
Private collection

290

**291 A raja worshipping a
Tīrthankara**
Deccan school, *c.* 1690
21 × 31cm
Bombay, J. P. Goenka collection

292 Rāja Sidh Sen as an ascetic
(see p.48)
Pahari school, *c.* 1725
From Mandi, 22 × 14cm
*Hyderabad, Jagdish and Kamla Mittal
Museum of Indian Art, 76.260*

**293 Rāja Sidh Sen of Mandi
meeting Shiva and Pārvatī** *(not
illustrated)*
Pahari school, *c.* 1720–30
From Mandi, 36 × 27cm
*Hyderabad, Jagdish and Kamla
Mittal Museum of Indian Art, 76.258*

294 Raja visited by two monks
(not illustrated)
From a Kālakāchārya manuscript
Jain school, *c.* 1430
From western India, 6 × 5cm
Bombay, J. P. Goenka collection

291

295

295 *Yogīs* and *yoginīs* in a palace setting
Artist: Hūnhār II
Provincial Mughal school, *c.* 1760
From Lucknow, 33 × 43cm
London, Victoria and Albert Museum,
D1203–1903

296 Devotee holding a *chaurī* (fly whisk)
(see p. 56)
Maitraka period, 8th century
From Akota (Gujarat)
Bronze, 24 × 8cm
Baroda, Museum and Picture Gallery, AR547

297 Elderly *yoginī* and princess *(see p. 42)*
Mughal school, *c.* 1640
22 × 14cm
Dublin, The Chester Beatty Library and
Gallery of Oriental Art, Ms. 55.4

WOMEN AND RELIGION

While Indian women do not have access to brahmanical
salvation because they are on a lower scale in the system of
reincarnation than men, they are often deeply devoted and can
find ways of leading religious lives. Like men, they can become
ascetics, especially in old age, as illustrated by a dignified
yoginī seated outside her hut leaning on a short crutch
traditionally used for meditation and accompanied by a young
acolyte (**297**). A portrait of a formidable saintly lady from the
Pahari area honoured by a group of other women while
reading a scriptural text (**299**) shows the respect that could be
earned by women for a religious life. The contribution of
women to religious philosophy is, however, virtually non-
existent, and their literary output has been small. An exception
is the famous Rajasthani poetess Mīrābāī, who left her family
home as a young widow for a life of total devotion to Krishna.
Despite intense opposition, she eventually won admiration for
her Rādhā-like life.

In contrast to Mīrābāī's deep passion, it was a custom for
courtly women sometimes to feign devotion. In a painting by
Hūnhār II (**295**), India's traditional polarities of asceticism and
graceful human life are clearly exemplified. In a rich palace
setting lit with candles for a religious observance, beautiful
women sit among emaciated ascetics. A royal *yoginī* leaning on
a meditation swing contrasts to the Jain nun in white wearing

a face mask to prevent her from the sin of accidentally inhaling
and killing insects in the night air.

Most Indian women undertake simple devotional tasks
which are akin to household duties; these often take place
within the home and give an air of gentle, modest sincerity to
religion. For example, many women tend a household *tulsī*
plant placed in a tall container reminiscent of the ancient
platforms erected around sacred trees. The pleasantly aromatic
shrub is circumambulated, watered and marked with
sandalwood paste. The devotee here (**298**) is shown as a bare-
breasted ascetic, who carries a rosary, rather than as just a
simple householder. Usually considered sacred to Vishnu, the
tulsī is sometimes also associated with the worship of Shiva, as
is suggested by the presence of his bull, Nandin.

Women are excluded from the religious ceremonies of
greatest import. They are, however, not only allowed to
celebrate such sacred activities as festivals and fasts but can be
the most significant participants. For example, women carry
on the worship of other sacred trees in addition to the *tulsī* on
special days. The *āmlā* tree bears fruits similar to gooseberries
and is believed to be an embodiment of Vishnu; a Kotah
miniature (**300**) pictures three women making offerings to
these trees on a fast day. Many beliefs, such as the worship of
the *āmlā*, have been taken into formal Vishnu or Shiva
worship, but are so ancient that the true reasons for their
existence are obscured. Women, however, have gracefully
retained such observances of traditional custom.

301 Sarūp Singh at the Holī festival *(detail)*
Rajasthan school, *c.* 1854
From Mewar, 80 × 112cm
Udaipur, Zenana Museum

298 *Yoginī* waters a *tulsī* plant
Rajasthan school, 18th century
From Jaipur, 20 × 13cm
London, Trustees of the British Museum, 1921 1–11 03

299 Woman devotee chants the scriptures
Pahari school, *c.* 1760
From Nurpur, 17 × 28cm
London, Trustees of the British Museum, 1966 10–10–011

300 Women worshipping *āmlā* trees *(see p. 45)*
Rajasthan school, *c.* 1670
From Kotah, 22 × 18cm
Hyderabad, Jagdish and Kamla Mittal Museum of Indian Art, 76.129

FESTIVALS

The traditional Hindu week did not include days of rest, but two days in each month were fast days on which most people did no work, such as the *āmlā ekādashi* (**300**). In addition, India has a great many festivals which are kept as holidays. Among the best-loved are the spring observance of Holī, the early autumn Dashera festival, sacred to Durgā, and the late autumn Divali or 'Festival of Lights'.

Holī is an exuberant even roisterous period during which the social formalities are overturned. In the Mughal period, those considered low in status became jokingly rebellious in ways which would not otherwise have been tolerated, and even Rājput rulers were sprayed with coloured water and visited by crowds of raucous singers. The red water and powder which are thrown very freely probably symbolize the blood or energy of life reaffirmed in the spring.

A large Mewar painting of Holī (**302**) depicts Mahārāna Pratāp Singh II (ruled 1751–4), with his heir apparent and nobles, decorously celebrating Holī as if he were thoroughly conscious of his obligation to enter into the frivolity of the festival. (The high-ceilinged room with a balcony is clearly rendered from direct observation though it does not exist today: above the wall panels of fighting elephants are two Chinese pictures which, like other Udaipur decorative items, show contacts between Rajasthan and the Dutch East India

303 Sangrām Singh at the Gangaur festival (*not illustrated*)
Rajasthan school, *c.* 1720–30
From Mewar, 72 × 70cm
Udaipur, Zenana Museum

304 Krishna's marriage
From a *Mahābhārata* manuscript
Pahari school, *c.* 1810
From Garhwal, 37 × 51cm
Private collection

305 Boy on a swing (*not illustrated*)
Rajasthan school, 1887
From Mewar, 14 × 21cm
Chandigarh, Government Museum and Art Gallery, 2437

304

302 Pratāp Singh II celebrates the festival of Holī in his palace
Rajasthan school, 1753
From Mewar, 55 × 38cm
New Delhi, National Museum, 50.14/15

302

Company.) Pratāp Singh, with a halo, is shown once on his throne before a large tank of coloured Holī water and again in the foreground, involved in a mock battle between his nobles. Four large water guns, elaborately worked in silver and gold, are arranged in front of him. In a much livelier Holī scene, Mahārāna Sarūp Singh of Mewar (ruled 1842–61) is shown several times on horseback with arcs of red powder swirling around him (**301**). Though the artist Tārā, who was Sarūp's best and more prolific painter, has conventionalized the setting, the Udaipur palace courtyard is easily recognizable.

Weddings were particularly beloved celebrations: women, especially, delighted in them because they provided freedom to have a lively time and hear community news. In a Garhwal night scene (**304**) Krishna and his bride move toward the brahmanical fire and the *pandal*, or small hutlike structure constructed for the most eventful moments of the marriage.

During the Gangaur festival, lavishly celebrated in Mewar, unmarried girls petitioned for a husband like the god Shiva at worship ceremonies over a two week period. At the climax of the festivities, clay images of Shiva and Pārvatī were placed in the lake at Udaipur by a procession of devotees, while the regularly worshipped images were immersed and then taken home. During the accompanying fireworks, parties of women danced by the lake and at the Udaipur palace. Here (**303**) the artist has managed to combine all these complex activities with many figures into a large scene which – like many Rajasthani miniatures – shows the raja several times. The night effects, rendered here with subtle tones rather than as a flat black background, were an unusual challenge for the artist.

During many festivals and on special occasions, women made wall paintings on houses using rice flour and coloured powders. A miniature (**305**) of an unidentified celebration concerning a child shows him in a swing, a popular object expressing joy and fertility which is celebrated in a spring *rāga*.

सम्बोधि

7

ENLIGHTENMENT

Two opposite extremes must not be entered into: indulgence in sensual pleasure and self-mortification. Between these two lies a middle way which, if followed, bestows peace, higher wisdom, enlightenment and the extinction of those attachments which obstruct such a state. The middle way is like a road having eight parts – outlook and aspiration, speech and action, livelihood and effort, mindfulness and concentration – which must all be conducive to the extinction of suffering.

Suffering is an immutable fact. It is manifest in the following forms: birth, ageing, disease, dying, involvement with the unpleasant, separation from the pleasant, and non-attainment of the desirable. In other words suffering is an inherent function of our very existence which by nature clings to itself. I have seen the significance of the existence of this fact of suffering; I have recognized the need to understand suffering; and I have made it understood to myself.

That suffering has an origin is a fact. Its origin lies in the thirst that is bound up with rebirth – a thirst that is accompanied by delight and passion, that slakes itself haphazardly. The origin of suffering is the thirst which is desire, the thirst which is living, the thirst which is procreation. I have understood the fact of the origin of suffering; I have seen that it must be rejected; and I have rejected it.

That suffering has an end is equally a fact. Its end is the utter destruction, with dispassion, of the thirst that is the origin of suffering; it is the abandonment, the letting go, of that thirst; it is the independence and release from that thirst. I have been enlightened by the fact that suffering has an end; I have known that this fact should be realized; and I have come to that realization.

That there is a way to the end of suffering is also a fact. That way is the road with eight parts, the middle way (as I have described it). I had the wisdom to comprehend the fact that there is a way to destroy suffering, and to formulate it using the metaphor of a road; I knew that this fact required fostering; and I have fostered it.

It has been difficult to order these meditations into the four immutable facts and to establish the three stages by which each was to be fully internalized and clearly realized. But having done so, I am certain that my mind is free; this is to be my last life on earth – there is now no more rebirth for me. I am completely enlightened.

These words, according to the ancient Pāli scriptures preserved in Sri Lanka, are those of a thirty-five-year-old man speaking to five ascetics, his erstwhile companions, in the Deer Park near Varanasi around the year 528 BC. The man was Siddhārtha, of the house of Gautama in the tribe of the Shākyas who lived to the north, just within the modern frontier of Nepal, between the Ganges and the Himalayas. On the basis of this statement and his subsequent teachings, he became known as the Buddha, 'The Enlightened'.

Some ten or twelve years earlier, according to legend, a boy had been born in the Jnātrika clan of the powerful Licchavi tribe near their city of Vaishali north of the capital of the kingdom of Magadha, where the Buddha mostly preached. The Jnātrika boy was named Vardhamāna, of the house of Siddhārtha Kāshyapa. The Kāshyapa family followed the teachings of a sage called Pārshva, who had died about 200 years previously; and when Vardhamāna renounced home and family to lead a wandering ascetic life – as the Buddha had done – he soon fell in with a group of wandering ascetics who were committed to achieve salvation through the methods taught by the same Pārshva his parents had revered. The group obeyed four basic rules: no violence, true speech, no stealing, no acquisitiveness. At the end of his first year of wandering, his only loincloth was threadbare; Vardhamāna simply cast it aside, and for the rest of his life he went naked. For thirteen years his wanderings continued until, near the hill where Pārshva was said to have died, he came to a village called Jrimbhika beside a river, where he sat under a *sal* tree close to an ancient shrine. It was here that his meditations led him into a state called *kevala* (literally, 'alone'), which is the complete isolation of the real inner self from all earthly influence, from one's past lives or from the present. He was forty-five years old when he achieved this state, a moment in his life equivalent to the enlightenment of the Buddha. He then left the forests and taught among the peoples of his own and the Buddha's tribes and in the Gangetic kingdoms. Vardhamāna was now known as Mahāvīra, 'Great Hero', and given the title of Jina, 'Conqueror', from which the name of the religion which he established – Jainism – is derived.

The peoples to whom the Buddha and the Jina preached along the Ganges plain were becoming increasingly urbanized

306

306 A Jain Tīrthankara
Gupta period, *c.* 5th century
From Uttar Pradesh
Red sandstone, 71 × 54 × 56cm
Mathura, Government Museum, B.61

and increasingly subject to the *brāhman* priesthood, whose religious outlook stemmed from the *Vedas* and the rigid ritualistic reformulations of them. These two men, both born into the warrior caste to which the ruling military aristocracy also belonged, spoke before powerful kings and princes as well as to the multitudes; their message was that the individual should seek his own path to salvation, independent of the priests. Like the ancient seers of former times, they were visionaries from the forest; they were heard with reverence, and became connected in men's minds with the tradition of the forest sages. The Buddha was said to be one teacher in a succession of great spiritual leaders called Tathāgatas; the Jina was considered the new Tīrthankara, successor to Pārshva. Their impact upon class-divided city-dwellers was tremendous. Men of high social position gave away their wealth and joined the *sangha* – the monastic community – of Buddhists or Jains, and many *brāhman* priests deserted their inherited ritual posts to follow the new leaders, bringing with them their wealth of scholarship. The two new movements grew rapidly and both the Buddha, after fifty years of teaching, and the Jina, who preached for thirty years before fasting to death, left behind them substantial followings. The religious systems formulated by their disciples and later dialecticians are the creeds of millions of people today.

DIAGRAMS OF COSMIC ORDER

At the physical death of the Buddha, the body was cremated; the remains were divided and interred as sacred relics in artificial hemispherical mounds called *stūpas*. Both Buddhists and Jains erected brick and stone *stūpas*, which in time became the foci of religious complexes which included monasteries, universities, meditation cells, secluded concourses for contemplation and temples for worship.

The principal element in *stūpa* symbolism is the axis, which rose from beneath the earth into the world of man, where a platform was built, its four sides representing the main directions of space. With the axis as its centre, a circle was described around it within the square, which was divided into eight equal segments by lines indicating the cardinal and intermediate directions, like the spread petals of a great lotus rising from the fundament. Upon this circular, diagrammatic lotus rose the hemispherical dome of the *stūpa*, facing the whole arc of the atmosphere and the heavens from ground level to zenith. The *stūpa* was thus far more than an earthen tumulus or the remains of the Buddha; it was a monumental sign of his presence and his doctrine.

Relief carvings sometimes depict these *stūpas* in elevation. They show the dome entwined by the coils of a giant serpent (Muchilinda, king of the *nāgas*) which shelters the symbol of the departed Teacher. The tree beneath which the Buddha sat on that momentous occasion rises behind the *stūpa*, its trunk a projection of the axis, its foliage burgeoning like a canopy above the followers of the doctrine (**308**). In other depictions of the *stūpa*, it appears surrounded by a king, with all the regalia of temporal power, lay devotees, and spirits of the air flying towards a little altar provided for them on the summit, often bearing garlands as offerings (**309**).

The concept of an ordered and stable cosmos could also be expressed in small diagrammatic panels, the most exquisite of which were the votive plaques intended to augment the glory of a *stūpa*; these were individually sponsored and offered by devotees as acts of piety. These Jain panels consist, typically, of a square containing a circle which encloses a *svāstika* with another circle at its centre (**307**). In place of spokes, this wheel is connected to the centre by a *svāstika* of vines, tendrils and blossoms – the natural world tamed and made into an emblematic, almost heraldic, device. The curving tendrils, like the petals of the lotus in later *mandalas*, frame specific symbols. These are called *mangalas* (auspicious signs) – such as the pair of fish representing increase and growth and the *shrīvatsa* (fortune's favourite) a good-luck symbol – and were considered powerful protection against evil or distracting influences. The inner circle is framed with four trident-like symbols, the *triratna* (three jewels) of the religion, representing an essential triune concept consisting of the Teacher himself, the doctrine, and the monastic order; this is used by all Jains and Buddhists to symbolize their vows of knowledge, belief and conduct.

The importance of the lotus was directly connected to the Buddhist need to associate the Buddha as a man, or as Man, with an historical succession of great teachers. It was felt necessary to establish the doctrine upon undeniable authority other than that of the *Vedas*, the fundamental scriptures of the ritualistic priesthood whose activities both the Buddha and the Jina regarded as misleading.

311

308

307 Jain cosmic diagram (*Ayāgapatta*)
(see p.61)
Kushāna period, 1st century AD
From Mathura (Uttar Pradesh)
Red sandstone, 89 × 92cm
Lucknow, State Museum, J.250

308 *Stūpa* and tree
Sātavāhana period, 1st–2nd century AD
From Chandavaram (Andhra Pradesh)
Limestone, 136 × 94cm
Hyderabad, State Museum
This panel and **309** formed part of the
decoration of actual *stūpas* which they
represented in miniature form, adding
earthly and mythical devotees.

309 *Stūpa* and figures *(see p. 62)*
Sātavāhana period, 2nd century
From Nagarjunakonda (Andhra Pradesh)
Limestone, 151 × 97 × 15cm
New Delhi, National Museum, 50.25

310 Model of *stūpa* *(not illustrated)*
Kushāna period, 3rd–4th century
From Gandhara (Pakistan)
Copper repoussé, 50 × 15 × 15cm
London, Spink & Son Ltd

**311 Diagram showing continents
separated by oceans centred on Mount
Meru**
Jain, mid-18th century
From Rajasthan
Gouache on cloth, 84 × 84cm
Jean Claude Ciancimino collection

**312 Diagram showing continents
separated by oceans centred on Mount Meru**
Late 15th century
From Gujarat
Gouache on cloth, 58 × 55cm
Jean Claude Ciancimino collection

312

313

314

313 Procession of worshippers
Kushāna period, 2nd century AD
From Máthura (Uttar Pradesh)
Red sandstone, 101 × 92 × 13cm
New Delhi, National Museum, J.555
This fragment of an architrave probably served as part of an entrance gateway to a Jain temple or *stūpa*. The worshippers entering the sacred space would have been greeted by similar depictions of courtly and celestial devotees.

314 Siddhártha and companions on the way to school
2nd–4th century
From Gandhara (Pakistan)
Grey schist, 32 × 36cm
London, Victoria and Albert Museum, IS 51–1948
This small figure of Siddhártha with a halo sits in a child's cart drawn by rams. His companions hold writing palettes.

LIFE OF THE BUDDHA

Much as the early Buddhist community revered Siddhártha as Teacher, Lord and Buddha, the later Buddhists were clearly more interested in the ideal that he embodied than in his transient human person. Everything known about the Buddha has either been recorded incidentally in relation to his teachings, or has been deliberately told about him to prove his Buddha-nature. The important episodes in the life of the Buddha were arranged very early into two sets of four: (1) the four stages of his progress – birth, enlightenment, first preaching, and final *nirvāna* (associated respectively with Lumbini, Bodhgaya, the Deer Park near Varanasi, and Kushinagara), and (2) the four miracles that occurred in the towns of Shravasti, Rajagriha, Vaishali and Sankashya. These eight places all became places of pilgrimage. It is quite possible that a deliberate collection of stories and legends connected with these places provided the first incentive towards the production of a full-scale biography of Siddhártha. Two such early biographies are the *Lalita Vistara* ('An Extended Version of the Display') and the *Mahāvastu* ('The Great Matter').

The earliest depictions of scenes from the life of the Buddha did not include the Master himself; however, his invisible presence is always implied in the empty throne beneath the tree (**319**), in the riderless horse, or in the ladder with footprints. By the 1st and 2nd centuries AD, under the patronage of the Kushāna rulers of central India and the Gandhara region, the first images of the Buddha were created. Many of these came to be incorporated into narrative scenes which also depicted everyday life. Thus the life and teachings of the Buddha take place in crowded townscapes and idyllic groves. Probably the most elaborately conceived evocations of contemporary courtly life which include the prince Siddhártha are to be seen in the fluid compositions and vibrant colours of the Ajanta frescoes (see pp. 26–7).

Prince Siddhártha, for all his prosperity, was not inwardly happy. While riding out of the palace with his faithful charioteer, Channa, he saw the 'Four Signs' – which had been placed there by the gods. These were an aged man, a sick man, a corpse, and a wandering religious mendicant; the last, clad in a simple robe and carrying a small begging bowl, was peaceful and calm. Seeing the mendicant, Siddhártha realized where his destiny lay, and decided to become a forest wanderer himself. A relief from Gandhara (**314**) represents the moment of recognition: Siddhártha, seated in his chariot with Channa, sees the religious man, while the gods look on in the background.

The next great episode to find expression in sculpture is the moment of enlightenment. As the Buddha sat beneath the Tree of Wisdom he was attacked by the demon army of Māra, which tried to distract him with various temptations, as well as with a whirlwind, tempest, flood and earthquake. But he sat firm, cross-legged beneath the tree, protected by the hoods of the serpent king Muchilinda. Then Māra called on the Buddha to produce evidence of his goodness and benevolence; the Buddha touched the ground with his hand and the earth itself

316

315

319

315 Worship of the Buddha's relics
Ikshvāku period, 3rd–4th century
From Amaravati (Andhra Pradesh)
Limestone, 92 × 89 × 16cm
*London, Trustees of the British
Museum, 1880 7–9.8*

316 Life of the Buddha
Gupta period, 6th century
From Sarnath (Uttar Pradesh)
Sandstone, 146 × 38 × 17cm
Sarnath, Archaeological Museum, 262
Below, the enlightenment of the
Buddha, centre, the Buddha
teaching; above, the 'great *nirvāna*'.

**317 & 318 The birth of
Mahāvīra, and Mahāvīra
enthroned** *(not illustrated)*
From a *Kaplasūtra* manuscript
Jain school, 1404
From Gujarat, 9 × 8 and 9 × 7cm
London, Royal Asiatic Society

319 Life of the Buddha
Ikshvāku period, 3rd–4th century
From Ñagarjunakonda (Andra Pradesh)
Limestone, 181 × 95cm
*Nagarjunakonda, Archaeological
Museum, 52*
Below, the enlightenment of the
Buddha; centre, the Buddha
receives offerings; above, the
Buddha at Sarnath.

spoke with a voice of thunder, 'I am his witness.' This act is
usually shown in sculpture by the right hand which rests on
the leg, the fingers touching the earth (**316**, **327**). The serpent
and the tree are also sometimes represented (**319**).

Leaving the Tree of Wisdom, the Buddha journeyed to the
Deer Park (the modern Sarnath) near Varanasi where his
former disciples had settled. To these ascetics the Buddha
preached his first sermon, or, in Buddhist phraseology, 'set in
motion the Wheel of the Law'. Illustrations of this episode
generally show the Buddha with his fingers held together in
the teaching gesture, 'untying the knot of delusion' (**316**), or
with one hand held up in the gesture of protection (**319**).

After his first sermon the Buddha gathered many disciples,
some of whom offered money, gifts and land to the Buddha
(**319**). Other followers of the Buddha are occasionally depicted
in royal processions (**313**).

The end of the Buddha's life came when he was eighty. He
spent the last few months of his life near the city of Vaishali,
then he and his followers journeyed northwards to the hill
country, the home of his youth. Having prepared his disciples
for his death, he lay down on his side and achieved the final
nirvāna or *parinirvāna* (**316**). After his death he was cremated
and his ashes were distributed among various peoples. In a
medallion from the Amaravati *stūpa* (**315**), both ordinary
humans and semi-divine *nāgas* worship a reliquary casket
placed on a throne. (Such a casket might have contained the
ashes of the Buddha, and have been buried deep within a
stūpa.) The devotees hold their hands together above their
heads or bow down before the throne.

321

320 The Buddha *(see p. 34)*
3rd–5th century
From Gandhara (Pakistan)
Grey schist, 21cm high
*London, Victoria and Albert Museum,
IS163–1949*

321 A Jain Tīrthankara
Kushāna period, *c.* 1st century AD
From Uttar Pradesh
Red sandstone, 52 × 54 × 13cm
Mathura, Government Museum, 8.37

322 The Buddha *(not illustrated)*
Gupta period, *c.* 5th century
From Gandhara (Pakistan)
Stucco, 31 × 22 × 27cm
Private collection

323 The Buddha *(not illustrated)*
8th century
From Kashmir
Ivory, 10 × 11cm
Patna, Sri Gopi Krishna Kanoria Collection

MEDITATION

Seated in the lotus position (*padmāsana*), his eyelids gently lowered, the saviour of the world gazes inwards, unravelling the mystery of all existence. Perhaps no other Indian image conveys more strongly the quest for eternal truth, the desire to escape the sufferings of this world, the pursuit of enlightenment. Yogic postures have been known in the Indian sub-continent since the time of the Indus Valley Civilization. A seal from Mohenjo-Daro (3rd–2nd millenium BC) depicts an equivalent of the lotus position, which suggests that in pre-history there was the same emphasis on controlling physical posture. Later, in Buddhism and Jainism, the lotus position appears again, signifying the physical and mental discipline (*yoga*) through which the Buddha and the Jain saints seek and discover truth. In the most favoured type of Buddhist and Jain image the body is immobile: the legs are folded one under the other with the soles upwards, the palms of the hands rest in the lap, the head is held straight, and the eyes see only inwards. The hair is generally made up of small curls, and sometimes there is a small protuberance or top-knot in the centre of the skull; the ears are long-lobed, the eyes slightly pointed; a small dot placed between them indicates beauty.

The earliest images of meditating saviours are from Mathura and Gandhara. In the early fragmentary torso from Mathura (**321**), the body of a Jain saint is seen, massive and unyielding; it conveys the quality of inwardly-held breath, and the auspicious symbol, the *shrīvatsa*, is imprinted on the chest. Though the Gandhara head shows the influence of western Classical sculpture – the modelling is softer and more rounded – the Indian emphasis on the sharply delineated eyes and inwardly fixed stare is preserved (**320**). By the Gupta period, the image of the seated saviour was perfectly realized, the cosmic dimension of his meditation indicated by the immense halo incorporating the vegetal decoration that carries with it all the symbolism of the natural world. Again, the solidity of the figure, with its tautly drawn skin and cylindrical limbs, expresses immobility (**324**).

Accessory figures are included in later sculptures of meditating saviours. The Kashmiri ivory (**323**) shows the Buddha crowded by groups of attendant disciples; on either side, walking Buddhas are framed in pseudo-Classical niches. The multi-headed serpent shelters both the meditating Buddha and the meditating Jain saint Pārshvanātha. In an inlaid bronze from western India (**325**), accessory figures and flying celestial beings are also included and the throne is supported on lions; the meditating saviour is the focus of a complete composition, itself a highly contrived geometric construction. A Deccani bronze (**326**) explores the same theme, repeating in miniature form the principal seated figure so as to create the impression of a universe filled with meditating saviours, the figures forming the frame to an elaborate throne.

324

324 A Jain Tīrthankara
Gupta period, *c.* 5th century
From Mathura (Uttar Pradesh)
Red sandstone, 95 × 60cm
Lucknow, State Museum, J.118

325 Pārshvanātha, the 23rd Tīrthankara
Maitraka period, 9th–10th century
From Akota (Gujarat)
Bronze, 34 × 25 × 11cm
New Delhi, National Museum, 68.189

325

326

326 A Jain Tīrthankara
Western Ganga period, *c.* 11th century
From Karnataka
Bronze, 46 × 26 × 15cm
Mysore, Directorate of Archaeology and Museums

327 The Buddha
Pāla period, 11th–12th century
From eastern India
Basalt, 125cm high
London, Victoria and Albert Museum, 617–1872

327

SALVATION

Standing figures of the Buddha – the right hand raised in the gesture that bestows fearlessness or confidence (*abhaya-mudrā*), or lowered in the gesture associated with the dispensing of gifts (*varada-mudrā*) – are regarded as the saviours of man. Sculptured as a massive figure, with great folds of material gathered at the waist, Maitreya, a Buddha-to-be, assures man of ultimate salvation (**328, 331**). The bulk of the body, the immobile head with the great disc behind, give visual reassurance of the inevitability of the Buddha's message. Though Maitreya stands firmly on the ground, as if joined to the earth, his eyes gaze inwards, towards a realm far removed from the world of man.

   Later images of the saviour-Buddha convey a more gentle and lyrical message. The elegantly conceived robes, delicately cut in limestone or red sandstone, or even cast in bronze, reveal a subtly modelled figure combining solidity with grace: salvation is almost alluring (**329, 330, 332**). The swaying posture of the Sarnath Buddha illustrates well the emphasis on fluid modelling and gentle carving, typical of the Sarnath style. The eyes are shown almost closed; nevertheless, the gestures of the hands surely promise the salvation for which man yearns (**333**). Here the halo is replaced by a larger almond-shaped back-piece; the cloak is reduced to an almost transparent sheath.

   In the Gandhara sculpture (**335**) a Bodhisattva appears as a prince. The richly dressed hair, the flowing moustache, and the ornaments about the neck and chest indicate his royal stature. But the halo behind the head and the gentle but fixed expression once more reassure man of ultimate *nirvāna*.

328

329

330

328 Maitreya, a Bodhisattva
Kushāna period, 2nd century AD
From Ahicchatra (Uttar Pradesh)
Sandstone, 76 × 27 × 13cm
New Delhi, National Museum, 59.530/1

329 The Buddha
Ikshvāku period, 2nd–3rd century AD
From Uppukonduru (Andhra Pradesh)
Limestone, 92 × 35 × 15cm
Hyderabad, State Museum, P5388

330 The Buddha
Gupta period, 5th century
From Jamalpur (Uttar Pradesh)
Red sandstone, 112 × 23 × 61cm
Mathura, Government Museum, A.8

**331 A Bodhisattva
probably Maitreya**
Kushāna period, 2nd century AD
From Mathura (Uttar Pradesh)
Sandstone, 204 × 86 × 36cm
New Delhi, National Museum, A.40

332 The Buddha
Pāla period, 6th century
From Nalanda (Bihar)
Bronze, 36 × 13 × 9cm
Nalanda, Archaeological Museum

333 The Buddha *(see p. 63)*
Gupta period, 6th century
From Sarnath (Uttar Pradesh)
Sandstone, 105 × 49 × 20cm
*Sarnath, Archaeological Museum,
5512*

334 The Buddha *(not illustrated)*
Early Chālukya period, 8th century
From Buddhapad (Andhra Pradesh)
Bronze, 28 × 13cm
*London, Trustees of the British
Museum, 1905 12–18.3*

335 A Bodhisattva
3rd–4th century
From Gandhara (Pakistan)
Grey schist, 100 × 29cm
*London, Spink & Son Ltd,
SE2.1467*

332

331

335

**336 Avalokiteshvara,
a Bodhisattva**
Pāla period,
10th century
From eastern India
Bronze, 23 × 18 × 13cm
*New Delhi, National
Museum, 68.148*

**337 Avalokiteshvara, a
Bodhisattva**
10th–11th century
From Kashmir
Bronze inlaid with silver and
copper, 24 × 11cm
*London, Trustees of the British
Museum, 1969 11–3.1*

**337a Padmapāni
Avalokiteshvara**
(not illustrated)
c. 1100
Sandstone, 71 × 39 × 20cm
Lucknow, Government Museum, 0.255

336

COMPASSION

The Buddhist universe of Mahāyāna, the 'Great Vehicle' school, contains numerous Bodhisattvas. According to an older Buddhist doctrine, the Bodhisattva works in wisdom and love so that after many lives he may ultimately become a Buddha. Ordinary believers are encouraged to follow his example and so, eventually, achieve *nirvāna*. Yet the Bodhisattva is a being of immeasurable charity and compassion; while suffering individuals remain in the toil of transmigration he will not leave them without help. Though the Bodhisattva is to become a Buddha, he bides his time until even the most insignificant worshipper has reached the highest goal. In the same way, man strives to become like a Bodhisattva, and by the spiritual merit which he gains, to assist all living things on the way to perfection.

Clearly, the Bodhisattva is a spirit of compassion and suffering. In the 'Thunderbolt' scripture (*Vajradhvaja Sūtra*) the Bodhisattva pronounces:

I take upon myself the deeds of all beings, even those in the hells in other worlds, in the realms of punishment. I take their suffering upon me, I bear it, I do not draw back from it, I do not tremble at it, I have no fear of it. I must bear the burden of all beings, for I have vowed to save all things living, to bring

them safe through the forest of birth, age, disease, death and rebirth. I think not of my own salvation, but strive to bestow on all beings the royalty of supreme wisdom. So I take upon myself the sorrow of all human beings. I agree to suffer as a ransom for all beings, for the sake of all beings. Truly I will not abandon them. For I have resolved to gain supreme wisdom for the sake of all that live, to save the world.

Chief of the Bodhisattvas from the earthly point of view is Avalokiteshvara, 'The Lord Who Looks Down'. Invariably he holds a lotus, a symbol of perfection and knowledge; thus he is also known as the 'Lotus Bearer', Padmapāni. His special attribute is compassion, and his helping hand reaches even to the deepest and most unpleasant of the Buddhist purgatories. In sculpture, Avalokiteshvara appears as a youth, gently smiling; the palm-outward gesture (*varada-mudrā*) of his right hand indicates the giving of spiritual riches, peace and comfort. The left hand always holds the lotus by which the Bodhisattva is recognized. The torso is naked, though jewelled, while garments flow about the waist and legs. In the Kashmiri example (**337**), seated deer beneath Avalokiteshvara refer to the Deer Park where the Buddha first preached his essential doctrine. The six arms and flaming halo suggest the transformation of the original saviour into a divinity.
Some forms of Avalokiteshvara are seated on a lion, and armed with a trident.

338 Siddhaikavīra, a form of Manjushrī, a Bodhisattva
Pāla period, 8th–9th century
From Nalanda (Bihar)
Yellow sandstone, 116 × 38 × 17cm
New Delhi, National Museum, 59.528

339 Manjushrī, a Bodhisattva *(not illustrated)*
Bronze
Raipur, Archaeological Museum
The special activity of this Bodhisattva is to stimulate understanding.
Manjushrī is usually shown with a naked sword in one hand, to
destroy error and falsehood, and a book in the other, describing the
ten *pāramitās*, or great spiritual perfections, which are the cardinal
virtues developed by Bodhisattvas.

340 Bhrikutī, consort of Avalokiteshvara
From Achutrajpur (Orissa)
Somavamshī period, 10th century
bronze, 35cm high
Bhubaneshwar, State Museum, 274
Avalokiteshvara is sometimes provided with a consort, Bhrikutī, who
shares with her lord compassion for all that suffer. In this bronze the
ascetic form of the goddess is stressed: her garments are sparce and
diaphanous, her hair is formed into coiled locks that descend to her
shoulders, and she holds the ritual waterpot and rosary in her hands.

338

340

193

341

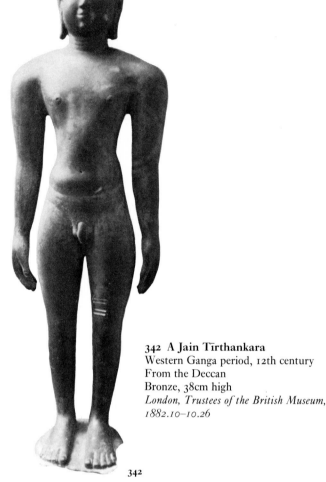

342 A Jain Tīrthankara
Western Ganga period, 12th century
From the Deccan
Bronze, 38cm high
London, Trustees of the British Museum,
1882.10–10.26

342

341 The first and last Jain Tīrthankaras, Rishabhanātha and Mahāvīra
Eastern Ganga period, 11th century
From Orissa
Schist, 69 × 36cm
London, Trustees of the British Museum, 1872.7–1.99

THE NAKED SAVIOUR

According to Jain cosmography, the universe is divided into an infinite number of cycles, each consisting of a period of improvement and a period of decline. Each period is basically like the last, and contains twenty-four Tīrthankaras or 'Ford-Makers' who occupy the highest position in the Jain pantheon, to whom the gods and goddesses – many of which are borrowed from Hinduism – are subordinated. The lives of the Tīrthankaras follow a canonical pattern of standard episodes and crises leading to a state of absolute perfection and enlightenment, and release from the bondage of transmigration. The twenty-fourth Tīrthankara, Mahāvīra, was a contemporary of the Buddha, and though legends about his life are even more formalized and unreliable than those about the Buddha, the fact he lived is scarcely to be doubted.

Jainism is fundamentally atheistic, denying any ultimate divinity: though the Tīrthankaras are adored, they have never been deified. They cannot intercede on behalf of man; their value is to provide objects for meditation.

Images of the Tīrthankaras show youthful naked ascetics decorated with crowns and ornaments (**341**). They stand stiffly, their arms hanging beside their bodies. The still unyielding posture, the tautly drawn body, and the small diamond-like *shrīvatsa* symbol on the chest are all characteristic; so is the fixed inward-looking gaze. Umbrellas above their heads symbolize the heavenly abode of the naked saviour. All the Tīrthankaras are represented exactly alike, except Pārshvanātha, the twenty-third, who has a serpent coiling up behind him, the multi-headed serpent head rearing up above the saviour (**344**). The Tīrthankaras are sometimes distinguished from one another by animals, trees, or flowers placed beneath the figures or *yakshīs* on either side.

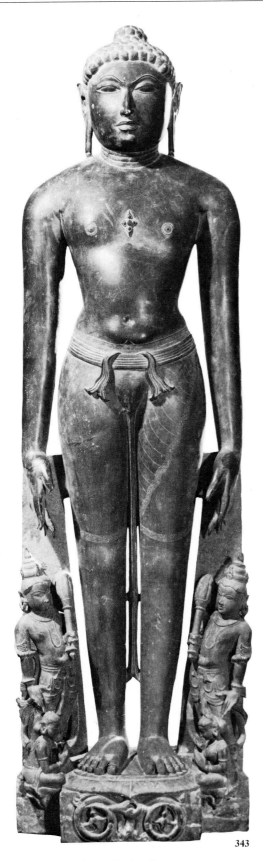

343

344

343 Neminātha, a Tīrthankara
Chāhamāna period, 12th century
From Narhad (Rajasthan)
Basalt, 119 × 37 × 22cm
New Delhi, National Museum, 69.132

344 Pārshvanātha, the 23rd Tīrthankara
Late Chālukya period, 12th century
From Gulbarga (Karnataka)
Black basalt, 150 × 66cm
London, Victoria and Albert Museum (store), IS931

वैष्णव इतिहास

8
MYTHOLOGY OF VISHNU

The deity with whom the concept of a stable universe has become most unequivocally associated is Vishnu. More than Shiva or the almost forgotten Brahmā, Vishnu embodies the ideas of the priesthood and the warrior-aristocracy. Vishnu, sustainer and preserver, is dedicated to the maintenance of *dharma*, universal order.

Throughout the varied forms of this god run dominant themes, expressing the underlying symbolism of the central principle of the cosmos. Perhaps the most important of these themes is the concept of the god as the universal axis. In the eternal cycles of cosmic renewal and destruction, the universe is conceived as Hiranya-garbha, the 'Golden Egg'. At the base lie the intertwined serpents of the subterranean waters which represent the primordial ocean upon which the cosmic egg floated after being impregnated by Svayambhū, the 'Self-Existent', (see p.92). Upon this serpent-ocean stands the upright figure of Vishnu, nearly as tall as the long axis of the egg, his outstretched arms representing the extension of space, his body symbolizing the mysterious primeval shape assumed by the primeval man, Svayambhū, born within the golden egg through his own desire. To make manifest the cosmic process engendered by his emergence from the oceanic void, three figures emanate from Vishnu upward, in direct continuation of the axis. First is Brahmā, the founder and maker of the stable universe, his four heads directed at the four quarters of space, each vigilantly overseeing the formation of the organized cosmos. Next arises Hayagrīva with a horse's head, embodiment of the fire than burns within the waters and rises each day as the sun from the eastern sea, his loud neighing on the battlefield like the chanting of the *Vedas*. Last is Shiva, wielding a trident to pierce the three horizontal strata of the universe, who will consume all in cataclysmic fire when the four ages of each great time-cycle have run their course and the sight and knowledge of the primeval being, of *dharma* and all religion, is stifled and obliterated by misunderstanding, negligence and wilful heresies. After this purification by fire, all is returned to the pure aquatic state and the cosmic wheel begins to turn anew. From this vertical axis of four great gods spring archetypes of the inhabitants of the universe, outspread like the foliage of the world-tree of which Vishnu is the trunk, rooted in water, his arms the branches. Those on the right represent the powers of light, such as seers, priests and famous warriors; while on the other side stand the dark forces of the demons, of those who would usurp the *dharma* of others and create instability. This division is necessary, for the universe is finely balanced; both men and gods must adhere to the righteous path laid down for them in the *Vedas* and repeatedly restore the balance whenever it is threatened from within.

Vishnu, the all-pervading cohesive force, maintaining a balance between destructive, disruptive powers and the life-processes of the universe, leads to another fundamental theme in the mythology of the god, the concept of incarnations. Vishnu is said to have come down to earth, in the form of an animal or man, on various occasions for the furtherance of creation and the well-being of the world; this act is called the 'descent' (*avatāra*). The number of *avatāras* is generally agreed to be ten. The first three incarnations – 1. the fish (Matsya), 2. the tortoise (Kūrma), and 3. the boar (Varāha) – embody various cosmic myths concerned with the creation of the earth, and were originally associated with Prajāpati-Brahmā, the creator-god of the *Vedas* and later texts. With the development of the cult of Vishnu these forms were absorbed as incarnations of the composite man-god Vāsudeva-Krishna. The man-lion (Narasimha) incarnation 4. depicts the god in his terrifying and vengeful form, and the dwarf incarnation (Vāmana) 5. embodies the Vedic god of motion, Trivikrama, known for the characteristic three strides by which he created the triple world (*triloka*) of earth, atmosphere and heaven. Next come the three Rāmas, the human incarnations – 6. Rāma with the axe (Parashurāma), 7. Rāma, the hero of the *Rāmāyana*, and 8. Balarāma, the eldest brother of Krishna. These latter forms of Vishnu are real 'descents' in that they come to live among men for the attainment of various ends. Krishna is not usually included in the ten incarnations, though he may on occasions replace Balarāma. Krishna is considered not so much an incarnation of Vishnu as a fundamental aspect or emanation of the god himself. The last two incarnatory forms of Vishnu are 9. the Buddha, and 10. Kalki, the horse-headed god who heralds the final destruction of the present era. The remarkable inclusion of the Buddha no doubt indicates an intention to discredit the Buddhists by depicting them as the victims of a false form of Vishnu created to delude demons.

345

347

345 Vishnu surrounded by *avatāras*
Chauhan style, 12th century
From Gadwala (Rajasthan)
Black marble, 113 × 95 × 21 cm
New Delhi, National Museum, L.39

346 Trivikrama
Stone, 44 × 37 × 19 cm
New Delhi, National Museum, 80.1375

347 Chakra-purusha, Vishnu's disc personified
Gupta period, 5th century
Sandstone, 43 × 10 cm
Bangalore, Government Museum, 133

348 Chakra-purusha, Vishnu's disc personified (*not illustrated*)
Patna, State Department of Archaeology

UNIVERSAL ORDER

The basic image of Vishnu is that of a standing or seated figure, eternally young as are most gods, the priest's sacred thread looped across his bare chest from left shoulder to right hip, wearing the crown and body ornaments of the warrior aristocracy. He holds a sharp-edged iron disc (*chakra*), a heavy wooden mace (*gadā*), and a conch shell (*shankha*), which he uses both as a war-horn on the battlefield and as a sacred instrument in ritual worship; his fourth hand is held palm outwards to signify reassurance, a gesture which is sometimes replaced by a lotus flower (**354, 353**). Eight-armed images of Vishnu hold other weapons: a bow and arrow, a sword and shield. As the bolt upright body of Vishnu was identified with the universal axis, the four or eight arms represented the directions of space, while various meanings were attributed to the weapons and the lotus held by the god. The sword, for instance, was seen as the weapon of *dharma*, while the spoked disc signified universal dominion. These weapons were sometimes made into godlings like the 'disc-man' (*chakra-purusha*), a small figure supporting a spoked wheel (**347**).

346

349 Vishnu as Vishvarūpa
(not illustrated)
Gupta period, 6th century
Red sandstone
Mathura, Government Museum, 42–43,2989

350 Trisandhya *(three panels, not illustrated)*
Gupta period, *c.* 5th century
From Garhwa (Uttar Pradesh)
82 × 30 × 17cm, 140 × 30 × 20cm and
180 × 28 × 25cm
Lucknow, State Museum

351 A fragment of Vishnu as Vishvarūpa *(not illustrated)*
Gurjara-Pratihāra period, 10th–11th century
From Gana Taman
Stone, 60 × 60 × 15cm
New Delhi, National Museum, 78.998

352 Vishnu as Vishvarūpa
(not illustrated)
1825–50
From Kashmir, 53 × 37cm
New Delhi, National Museum, 59.115/1

353 Vishnu *(not illustrated)*
Chola period, *c.* 950
From Kongunadu (Tamil Nadu)
Bronze, 30 × 20cm
London, Trustees of the British Museum,
1967.12–15.1

354 Vishnu
Pallava period, 8th century
From Tamil Nadu
Granite, 184 × 100 × 31cm
New Delhi, National Museum,
59.153/106

355 Head of Brahmā
11th century
From central India, Malwa
Sandstone, 46 × 32cm
London, Trustees of the British
Museum, 1880.8

354

356

356 Vishnu
Chola period, 15th century
From southern India
Copper, 66 × 25cm
London, Victoria and Albert Museum,
IM 127–1927

355

As the central principle of the universe Vishnu becomes Vishvarūpa, 'The Omniform' – the form of the universe made manifest. The various references to Vishvarūpa in the *Mahābhārata* and the *Purānas* make it clear that in this form Vishnu was intended to embody the totality of forces and manifestations present throughout the universe. In one figure of Vishnu as Vishvarūpa, the god is provided with weapons and a high crown; he stands upon writhing serpents, symbols of the ocean of dissolution from which all creation evolves and to which it returns; on either side of his head are the agents of darkness and destruction as well as the incarnations of the god himself.

In another image representing Vishnu as the supreme cosmic principle (**357**), the god appears at the centre of a triad, flanked on either side by Brahmā and Shiva. This triple image (*trimūrti*) is a potent Hindu symbol, representing the stability of the universe as a constant cyclical process. The triune concept embodies the creation of the universe by Brahmā, its maintenance by Vishnu, and its purification through destruction by Shiva. The three gods together are also linked to the three principal 'qualities' of material existence (*gunas*); Vishnu at the centre merely emphasizes his role as the fundamental force, the preserver of universal order.

357

VISHNU ON GARUDA

Vishnu is often seated on the great sun eagle Garuda, proverbial enemy of the serpents, pursuer of evil, and the embodiment of courage. Though the face and body of Garuda are often humanized, he has wings and a beak-like nose; his human hands are often joined together in worshipful homage to the god he serves (**359**). Vishnu is sometimes accompanied by his consort, Lakshmī, as he flies through the air on Garuda. In an example from Kashmir (**363**), Lakshmī appears as a diminutive figure.

It was also on Garuda that Vishnu descended to earth to free the elephant king, Gajendra, from the clutches of a crocodile demon who had dragged Gajendra into the deep waters of a lake. The elephant king prayed to Vishnu who compassionately appeared and killed the crocodile. In the sculpture and painting illustrating this episode (**360, 362**), Vishnu, with Lakshmī, is seated astride the shoulders of Garuda who is seen flying through the air; the elephant is entangled in lotus plants in the waters below; and a *nāga* king and queen pay homage to the miraculous event.

357 Vishnu with Brahmā and Shiva
Kalachuri period, 10th century
From Maukhedi (Deccan)
Buff sandstone,
140 × 40 × 18cm
Bhopal, State Museum, 775

358 Harihara (Vishnu and Shiva joined)
Pahari school, *c.*1730
From Basholi
New Delhi, National Museum, 60.1673

359

358

359 Garuda
11th–12th century
From eastern India
Schist, 41 × 20 × 20cm
London, Trustees of the British Museum, 1872.7–1.67

360

363

361

362

360 Salvation of the elephant king, Gajendra
Post-Gupta period, 6th century
Sandstone, 133 × 113 × 23cm
Deogarh, Archaeological Shed, A.S.I.

361 Garuda carrying Vishnu and Lakshmī
Hoysala period, 13th century
Soapstone, 160 × 78 × 67cm
New Delhi, National Museum, 265

362 Salvation of the elephant king, Gajendra
From the *Gajendra Moksha* manuscript
Rajasthan school, *c.*1700–20
From Mewar
Bombay, J. P. Goenka Collection

363 Vishnu as Vaikuntha on Garuda
11th century
From Verinag (Kashmir)
Grey granite, 88 × 39 × 22cm
Srinagar, Sri Pratap Singh Museum, 3080

364 Yoganarayana, Vishnu in a yogic pose *(not illustrated)*
Jodhpur, Sardar Museum

365

368

369

THE COSMIC OCEAN

At the end of each great time-cycle, when the old, blind universe has been destroyed, it returns to the formless, oceanic state. In the mythology of Vishnu, it is he who floats upon the waters of the ocean in a yogic trance-like sleep before the new creation. In images representing this pre-creation scene, the pause between one universe and the next, Vishnu appears lying upon the serpent Ananta, 'Endless', which symbolizes the waters, its multiple cobra-hoods curving up like a wave to shelter his head. Such images generally show a long-stemmed lotus growing from the coils of the serpent (directly from the waters) or from the god's navel (from the axial centre). The god Brahmā, the four-headed, usually sits on the blossom setting about the work of making and organizing the new universe. Vishnu's wife, Lakshmī, is sometimes also included in this scene, attentively rubbing the feet of the god. Around Vishnu are his discarded weapons, particularly the conch shell and disc. Related images of Vishnu depict the god in a waking state, seated on the serpent coiled beneath and behind him (**365**).

Other creation myths introduce the first two of Vishnu's incarnations, as the fish (Matsya) and the tortoise (Kūrma). Here the god undergoes transformations in order to restore universal harmony; in both incarnations he is closely associated with the cosmic waters. In the form of the fish, Vishnu rescues the *Vedas* and Manu, the patriarch and progenitor of all mankind, from the flood. Like the Biblical Noah, Manu is directed by Vishnu to build a ship; thus mankind, in its ordained religious and social groupings, is preserved from extinction.

In another creation myth connected with the restoration of universal balance, the demons (or 'anti-gods', *asuras*) have repeatedly defeated the gods; weakened, they pray to Vishnu for guidance. He promises them the drink of immortality, *amrita*, if they will enter into a temporary alliance with their foes. The ocean must be churned as if it were milk, using the mountain called Mandara as a churning stick, and the serpent Vasuki as the rope to wind around it. The gods and demons must then pull the serpent from opposite sides in turn to rotate the mountain and so churn the ocean. To support the Mandara mountain, Vishnu himself assumes the form of an enormous tortoise, whose shell serves as a pivot. In the course of the gigantic churning action, various supernatural objects are condensed and thrown up, until finally there appears the *amrita*. To prevent the demons, still more forceful than the gods, from taking this for themselves, Vishnu transforms himself into the entrancingly beautiful Mohinī, who bewilders the demons. During the confusion the cup of nectar is given to the gods; they drink it, and are again victorious over the forces of chaos (**366, 369**).

370

370 Varāha *(see p. 65)*
Chandella period, 11th century
From Khajuraho (Madhya Pradesh)
Sandstone, 145 × 37 × 34cm
Khajuraho, Archaeological Museum, 861

371

BOAR AND MAN-LION

The myths of Vishnu's transformations clearly make man dependent upon the grace of the gods; but they are also instructive, teaching forethought, preparedness and valour in the many situations when *dharma* – the universal order – is seen to be at risk.

The transformation of Vishnu into the truly enormous boar, Varāha, became necessary when the earth was submerged in the ocean – symbolically, in danger of being resolved into its constituent particles and so returned to the pre-creation phase before the time-cycles had naturally returned it there – and in desperate need of rescue. Though the forces of disorder seem thus to have most effectively dislocated time, Vishnu as the giant boar dives into the depths of the ocean and surfaces with the earth intact. The earth is symbolized by a beautiful goddess, Bhūdevī, who in sculptural representations of the myth (**370**) is held aloft by Vishnu, generally on his raised elbow. The boar-head of the god gently nuzzles the goddess, while the raised foot pressing down on the aquatic serpents represents the act of stepping out of the water, crushing the ocean demon who had held the earth prisoner. Celestial beings and others witness the miraculous event. Other boar-headed images of Vishnu, in seated or standing postures (**372**), illustrate this form of the god, though not always in the act of rescue.

Some illustrations of Vishnu as Varāha take a completely animal form. The body of the giant boar covered with tiny figures (**371**) refers to the myth in which the gods, demons and other representatives of *dharma* cling to his bristling coat and so survive to repopulate the world, losing none of their ancient wisdom.

As the fierce man-lion (Narasimha), Vishnu descends into a pillar in the palace of a heretical king and emerges from it to fight and disembowel the monarch who is opposed to true *dharma* (**375, 376**). In this bloodthirsty but effective act, Vishnu plays the part of a righteous warrior-aristocrat. Images of the Narasimha performing yogic exercises also associate him with the peaceful devotee (**374**). Even so, the savage head – with its protruding eyes and snarling mouth – are reminders of the fierce character of Narasimha.

These two metamorphoses of Vishnu are sometimes combined into a composite image, known as Vaikuntha, 'The Penetrating One'. (In Kashmir, this image became the focus of a particular cult, hence the popularity of Vaikuntha images from this region.) A stylized boar head (left), lion head (right) and human face (centre) are combined (**377**); usually a fourth demonic face is also added. Not only do these faces refer to the boar and Narasimha incarnations of Vishnu; they also symbolize the qualities of knowledge, power, strength and energy.

371 Varāha
10th century
From Uttar or Madhya Pradesh
Black basalt, 67 × 40 × 83cm
Oxford, Ashmolean Museum, 1969.43
Such animal representations of the boar incarnation are occasionally treated as the 'vehicle' of Vishnu, and in temples are given their own pavilions.

372

374

373 Prashurāma
(not illustrated)
Pahari school, *c.* 1730
From Bilaspur
New Delhi, National Museum,
47.110/335
The mythology associated with
Parashurāma, the first human
incarnation of Vishnu, clearly
indicates that he was a symbol of
the *brāhmans* against the
kshatriyas. The epics and
Purānas relate that he destroyed
the *kshatriyas* as many as twenty-
one times. He is shown
wielding his characteristic
weapon, the axe, while the arms
and hands of his victims lie
scattered about.

372 Varāha
Gurjara-Pratihāra period, 9th–10th century
From central India
Bronze, 13 × 9 × 6cm
New Delhi, National Museum, 67.107

374 Narasimha seated in a
yoga **posture**
Vijayanagara period, 15th
century
From Tamil Nadu
Granite, 116 × 55cm
New Delhi, National Museum,
68.1544

375

376

375 & 376 Narasimha
Pahari school, *c.* 1715
From Mankot, each 23 × 16cm
New Delhi, National Museum, 62.1770 and
62.1771
This narrative sequence showing Narasimha
coming out of the pillar and then
disembowelling the wicked king is unusual
(one other scene belonging to the series is
also known but there may originally have
been more); the disembowellment
composition alone is a common Pahari
theme repeated with the same details.

377 Vishnu as Vaikuntha *(see p. 64)*
Solankī period, 11th century
From Gujarat
Marble, 36cm high
Bombay, Prince of Wales Museum of Western
India, 95

THE RĀMĀYANA

Probably the most popular of Indian epics, celebrated throughout much of Asia, the *Rāmāyana* describes the story of Rāma and his abdication as heir to the throne. The prince acts in response to an unjust promise extracted from his father, the old king, by one of the latter's three wives. Rāma, his wife Sītā, and his brother Lakshmana, go to the forest for a period of exile. Despite the pleas of Rāma's half-brother Bhārata, who is the innocent object of his mother's ambitious desire to become queen mother, Rāma stands firm in his renunciation (385); he seems to sense his greater destiny and has made a vow to rid the world of all oppressive demonic forces.

Despite its vivid narrative the epic should be understood on a deeper level: Rāma represents the god Vishnu in perceptible form; he is the saviour of the universe and, throughout the tale, contact with him brings redemption. Rāma is also the embodiment of all princely virtues, while Sītā is the epitome of chastity and loyalty. In sculpture Rāma is depicted as the upright, noble prince, holding the bow that he bent and broke in order to win the hand of Sītā (378).

When Sītā hears of Rāma's proposed exile, she overrules his wish to leave her within the seclusion of the palace and accompanies him into the forest; thereafter, she endures all hardship in this spirit of devotion. Though physically difficult, life in the forest is tranquil and carefree, and the tale becomes more lyrical with the description of Rāma's journey away from the court (382). Throughout the epic, the kinship between man and animals is stressed; the miniature of the crow reciting the scriptures to the other birds (393) shows that all beings are meant to hear of the events of Rāma's life which have restored the balance, order and health of the universe.

The idyllic forest life of the three exiles is interrupted by the appearance of various demons (384). The most significant is the ogress Shūrpanakhā, whose brother is the many-headed demon Rāvana, ruler of the golden city of Lanka which can be identified as Sri Lanka. Lakshmana, characterized as being impetuous and unwise in contrast to Rāma, attacks Shūrpanakhā, cutting off her ears and nose (381). In retaliation Shūrpanakhā inspires Rāvana to abduct Sītā, which he does in his aerial chariot. Although Rāvana is described as a demon, on a deeper level he is understood as personifying ambition and lustful greed which upset the order of the cosmos including the sanctity of woman and the family. The demon is intercepted by the gallant vulture Jatāyu, but in the ensuing conflict Jatāyu is wounded too deeply to prevent Rāvana from flying off with Sītā in his aerial chariot (388).

Rāma's close relationship with the animal kingdom is also demonstrated not only by Jatāyu but by the monkeys and bears who agree to help him rescue Sītā. The energetic monkey general, Hanumān, is often depicted with his paws brought reverentially together waiting in attendance on Rāma (380). In their search for Sītā, the monkeys endure much privation; at one point they are restored by fruits from a miraculous garden hidden within a cave and tended by an ascetic (390). Ultimately, Hanumān is able to cross to Lanka and establish contact with Sītā.

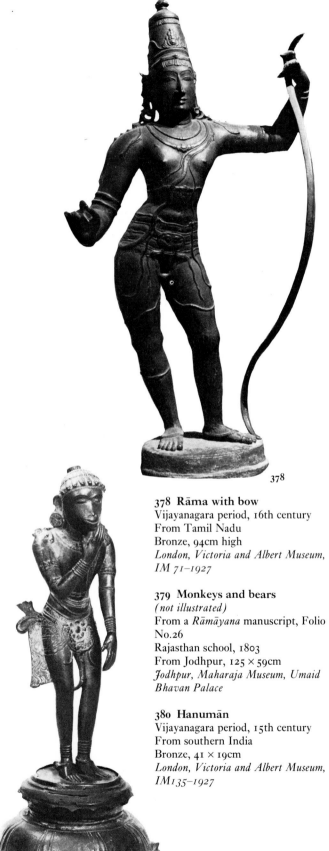

378

378 Rāma with bow
Vijayanagara period, 16th century
From Tamil Nadu
Bronze, 94cm high
*London, Victoria and Albert Museum,
IM 71–1927*

379 Monkeys and bears
(not illustrated)
From a *Rāmāyana* manuscript, Folio No.26
Rajasthan school, 1803
From Jodhpur, 125 × 59cm
Jodhpur, Maharaja Museum, Umaid Bhavan Palace

380 Hanumān
Vijayanagara period, 15th century
From southern India
Bronze, 41 × 19cm
*London, Victoria and Albert Museum,
IM135–1927*

380

381 Lakshmana disfiguring Shūrpanakhā
Gupta period, 5th century
From Deogarh (Uttar Pradesh)
Sandstone, 84 × 60 × 27cm
New Delhi, National Museum, 51.178

382 Rāma and Sītā in the forest
(see p. 82)
From a *Rāmāyana* manuscript
Sub-imperial Mughal school, *c.* 1600
New Delhi, National Museum, 56.114/5
This set of miniatures (damaged in a fire at one time) combines Mughal features with the decorative cloud forms and tilework characteristic of certain Sultanate paintings.

383 Vibhīshana presenting himself to Rāma and Lakshmana *(not illustrated)*
Rajasthan school, *c.* 1700
From Sawar, 67 × 45cm
Private collection
From the same series as **393**, here the Lanka demon allies himself with Rāma.

384 Demons in the forest
From an *Arsh Rāmāyana* manuscript, Folio 9
Rajasthan school, *c.* 1650
From Mewar, 20 × 33cm
Udaipur, Oriental Research Institute

388 Rāvana fighting Jatāyu
From the *Shangri Rāmāyana* manuscript
Pahari school, *c.* 1710
From Kulu, 18 × 28cm
New Delhi, National Museum, 62.2530

385 Bharata meeting Rāma and Lakshmana
From an *Arsh Rāmāyana* manuscript, Folio 24
Rajasthan school, *c.* 1650
From Mewar, 33 × 20cm
Udaipur, Oriental Research Institute

386 Test of Sītā *(see p. 73)*
From a *Rāmāyana* manuscript
Pahari school, *c.* 1725–30
From Kulu, 18 × 26cm
Hyderabad, Jagdish and Kamla Mittal Museum of Indian Art, 76.222

387 Rāma breaks the bow
(not illustrated)
From the *Adbhuta Rasa* manuscript
Early provincial Mughal, 1600
34 × 24cm
New Delhi, National Museum, 56.114/11

389 Hanumān fighting a demon
From a *Rāmāyana* manuscript
Central Indian school, *c.* 1635
From Malwa
Varanasi, Bharat Kala Bhavan Museum,
6785

390 Monkeys in the garden
From a *Rāmāyana* manuscript
Pahari school, *c.* 1720
From Nurpur, 16 × 27cm
Bombay, J. P. Goenka Collection
Although this set is generally identified as
coming from Mankot the human figures
identify it as Nurpur.

**391 Monkeys and bears crossing the
bridge to Lanka**
From a *Rāmāyana* manuscript
Central Indian school, *c.* 1700
From Malwa
Varanasi, Bharat Kala Bhavan Museum, 595

392 Attack on Lanka
From a *Rāmāyana* manuscript
Artist: Sahibdin
Rajasthan school, 1652
From Mewar, 18 × 36cm
London, The British Library

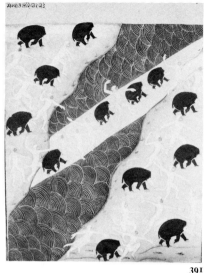

391

393 The crow reciting the scriptures
(not illustrated)
From a *Rāmāyana* manuscript
From Sawar, 65 × 39cm
Patna, Sri Gopi Krishna Kanoria
Collection
This painting is by the same artist and
from the same series as 383. Here
Garuda sits with his hands together in
the *anjali mudra* listening to the crow
while on the other side the gods and
rishis hear the word.

392

389

Despite being surrounded by demonesses and having to face
Rāvana, Sītā has maintained her serenity. Fortunately Rāvana
has been cursed so that he cannot rape a woman lest this
precipitate his doom. Nevertheless, he constantly harangues
Sītā, who with her heart fixed loyally on Rāma, remains
confident that her husband will rescue her. Despite this curse,
Rāvana has otherwise been given a boon that he cannot be
vanquished by gods or demons but only by a human being, a
class whose puny strength he is confident he can overcome.
This is the reason that the power of the god Vishnu must
appear through the human Rāma. The monkeys and the bears
lead Rāma across a land bridge to Lanka (391). In the long
battle that occurs Rāma's armies initially seem in danger of
defeat. The demon king, thinking that Sītā will capitulate if
she believes her husband is dead, tries to trick her into
despair; but although she is frightened almost beyond
endurance, Sītā withstands all his attempts.

Eventually Rāvana is killed, and Sītā is liberated from
Lanka. But this is only to face another trial, for Rāma states
that he cannot accept her back as his wife. Sītā then undergoes
a test of fire which proves her chastity without doubt (386).
This apparently cruel and unjust demand of the otherwise
gentle and sensitive husband is one which must be understood
symbolically: Sītā had undergone such emotional torment in
order to withstand the fiery, demonic assaults on her purity
that the physical fire simply corroborates her victory over
extreme adversity.

390

394

395

KRISHNA THE CHILD AND COWHERD

Though scenes from the complex narrative of Krishna's life as described in the *Bhāgavata Purāna* were occasionally carved on temple relief panels arranged in registers, the illustrated manuscript was a better vehicle for narrations. Numerous scriptural texts and poetry sets in addition to single scenes were prepared for Rājputs.

The events of Krishna's life are precipitated by the wicked king, Kamsa, who has heard a prophecy that the eighth child of his sister Devaki will overthrow him. This divine child, Krishna, and his older brother Balarāma are both miraculously saved from the murderous Kamsa's designs and spirited away to the village of Gokula, where they are brought up by a herdsman and his wife Yasodā. The juxtaposition of Krishna's status as a cowherd and as a member of a noble clan who finally becomes a ruler is interesting because the major emphasis of devotion is on Krishna's simple village life rather than the victorious ruler.

The child soon begins to demonstrate his god-like powers with spectacular results, but these deeds are generally in a context of childish mischief so that the villagers never perceive Krishna's status as a divine *avatāra*. In a well-loved and often illustrated episode, the prankish Krishna has become too much for the long-suffering Yasodā, who has tied him to a large mortar, a common custom in order to slow him down (**395**). But Krishna pulls the mortar between two trees, thereby

394 Krishna stealing the butter
Gupta period, 5th century
Red sandstone, 52 × 23 × 15cm
Varanasi, Bharat Kala Bhavan Museum, 180

395 Krishna pulling the mortar
From a *Harīvamsha* manuscript
Mughal school, *c.* 1590
23 × 19cm
London, Victoria and Albert Museum, IS2–1970

396 Krishna breaking the cart
From the Issarda *Bhāgavata Purāna* manuscript
Early Hindu school, *c.* 1570
14 × 24cm
Bombay. J. P. Goenka Collection
This manuscript follows the pre-Mughal Hindu style, but is one of the group that was produced after the Mughal conquest and has faint traces of this influence.

396

397

398

397 Krishna subduing the serpent
(see also p.87)
From a *Bhāgavata Pūrana* manuscript
Pahari school, *c.* 1775
From Kangra, 23 × 29cm
New Delhi, National Museum, 58.18/19

398 Brahmā kneeling to Krishna
From a *Bhāgavata Purāna* manuscript
From Kangra, 21 × 30cm
New Delhi, National Museum, 58.18/8
397 is from the same series, one of the
earliest and most elegant commissioned by
the Krishna devotee Sansār Chand.

**399 Cowherds wrestling around
Krishna**
Pahari school, *c.* 1710
From Kulu, 15 × 25cm
*Hyderabad, Jagdish and Kamla Mittal
Museum of Indian Art, 76.243*

399

uprooting them and releasing two cursed youths. The villagers
are shown as astonished by the incident: men and women
gesticulate wildly, putting their hands to their mouths in the
traditional gesture of wonder. Krishna's puzzled foster parents
stand expostulating before him, while his brother Balarāma is
shown behind. In the background, a woman is churning butter
in the customary fashion which relates to other popular
Krishna stories in which he successfully steals butter from
Yasodā (**394**). Widespread worship of the baby Krishna is an
accentuation of the love felt for all the spontaneity of human
children. His divine name meaning 'Butterlover' indicates how
his devotees love and honour his childhood pranks. A further
anecdotal painting (**396**) shows the young Krishna lying on his
small bed happily kicking a cart to pieces.

When the portents of danger created by the wicked Kamsa
become foreboding, Krishna's foster parents move to the
remote village of Brindaban where Krishna grows up as a
cowherd (*gopa*). Here he plays all kinds of games with the
other *gopas*, which are recorded in exuberant paintings since
joy is one of the main aspects of Krishna devotions (**397**).
Though they always call on Krishna in moments of peril and
are aware that he saves them repeatedly, the cowherds are
never quite aware of his identity. When Krishna saves them

from a forest fire, for example, they all have their hands over
their eyes so that they do not see him swallowing the fire and
are merely awestruck that it is suddenly gone (**403**).

In many instances, Krishna fools the gods, demonstrating
playful irreverence towards older forms of religion. One
incident occurs when Krishna and the cowherds are picnicking
(**404**). Krishna leaves to search for stray cows and on his
return finds that Brahmā has spirited the boys away. Krishna
simply replaces them with duplicates for a year until Brahmā
finally acknowledges Krishna's power and releases them (**398**).
In the meantime, no one notices the deception and the boys
themselves have no recollection of the event. In the tale of
Krishna and Mount Govardhana, the villagers have been
worshipping Indra to ensure rain. Krishna convinces them
that it is more appropriate for them as herders to pay tribute
to the mountain. Furious Indra then sends floods of rain, but
Krishna picks up Mount Govardhana and shields the villagers
with their cows until Indra acknowledges his supremacy. On
another occasion Krishna dances on the head of the serpent
Kāliya, who lives in a deep pool with his many wives, in order
to subdue him (**402**). Both this tale of the serpent (*nāga*) and
the story of picking up Mount Govardhana seem to represent
the dominance of Krishna worship over older nature spirits.

400

406 Rādhā and Krishna seated on lotuses   406
Pahari school, *c.* 1715
From Basohli
Varanasi, Bharat Kala Bhavan Museum

400 Krishna holding up Mount Govardhana
c. 18th century
From Orissa
Wood, 84 × 43 × 21cm
New Delhi, National Museum, 79.459

401 Krishna, Balarama and Parashurāma at the mountain (*not illustrated*)
From a *Bhāgavata Purāna* manuscript
Pahari school, *c.* 1825
Chandigarh, Government Museum and Art Gallery, 3171

402 Krishna subduing the serpent demon, Kāliya
(*see p.70*)
Chola period, 10th–11th century
From Tamil Nadu
Bronze, 59 × 23 × 16cm
New Delhi, National Museum, 70.11

403 Krishna swallowing the forest fire (*see p. 86*)
From a *Bhāgavata Purāna* manuscript
Pahari school, *c.* 1660
From Mandi, 20 × 29cm
New Delhi, National Museum, 62.2375

404 Krishna and the cowherds picknicking
(*not illustrated*)
From a *Bhāgavata Purāna* manuscript
Maratha school, late 18th century
From Nagpur, 14 × 13cm
Bombay, Prince of Wales Museum of Western India, 54.2/1

405 Akrura presents the jewel to Krishna (*not illustrated*)
From a *Bhāgavata Purāna* manuscript
Early Hindu school, *c.* 1525
From northern India, 18 × 23cm
London, Victoria and Albert Museum, IS2–1977

KRISHNA THE LOVER

Besides the worship of Krishna as a baby, it is the sweetness of Krishna the young lover which is a focal point of *bhakti* – fervent devotion to a personal god, through which salvation can be attained. Each worshipper, male or female, can play the role of Rādhā, the ultimate devotee. She is described in different ways by countless poets and appears variously as the only *gopī* loved by Krishna, as having to share his love with the other *gopīs*, as unhappily married to someone else, or even as dominated by a selfish Krishna. Each of these situations reflects the particular way in which different poets have surrendered to ardent devotion. It can be said that *bhakti* in its highest expression required total humility resulting in a warm and unselfish yielding of the ego whereas *bhakti* rendered with a purely emotional response is a totally unreasoned and impassioned abandonment of the self.

The basis of poetic elaborations of Krishna the lover is the scriptural text of the *Bhāgavata Purāna* which relates stories of Krishna's exploits with the *gopīs*. Rādhā's character was brought out by the Bengali poet Jayadeva who provided the foundation for further poetic descriptions of Rādhā's complex emotional relationship in his *Gīta Govinda*.

The Krishna of the *Bhāgavata Purāna* is fairly light-hearted and irresponsible; he begins his career of charming women at

407

408

an early age. All the village women adore and pamper him, finding his pranks endearing. When he grows up, the *gopīs* are attracted by the same careless wildness: though they appear to be a bit shocked by his provocative daring and by his flute-playing, they are also utterly captivated by it. Krishna takes the *gopīs'* clothes while they are swimming, and they only pretend to be angry. He teases them, swims with them, embraces them, and his uninhibited nature always compels their attention (412). They are perpetually ready to minister to his desires (406). He calls them away from their homes and their husbands on the night of the *rāsamandala* circle dance, and they go out yearning for him. Krishna then makes them believe that each is dancing with him. This image as it is generally conceived can either show a giant circle with Krishna beside each *gopī*, or a circle of *gopīs* with a symbolic Krishna figure in the centre (407, 408). This difference in composition seems to arise from two interpretations of the story – the first more literal and the second incorporating a more profound idea of *bhakti*, which visualizes Krishna as a presence in every human heart. In either version, the red ground indicates the importance of the emotional vitality in the relationship.

In the passionate duets between Krishna and Rādhā described in the *Gīta Govinda* and later poetic narratives, Rādhā faces many uncertainties. She seems to be left alone and to have lost Krishna; without her companion-mediator (*sakhi*) she would undoubtedly be frozen in isolation. The *sakhi*, however, patiently cajoles the two lovers and finally reunites them (410). Such struggles are quite removed from Krishna's superficial encounters with the *gopīs* and reveal a new and compelling type of emotional relationship.

Krishna's legend provided an answer to deep social as well as spiritual needs. In matters of love, the god stands for the choices of the heart, disregarding authority and overriding convention. He also stands for the right of youth to be carefree in an environment of child marriage and early responsibility. Finally, Krishna's intense emotional and physical relationship with Rādhā seems to stand for intimacy and privacy in contrast to an impersonal life within the large family.

407 Krishna dancing with the *gopīs*
18th century
From Bengal
Terracotta, 24 × 22 × 7cm
Calcutta, Asutosh Museum of Indian Art, Case 109

408 Krishna dancing with the *gopīs*
From a *Rasikapriyā* manuscript
Rajasthan school, *c.* 1630–40
From Mewar
Jodhpur, Rajasthan Oriental Research Institute

409 Dancing Krishna (*not illustrated*)
6th century
From Mathura (Uttar Pradesh)
Green stone, 30 × 14cm
Jean Claude Ciancimino Collection

410 Rādhā's confidante talking to Krishna (*not illustrated*)
From a *Gīta Govinda* manuscript
Rajasthan school, *c.* 1600
From Mewar
New Delhi, National Museum, 56/147/4

411 Illustration to *Gīta Govinda* manuscript (*not illustrated*)
Rajasthan school, 1745
From Mewar, 22 × 40cm
Varanasi, Bharat Kala Bhavan Museum, 11562

412

414

416

412 Krishna bathing with the *gopīs* *(see p.80)*
From a *Rasikapriyā* manuscript
Rajasthan school, *c.* 1630–40
From Mewar
Jodhpur, Rajasthan Oriental Research Institute

413 Krishna and Rādhā sheltering from rain *(not illustrated)*
Rajasthan school, 18th century
From Mewar, 19 × 21cm
Varanasi, Bhavat Kala Bhavan Museum, 1827

414 Krishna with the *gopīs* in a garden
From a *Rasikapriyā* manuscript
Rajasthan school, *c.* 1630–40
From Mewar
Jodhpur, Rajasthan Oriental Research Institute

415 Krishna as Rādhā, and Rādhā as Krishna *(not illustrated)*
Rajasthan school, late 18th century
From Mewar, 20 × 16cm
Varanasi, Bharat Kala Bhavan Museum, 65.98

416 Rādhā and Krishna in a tent
From a *Rasikapriyā* manuscript
Rajasthan school, *c.* 1630–40
From Mewar
Jodhpur, Rajasthan Oriental Research Institute

417 Krishna and Rādhā in a meadow
From a *Gīta Govinda* manuscript
Pahari school, *c.* 1785
From Kangra
Baron and Baroness Bachofen von Echt collection

417

418

421

424

418 Rādhā with *gopīs*
From a *Bhāgavata Purāna* manuscript
Rajasthan school, *c.* 1610
From Bikaner, 17 × 25cm
Bombay, J. P. Goenka Collection

419 Krishna with his wife *(not illustrated)*
Pahari school, late 18th century
From Kangra, 23 × 37cm
New Delhi, National Museum, 63.1183

420 Rādhā and Krishna in a pavilion
(see p. 44)
Rajasthan school, *c.* 1695
From Bundi
Varanasi, Bharat Kala Bhavan Museum, 594

421 Rādhā swooning
From a *Rasmanjari* manuscript
Pahari school, *c.* 1680
From Basohli, 23 × 33cm
London, Victoria and Albert Museum, I.S. 122–1951

422 Krishna painting Rādhā's feet
(not illustrated)
Pahari school, late 18th century
From Kangra, 28 × 23cm
New Delhi, National Museum, 49.19/290

423 Krishna on a lotus bed *(see p. 46)*
Pahari school, *c.* 1690
From Bilaspur
New Delhi, National Museum, 47.110/456

424 Krishna playing the flute
c. 19th century
From Kansat (West Bengal)
Wood, 141 × 47 × 35cm
Calcutta, Asutosh Museum of Indian Art

**425 Illustration to the *Gīta Govinda*
manuscript** *(not illustrated)*
Rajasthan school, 17th century
From Mewar, 24 × 20cm
Varanasi, Bharat Kala Bhavan Museum, 10854

शैवशाक्तिक इतिहास

9
MYTHOLOGY OF SHIVA AND THE GODDESS

Shiva is perhaps the most powerful of the major Hindu cult-gods. Elements of iconography and ritual systems associated with this god have penetrated the worship of Vishnu and of The Goddess since the early centuries AD. When the Vishnu cult first created an image of its greatest conception of god, Vishvarūpa, 'The Omniform', in the 5th century, it encircled the multi-headed god with a host of lesser divinities; but encompassing all was carved a ritually protective boundary consisting of the ferocious Eight-Bhairava heads of Shiva.

Shiva is a god of paradoxes: withdrawn ascetic/universal progenitor; the male principle/man and woman in one; wild huntsman of the forests/teacher of the arts and sciences in the mountains; creator/destroyer; naked wanderer in the wilderness carrying a skull, frightener of men and lover of women/the supreme dancer who leads man to salvation. All these oppositions are resolved and accounted for in his mythology. One of the medieval commentators on a Shiva scripture summed up the god's nature in a single phrase: 'even his ugliness is an ornament' – for who could see a flaw in one who suffers for the sake of mankind? In the beauty of his images we see terror, in their horror is divine grace.

Shiva is the despised god, outcast, with matted hair and skin covered in ashes from the cremation grounds. He ignores the rules of the *brāhman*-priests, overturns and confutes them. Yet, like Vishnu, the *brāhmans'* god *par excellence*, he becomes incarnate in every universal time-cycle: the present saviour is Lakulīsha, 'Lord of the Staff', who entered an unclaimed corpse in the graveyard at Karvan in Gujarat some 2,000 years ago. With all his attendant grotesqueness (personified as the *ganas*, his troupe of deformed dwarfs), Shiva is the friend of man, manifesting both the demonic and the divine potential latent in us all. His images often show bone and blood, the skull and animal-skin; before him everyone is naked, pierced through the physical body of skin, blood and bone to the core, to the illusion of men's imagined selves, where he challenges the most basic assumptions of man's very humanity. This penetration is the act of the closest and truest of friends. Unlike any of the other gods, he has walked the earth as a man, not in part, but in his entirety. He is not aloof; there is none too wretched to escape the closeness of Shiva.

The development of the Hindu cult of The Goddess, more usually referred to as *shakti* worship, was contemporary with that of Shiva. A composite Goddess concept evolved, incorporating various components, such as motherhood, elements of goddesses invoked in the earlier *Vedas*, and several indigenous strands unknown in Vedic religion. This is borne out by the sometimes bewildering variety of names and different forms attributed to The Goddess. Thus The Goddess is considered the creative energy or power (*shakti*) of the male deities, and is associated with a number of gods, in particular with Shiva with whom she shares many characteristic features. The Goddess is often regarded as dynamic, while Shiva remains passive; as such the Devī symbolizes the female principle, the supreme deity of the followers of The Goddess (known as *shāktas*). Devī may be conceived of as the *kundalinī* (serpent power) *shakti*, inherent but dormant in man, which has to be awakened through yogic and other processes so that the devotee may achieve spiritual liberation. In the later development of both Hindu and Buddhist Tantrism, Shakti-Devī is considered the formless, absolute principle immanent throughout the universe.

The Goddess assumes numerous forms symbolizing the different ways in which she is conceived. As the *shakti* of Shiva, The Goddess as creative energy is identified with procreation, the power of lust and, ultimately, with spiritual liberation. The eternal couple, Shiva-Shakti, is represented in the male and female emblems, the *linga* and the *yoni*; also in such iconographic forms as the union of Shiva and Shakti in the figure of Ardhanārīshvara.

In her permanent and peaceful aspect, The Goddess is worshipped as Pārvatī ('Daughter of the Mountain'), Umā, ('Light, Beauty') or Gaurī ('The Fair One'). Here she appears with her lord Shiva, embodying his tranquil, benevolent and artistically creative nature. In her forceful role as Durgā, the destroyer of the buffalo demon who had threatened the gods, The Goddess is depicted as the antagonist of all evil in the eternal cosmic struggle. As the personification of righteous wrath, the terrifying Chāmundā-Kālī becomes the supreme deity of the *shāktas*; though sometimes linked with the frightening aspect of Shiva (as Bhairava), she is mostly conceived as an independent deity.

426 Linga *(not illustrated)*
Kushāna period, 1st century AD
From Kankali mound, near Mathura (Uttar
Pradesh)
Sandstone, 100 × 30 × 23cm
Lucknow, State Museum, H.1

427 Four-faced *(chaturmukha) linga*
Gupta period, *c.* 5th century
From Kosam (Uttar Pradesh)
Sandstone, 97 × 30 × 30cm
Lucknow, State Museum, H.3
The roughly finished lowermost square
section of these *lingas* would have been
concealed within a supporting pedestal.

428 One-faced *(ekamukha) linga*
(see also p.68)
Gupta period, 5th century
From Khoh (Madhya Pradesh)
Red sandstone, 96 × 24 × 27cm
New Delhi, National Museum, 76.223

429

429 Miniature *linga* **and** *yoni*
8th century
From Kashmir
Black stone, 5 × 7cm
Private collection

430 Miniature *linga* **and** *yoni*
(not illustrated)
8th century
From Kashmir
Crystal
Jean Claude Ciancimino Collection

427

THE LINGA

The oldest symbol by which Shiva is recognized is the *linga*.
Stones, shaped by water and abrasion, with natural markings
on them, some resembling the three horizontal strokes painted
on the forehead by devotees of Shiva, or the three prongs of
the god's trident, were the first *lingas*. These stones are set
upright in pedestals of stone or brass and honoured as the god
himself. This is a very ancient cult practice which has its roots
in prehistoric tribalism.

From the 2nd or 1st century BC, the *linga* was copied in
more tractable stone by sculptors, with added octagonal and
square sections beneath it; it was embedded in the earth, at
first in stone-railed open-air shrines beneath a sacred tree. A
few centuries later, the same shape was copied for installation
in the dark sanctuary – called the *garbha-griha* or 'womb-
house' – of temples dedicated to Shiva. The phallic symbolism
is obvious, especially in the early sculptured *lingas* (**426**);
indeed, there are several myths which tell of Shiva's self-
castration, leaving his phallus to be copied as an image of his
power and worshipped as his emblem.

The basic tripartite form of the *linga* and its omni-
directional symbolism indicate that the whole shaft imitates
the universal axis. But just as images of Shiva in human form
display representational symbols of time (such as the sun and
moon, or the drum and the fire, with the figure of the god
between them), the *linga* also demonstrates the three phases of
the time-axis: from the square to the octagon to the circle.
Buried in the ground, the lowest part is cubic like the
sanctuary, four-sided and thus stable as the earth itself. From
this projects an octagonal zone, its eight facets directed at the
cardinal and intermediate points of horizontal space. This zone
is above ground level, but concealed within a stand which

serves to drain away the water with which the top of the *linga*
is lustrated; this is called, symbolically, the *yoni-pītha* or
vagina-pedestal, as the central zone of the shaft penetrates it.
Rising above the octagonal section is the cylindrical domed top
of the shaft which, like the *stūpa*, faces the entire circle of the
horizon and all angles from it to the zenith. The *linga* thus
emanates from the mysterious depths of the earth and the
subterranean waters, and rises, facing the whole physical world
of *māyā*, to culminate in the dome which points at the
heavens; wherever it is situated, a Shiva *linga* becomes an
imitation of the *axis mundi*. The whole universe as time and
space is thus symbolized by this simple cult object.

On the side of the cylindrical top section of the *linga* a mask
of Shiva is sometimes carved, showing that the *linga* is the
primary symbol from which the god in his recognizably human
form originates (**428**). First comes the plain inflexible axis;
only secondarily does the articulate deity with seemingly
human characteristics appear. This concept of the primacy of
the *linga* finds graphic expression in the myth of Shiva's birth
from the *linga*. Here Shiva appears out of a fiery *linga* to prove
to Vishnu and Brahmā that he is the supreme lord (**431, 432**).
Neither extremity of this *linga* can be found by Vishnu or
Brahmā.

The four-faced *linga*, each face looking in one of the
cardinal directions of horizontal space, carries the inherent
symbolism of the *linga* much further (**427**). The faces are said
to be emanations, or sons, of Shiva, and each has two names,
the first elemental, the second devotional. The elements
represented are earth, water, fire and air, the axial *linga* being
referred to as 'The Lord, the Eternal Shiva'. These four
aspects of Shiva penetrated by the *linga* itself are said
symbolically to be composed of the four colours – black,
yellow, red and white – which are those of the four cosmic
eras, each ruled by one of the four faces.

428

431 *Linga* **with Vishnu and Brahmā** *(not illustrated)*
Gurjara-Pratihāra period, 10th century
From Harsha Giri, Sikar (Rajasthan)
Sandstone, 113 × 48cm
Ajmer, Rajputana Museum, I(27)374

432 Shiva appearing from the fiery *linga* *(not illustrated)*
Late Chola period, 12th–13th century
From Mudiyannur (Tamil Nadu)
Granite, 120 × 3 × 28cm
Madras, Government Museum, 90–8/38

433 One-faced Shiva *linga*
Early Pāla period, 7th century
From Bihar
Basalt, 70cm high
Private collection

434

434 Nandin
13th–15th century
From Karnataka or Tamil Nadu
Basalt, 58 × 33 × 78cm
Oxford, Ashmolean Museum, O.S.77

433

THE BULL

Nandin (usually pronounced as Nandī) is the name of Shiva's bull; it means 'causing gladness' and hence 'a son'. As a horse to a warrior, so the bull gives pleasure to Shiva. Probably the original reason for associating the bull with this god was simply the great masculine potency which each embodies, and the rage and physical power of which both are capable. In images of Shiva with Nandin, the bull is invariably quiet and docile. Unlike the animal 'vehicles' of other deities – such as the eagle of Vishnu or the lion of The Goddess – the bull is not represented as participating in the battles of his master. In the presence of Shiva, who represents virility without giving sexual expression to it, the bull becomes gentle. Nandin is also a symbol of *dharma*, four-footed and steady as a rock, for Shiva's ability to burn away sloth, ignorance and evil ensures the constant renewal of fertility, correct motivation, and religious aspiration; thus he perpetuates the conditions in which all levels of *dharma* can flourish.

Images of Nandin, often life-sized or colossal, are set in their own pavilions outside Shiva temples, facing the *linga* or the image of the god through the entrance doorway. Nandin is said to be always alert to his master's call, ever prepared to carry him wherever the god wishes in the three worlds. Although treated with due ritual respect, images of Nandin are usually extremely likeable, and no-one objects to children swarming all over him, adding by their play to the original glossy stone finish given to his smooth and shining hide.

THE LORD WHO IS HALF WOMAN

*The Lord who, though he stands in that sole sovereignty
    which holds many rewards for his devotees,
    himself wears only an animal-skin
– Who, though his body is conjoined with that of his beloved,
    is yet superior to ascetics whose minds are free
    from material desires
– Who, though he supports the whole world in his eight forms,
    is yet not proud
– May he lead you from the path of darkness,
    that you see the way of goodness.*

This benedictory verse of the god Shiva was written by the
Sanskrit poet and playwright, Kālidāsa, in the 5th century AD
as a prologue to one of his dramas. The 'eight forms' referred
to are explained by the commentator, Katyavema, as meaning
the five elements – earth, water, fire, air and space –
mentioned in connection with the *linga*, plus the visible
symbols of time, the sun and moon, and the god's devotee
himself, who is the eighth form of Shiva. The second line
might appear to suggest that the god is imagined as joined in
sexual intercourse with his consort, Pārvatī; but actually he is
never represented thus. The poet is referring to a particular
image of the god, which was iconographically established two
or three centuries before Kālidāsa, representing the god in
androgynous form. Sculptures representing this conception of
Shiva are divided into male and female halves, the left half –
always symbolically female – appearing as the goddess
Pārvatī, the right half as the god himself. Great artistic skill is
evident in many such sculptures, for only a master could
integrate the male and female halves into an aesthetically
convincing and pleasing whole (**436**).

   In origin, this image derives from the concept of the
hermaphroditic act of creation by a single creator.
Mythologists of the Vishnu cult introduced a goddess as the
personification of that god's trance-like sleep upon the waters
at the instant of creation. The introduction of a female
principle became necessary to lend credibility to the creation
myth, though it was for as long as possible subordinated to the
idea of an exclusively male creative power. Although in the
androgynous images the female half is of equal physical stature
to the male half, the name of these icons suggests that we are
looking at the god Shiva, whose generative force, when he
assumes the role of universal creator, requires a female
presence. In fact, the name of the image is Ardhanārīshvara,
which means 'The Lord Who is Half Woman' – a masculine
concept which incorporates a female aspect, not a male-female
partnership. This is borne out by another verse of Kālidāsa, in
which the poet again invokes Shiva in his androgynous form:

*Homage to the father-and-mother of the world,
    to him whose left half is his wife –
Whose left eye shrinks from the mere glance of the right.*

These sculptures are not fanciful depictions of the ideal couple
wedded together in matrimony; that is represented in other,
more conventional tableaux. The Ardhanārīshvara image is
indisputably bisexual in appearance, but the cosmogenetic
concept which it expresses is essentially and dominantly
masculine.

435

435 Ardhanārīshvara
Gurjara-Pratihārā period, *c.* 7th century
From Rajasthan
Sandstone
Jhalawar, Archaeological Museum

436 Ardhanārīshvara (*not illustrated*)
Gurjara-Pratihāra period, 9th century
From Abaneri (Rajasthan)
Sandstone
*Jaipur, Collection of Maharaja Sawai Man
Singh II, Rajasthan*

THE DIVINE MARRIAGE

When in each other's company, both Shiva and The Goddess are at peace. Their marriage was, indeed, an alliance of two mighty powers. The form of The Goddess whom Shiva married was Pārvatī, 'Daughter of the Mountain', for her father was Himavan himself, the personification of the mighty snow-clad Himalaya range, the abode of the gods. Four-headed Brahmā, the god best versed in ritual lore, officiated as priest at their marriage under the eyes of the immortals from their mountain fastnesses.

When standing or seated together, Shiva and Pārvatī present the very image of conjugal happiness, sometimes alone and sometimes attended by other gods and sages. On one occasion, the multi-headed demon, Rāana, attempted to dislodge them from their particular mountain, Kailāsa, just inside Tibet, by shaking its foundations; but Shiva merely pressed down with one toe, and the quaking caused by the demon was suppressed. At other times they are depicted seated upon the bull Nandin, while their son, the infant Skanda, dances before them (444).

Probably the most celebrated images of the divine parents with their son are the southern Indian bronzes (446); here their peace and contentment are manifest, while their separate inherent powers, though understated, are clearly perceptible. Shiva and Pārvatī are seated; between them stands their baby son, Skanda. The powerful modelling of these figures, and the serene expressions of the divine parents, are fully expressive of their contentment, which derives from the union of male and female principles in a graceful yet dynamic balance.

438

443

437 Head of Shiva *(see p.51)*
Gupta period, 5th century
From Varanasi (Uttar Pradesh)
Terracotta, 14 × 7 × 14cm
Varanasi, Bharat Kala Bhavan Museum, 1605

438 Shiva and Pārvatī
Pallava period, 8th century
From Pachur (Tamil Nadu)
Granite, 147 × 75 × 33cm
Madurai, Thirumalai Nayak Mahal Museum, 11/76

439 Shiva *(not illustrated)*
Pāla period, 8th century
From eastern India
Bronze, 16 × 9cm
Private collection

440 Shiva and Consort (Vrishabhāntika and Devī)
(see pp. 66 and 67)
11th century
From Truvenkadu (Tamil Nadu)
Bronze, 108 × 47 × 28cm and 93 × 37 × 30cm
Thanjavur, Thanjavur Art Gallery, 86/87

441 Shiva and Pārvatī
(not illustrated)
Dated 1283
From western India
Brass, 24 × 19 × 11cm
Oxford, Ashmolean Museum, 1965-5

442 Shiva and Pārvatī
(not illustrated)
16th century
From Saharan (Himachal Pradesh)
Bronze, 21 × 16 × 8cm
Simla, State Museum

443 The marriage of Shiva and Pārvatī
Nāyaka period, 18th century
From Tamil Nadu
Ivory, 16 × 11cm
London, Victoria and Albert Museum, IM17-1930

444 Shiva and Pārvatī
10th century
From Hinglajgarh (Madhya Pradesh)
Sandstone, 69 × 54 × 26cm
Indore, Central Museum

445

446

445 Pārvatī
10th century
From Hinglajgarh (Madhya
Pradesh)
Sandstone, 90 × 56 × 24cm
Indore, Central Museum

446 Shiva and Pārvatī with Skanda
Chola period, 10th–11th century
From Pattiswaram (Tamil Nadu)
Bronze, 51 × 62 × 31cm
Thanjavur, Thanjavur Art Gallery, 112

447 The marriage of Shiva and Pārvatī *(not illustrated)*
From a *Shiva Purāna* manuscript, no.15
Rajasthan school, *c.*1820
From Jodhpur, 123 × 45cm
Jodhpur, Maharaja Museum, Umaid Bhavan Palace

GODDESSES OF DESTRUCTION

In Hinduism there can be as many goddesses as there are
gods: each deity requires his *shakti* (energizing female
counterpart or consort), who may be worshipped together
with, or independently from, the god whom she accompanies.
Cults which elevate the female principle above the male, at all
levels from the cosmic to the terrestrial, are termed *shākta* or,
in more specific applications, *tāntrika* (tantric). In such a cult,
the many and various goddesses become, in effect, facets of the
one female principle, personified as The Goddess. Images of
her often portray a beautiful Amazonian figure standing upon
a buffalo, clearly symbolic of her aggressive pre-eminence, or a
skeletal hag. She then assumes the roles which the gods have
in male-dominated cults; it is a complete reversal of the
orthodox symbolic terms of philosophical and religious
thought. Thus the female principle becomes the first principle,
the energizing force that stimulates the masculine potential,
which is seen as dormant – or even dead – without her. In the
words of a famous *shākta* saying: 'Shiva without his *shakti* is a
corpse (*shava*)' – a play on the words Shiva and *shava*.

However, there is one goddess who is not the female
equivalent of a god. Her name, Chāmundā, is said to be
derived from the combination of Chanda and Munda, the two
male demons whom she slew and decapitated. Chāmundā was
created by the goddess Durgā, slayer of the buffalo-demon
(Mahishāsuramardinī); the gory myth of her rise to power over
the gods is related in the scripture called the *Devīmāhātmya*
(448). The gods are said to have been impotent to quell a
powerful demon in the guise of a black water-buffalo. When
their combined wrath condensed, it became a female – the
goddess Durgā. To her each of the gods gave his most
powerful weapon. And not only did she decapitate the buffalo-
guise of the demon and then slay the devil within, but she also
called forth all the consorts of the gods from their masters and
incorporated them into herself, so establishing her
independent supremacy over gods and demons alike. This
multiple and dominant female is often shown plunging a spear
or trident into the buffalo-demon, whom she holds up by the
tail (452). Sometimes the humanized demon is depicted
emerging from the body of the decapitated buffalo; he, too, is
violently slain (450). A large range of fearsome weapons is
carried by The Goddess, but despite her aggressive nature she
always appears as a beautiful woman.

448 Exploits of The Goddess *(detail)*
From a *Devīmāhātmya* manuscript
Early Rajput school, *c.* 1550–70
From Punjab hills
Simla, State Museum

448

449

449 Durgā
Early Chālukya period, 8th–9th
century
From Raichur district (Andhra
Pradesh)
Sandstone, 95 × 72 × 25cm
Hyderabad, State Museum, 7579

**450 Durgā killing the buffalo
demon**
Hoysala period, early 13th
century
From Karnataka
Soapstone, 148 × 76cm
*London, Victoria and Albert
Museum, IS77–1965*

450

451

453

451 Chāmundā (Kālī)
9th–10th century
From central India
Khondalite, 53cm high
London, Trustees of the British Museum, 1872.7–1.84

452 Durgā *(see p. 36)*
Early Chālukya period, 8th century
From Alampur (Andhra Pradesh)
Red sandstone, 84 × 65cm
Alampur, Archaeological Museum, 40

453 Kālī
Chola period, 11th century
From Tamil Nadu
Bronze, 14 × 11 × 5cm
New Delhi, National Museum, 70.10

454 Demons defiling the sacrifice made by an ascetic *(not illustrated)*
From *Vibhasta Rasa* manuscript
Pahari school, 1725
From Kulu, 22 × 32cm
New Delhi, National Museum, 62.2437

455 Consort of Sadāshiva
(see p. 71)
10th century
From Himachal Pradesh
Bronze, 37 × 24 × 7cm
New Delhi, National Museum, 64.102

456 Durgā killing the buffalo demon *(not illustrated)*
Pahari school, c. 1760
From Nurpur, 20 × 28cm
London, Victoria and Albert Museum, IS460–1950

457 Kālī fighting the demons *(not illustrated)*
From a *Vaudra Rasa* manuscript
Pahari school, late 18th century
From Guler, 28 × 39cm
New Delhi, National Museum, 60.168

458 Durgā fighting the buffalo demon *(not illustrated)*
From a *Vīra Rasa* manuscript
Pahari school, late 18th century
From Guler, 28 × 19cm
New Delhi, National Museum, 47.110/453

The creation of Chāmundā, or Kālī as she is more popularly known, is vividly described in the *Mārkandeya Purāna*:

From the forehead of Durgā, contracted with wrathful frowns, sprang swiftly a goddess of black and formidable aspect, armed with a scimitar and noose, bearing a ponderous mace, decorated with a garland of dead corpses, robed in the hide of an elephant, dry and withered and hideous, with yawning mouth, lolling tongue, and bloodshot eyes, and filling the regions with her shouts.

Sculptures of Kālī are remarkably similar to this description (451); though she frequently retains something of her more beautiful creator (453). As the counterpart of Shiva with five faces, Sadāshiva, the conception of The Goddess is occasionally even further elaborated. Here the five-faced and ten-armed goddess appears seated on the shoulders of Nandin, represented as a male figure (455). The terrifying aspect of the goddess is suggested by her fifth grinning face and the flames shooting up from the crown. She holds various weapons: a skull, a lotus and a book. Miniature figures of Ganesha and Shiva, both in dancing postures, are positioned below at either side.

459

459 Kālī at the burning ground
Pahari school, c. 1710
From Chamba, 133 × 188cm
London, Victoria and Albert Museum, IS126–1951

460 Durgā *(see p.38)*
19th century
From Bengal
Ivory, 50 × 41cm
London, Victoria and Albert Museum, 1070–1852

461

461 **The Seven Mothers dancing with Shiva**
Gurjara-Pratihāra period,
9th–10th century
From Uttar Pradesh
Sandstone, 53 × 136 × 17cm
New Delhi, National Museum

462 **The Seven Mothers**
(not illustrated)
From Rajasthan
Sandstone
Jaipur, Central Museum

463 **Head of Vārāhī**
Gurjara-Pratihāra period,
9th–10th century
From Madhya Pradesh
Yellow sandstone, 35 × 49cm
Gwalior, Archaeological Museum, 17/126

464 **The Mothers**
Maitraka period, 7th century
From Gujarat
Stone, 58 × 45 × 17cm
New Delhi, National Museum, 68.192

463

464

THE MOTHERS

As the activating *shakti*, The Goddess assumes as many
counterpart forms as there are gods, and more. These are
sometimes standardized into groups of mothers, usually seven
or eight in number. In collective sculptures of these 'Seven
Mothers' (Saptamātrikās) there are seen the female versions of
Indra (as Indrānī); Varāha, the boar incarnation of Vishnu (as
Vārāhī); Vishnu himself (as Vaishnāvī); Kumāra, the warrior
son of Shiva and Pārvatī (as Kaumārī); Shiva (as Maheshvarī);
and Brahmā (Brahmānī). The seventh Mātrikā, Chāmundā,
has no male counterpart. Often Shiva, playing the long-
stringed *vīnā* as the supreme master of music and dance, leads
them in a weird processional dance (**461**). Ganesha often
brings up the rear. The legend that accounts for the
appearance of these Mātrikās describes the *shaktis* of the
principal gods as helpers in the fight of the great goddess
Durgā against the demons who threaten the peace of the
universe. Each of the Mātrikās is characterized by the
respective forms, ornaments, weapons, and animal or bird
mounts, of each god. Thus Vārāhī reproduces the boar head of
Varāha, and Brahmānī the four heads of Brahmā.

465 Bhairava
Hoysala period, 12th century
From Halebid (Karnataka)
Soapstone, 138 × 61 × 27cm
*Bangalore, Government Museum, Venkappa
Art Gallery, 8*

466 Bhairava
Chola period, 12th century
From Central India
Sandstone
Private collection

467 Bhairava *(not illustrated)*
Hoysala period, 12th century
From the Deccan
Soapstone, 58 × 52cm
*London, Trustees of the British Museum,
1966.10–14.1*

468 Bhairava *(not illustrated)*
Late Chālukya-Hoysala period, *c.* 10th
century
From Belgur (Karnataka)
Granite, 76 × 48 × 20cm
*Bangalore, Government Museum, Venkappa
Art Gallery, 48*

469 Bhairava
Eastern Ganga period, 13th century
From Orissa
Bronze, 50 × 32cm
Private collection

465

466

GOD OF TERROR

The horrific skeletal forms of The Goddess, such as
Chāmundā, are female parallels to a form of Shiva usually
known as Bhairava, 'The Frightening' or 'The Terrible'.
Bhairava appears as a result of Shiva's horrendous crime of
killing a member of the priestly class. In fact, Shiva severed
the fifth head of Brahmā, the archetypal *brāhman* priest, thus
symbolically depriving him of his rulership of the universe (the
fifth and central head of Brahmā represented the centre of the
cosmic pentad, the universal axis). Shiva thereby achieved
divine status, but was condemned to expiate his crime by
wandering the earth as Bhairava, in the shape of a human
ascetic, the severed head or skull stuck firmly to his hand as a
sign of his truly cosmic criminality. Sometimes Bhairava is
depicted in this form carrying the severed head or skull on a
stick as he roams through the land (**467**). His eyes bulge and
fangs protrude from his mouth; around his neck is a garland of
skulls while his hair is long and matted, sometimes done up in
an elaborate coiffure. He wears the wooden sandals of the
ascetic while a dog, the animal associated with cremation
grounds, accompanies him (**466**). This form of the god derives
ultimately from the oldest mask of the four-faced *linga*, the
terrifying face of Bhairava on the southern side, ruler of the
most ancient aeon in the cycles of time, the Dark Age
following Shiva's acquisition of the universal axis. In fact,
many such ashen, skeletal figures are still to be seen in India
today; these are the *sannyāsins*, atoning for their sins by
imitating Shiva's great act of penance.

469

470 Kārttikeya
Gurjara-Pratihāra period, 8th century
Sandstone, 79 × 72 × 30cm
Bhopal, Birla State Museum, 124

471 Ganesha
9th century
From Ashpuri district, Madhya Pradesh
Sandstone, 84 × 47 × 22cm
Bhopal, Birla State Museum, 149

THE WARRIOR SON

The numerous names of this god – Skanda, Kārttikeya, Kumāra or Subrahmanya – indicate that many allied concepts were at the root of the later unified idea of a warrior deity sometimes considered the son of Shiva. This is borne out by the many different accounts in the Epics and *Purānas* about his origin. Shiva and Agni are both sometimes said to be his father; Gangā, Svāhā the wife of Agni and the six stars of the constellation Pleiades (*krittikās*) are variously described as the mother. For this reason he is often referred to as Shanmukha, 'the Six-Faced', and images of him with six heads exist. His association with the *ganas*, and the close connection between his followers and those of Kubera, indicate an underlying folk element.

Skanda-Kārttikeya-Kumāra was created to defeat the powers of evil, sometimes represented by Tāraka, the blind demon; thus he is the chief battle god, the head of the celestial armies. Frequently said to be chaste – his only wives are the personified army, Devasenā, and his female counterpart, the virgin Kaumarī – the god represents the virile power of chastity in the form of an innocent youth. The epic tradition that created Skanda-Kārttikeya as an eternally youthful sage-god is also at the root of another development in southern India, namely that of the Subrahmanya, the 'instructor-god', the son of Shiva.

From the earliest periods of Indian sculpture Skanda-Kārttikeya is shown holding the spear and cockerel, riding a peacock; occasionally he is shown slaying the demon.

GANESHA

As the impish dwarf attendants of Shiva, the *ganas* are popular in Indian art; sometimes they even imitate the great god. In this large-scale sculpture (**473**), a *gana* has taken the headdress (long locks decorated with crescent moon and skull) and the single large earring of Shiva; he also wears a snake anklet.

The lord of the *ganas*, Ganesha or Ganapati, is the destroyer of obstacles and is in every sense auspicious; he is invoked at the beginning of any enterprise, that he may make the way smooth, remove distractions, and protect one from evil. He is also the bestower of earthly prosperity and well-being. As the god of good beginnings he is immensely popular throughout India, among both Hindus and Jains.

There are various myths about the origin of Ganesha: he is described as the son of Pārvatī alone, as the son of both Shiva and Pārvatī, or as having independent origin. This suggests the attempt of later mythologies to bring this popular folk deity in line with the more important cult divinities, Shiva and The Goddess. However, Ganesha's original affiliation was mainly with the *ganas*, who have primitive non-Āryan characteristics. The most distinctive features of Ganesha are the elephant head and pot belly. He may hold an axe, an elephant-goad, sweetmeats or a tusk, and is usually seated alone or with his consort (**475**); however, Ganesha also dances in imitation of Shiva (**471**), sometimes in company with the Mātrikās. The tusk that he holds is one of his own, which is seen to be broken off, an honourable blemish sustained in defence of Shiva.

472 *Ganas (not illustrated)*
Gupta period, 5th century
From central India
Terracotta, 21 × 31cm
Private collection

473 *Gana (see p.69)*
Gupta period, 5th century
From Nagpur (Maharashtra)
Red sandstone, 85 × 65 × 40cm
New Delhi, National Museum, L.77.2

474

475

475 Ganesha with his consort
16th–17th century
From Kerala
Bronze, 24 × 22 × 7cm
New Delhi, National Museum, 66.87

476 Ganas in foliage *(not illustrated)*
Eastern Ganga period, 11th century
From Bhubaneshwar (Orissa)
Chlorite, 42 × 23 × 10cm
Bhubaneshwar, Orissa State Museum AY-119

477 Ganesha being honoured
(not illustrated)
From a *Sudama* manuscript
Pahari school, *c.* 1780
From Garhwal, 19 × 27cm
*Dublin, Chester Beatty Library and Gallery of
Oriental Art*
A picture of Ganesha, considered auspicious,
was often the first leaf in a manuscript.

478

474 Ganesha
Gupta period, 6th century
From Mathura (Uttar Pradesh)
Sandstone, 50 × 39cm
London, Spink & Son Ltd, A920

478 Ganesha
From a *Mrigāvat* manuscript
Pre-Mughal school, *c.* 1520
*Varanasi, Bharat Kala Bhavan Museum,
7991*

479 Ganesha
Early Chola period, 10th century
From southern India
Sandstone, 102 × 47 × 33cm
New Delhi, National Museum, 72.467

LORD OF THE DANCE

Time has three divisions as far as man is immediately concerned, as are expressed in the structure of his language. The three tenses, past, present, and future are real to mankind, but in divine terms they are fragments of one Time, called Mahākāla; this is one of the names of Shiva, for in him they are united. Many different types of image express this concept, but the most celebrated is undoubtedly that of Shiva as Natarāja, 'Lord of the Dance', which was perfected, with the inclusion of many other symbolic levels of meaning, in southern India. In his upper right hand, the dancing god holds a drum (*damaru*) shaped rather like an hour-glass, the skin stretched across the two extremities; it is sounded by a rapid rocking motion of the hand, producing a loud, staccato noise. The basic word for sound is *shabda*, and it is often considered the subtle continuum which is eternity; the *shabda-brahman* essentially consists of the sacred words of the Vedic hymns, the essence and origin of *dharma*, the oldest entity of the universe, condensed in the sacred syllable *aum* which is itself threefold (*a-u-m*). By sounding the drum, therefore, Shiva continuously echoes the primeval sound from the infinite depths of time past; and in so doing, he provides his own musical accompaniment for the dance, which is the very dance of time and all that comes to pass – for all things happen in time, which must exist before space can be extended. The dance takes place in one spot, and that is the central, dynamic axis of the universe and of man. It is the rhythms and dynamics of this dance of Shiva which govern the inherent power and organization of the universe.

In his opposite left hand the god holds fire. This is not a threat, but a symbol of the inevitable destruction of all that exists, the cataclysmic fire in which the universe will, in future time, be purified so that it may be renewed. This cycle of time, from the remote past to the remote future, runs in the great fire-cycle within which the god dances, filling it in every direction. Between past and future is man's present, and to this mortal condition the god addresses the remaining symbolism of his dance.

To allay fear, his right hand is raised in the gesture of reassurance, *abhaya-mudrā*, while his right foot crushes with all his weight a deformed, squirming dwarf which represents unenlightened man. While symbolically destroying this grotesque and grasping creature, Shiva indicates with his extended left hand the rising of his left foot, which is directed out of the circle in another dimension, through the cycle of time-conditioned existence to the eternal axis wherein lies the freedom of the spirit called *moksha*. The dance takes place within man, in the shape of spiritually liberated man, who is co-extensive with the measured rhythms of the universe.

480 Shiva dancing on Nandin (*not illustrated*)
12–13th century
From Awbari, 235 × 133 × 46cm
Gauhati, Museum, 3372

481 Lord of the Dance, Natarāja (*not illustrated*)
Chola period, 10th century
From Tiruvarangalam (Tamil Nadu)
Bronze, 225 × 86 × 72cm
Madras, Archaeological Survey of India

482 Dancing Shiva (*not illustrated*)
8th–9th century
From Hinglajgarh (Madhya Pradesh)
Sandstone, 84 × 52 × 21cm
Indore, Central Museum

483

483 Dancing Shiva
Early Chālukya period, 8th century
From Alampur (Andhra Pradesh)
Red sandstone, 122 × 71cm
Alampur, Archaeological Museum, 5

484

484 Shiva dancing on Nandin
13th century
From south India (Andhra Pradesh)
Stone, 41 × 41 × 16cm
New Delhi, National Museum

487

485 Shiva's Heaven *(not illustrated)*
Western Indian school, *c.* 1800
99 × 89cm
London, Victoria and Albert Museum,
IS09322

486 Shiva destroying the triple citadel
of the demons
Chola period, 11th century
From Tamil Nadu
Sandstone, 113 × 66 × 29cm
New Delhi, National Museum, L.55/17

487 Lord of the Dance, Natarāja
Chola period, 10th century
From Tamil Nadu
Bronze, 86 × 72 × 22cm
New Delhi, National Museum, 57.16/1

GLOSSARY

Agni Vedic fire god, intermediary between the gods and men.

ākāsha Space, one of the five universal elements.

Ālvārs Tamil worshippers of Vishnu, composers of devotional hymns.

amrita Drink of immortality, one of the divine treasures lost in the cosmic flood.

ānanda State of bliss; also the name of the Buddha's principal disciple.

Ananta 'Endless', the serpent on whom Vishnu sleeps or is seated.

anda Egg; hence Brahmānda, the cosmic egg.

apsaras Beautiful nymph; courtesans of the gods and seducers of men.

Ardhanārīshvara Form of Shiva in which half the figure is the god and the other half Pārvatī.

Arjuna Hero of the epic, *Mahābhārata*; Krishna is his charioteer in the *Bhagavad Gītā*.

artha Wealth and power, one of the four goals of life; also 'polity'.

Aruna Charioteer of the sun god Sūrya; symbol of the dawn.

arūpa Formless.

ashoka Flowering tree.

āshrama One of the four stages of life – student (*brahmachārin*), householder (*grihastha*), hermit (*vānaprastha*) and homeless wanderer (*sannyāsin*).

asura Anti-god, demon.

ātman The Self, the soul, identical with *brahman* the world spirit.

Avalokiteshvara 'The Lord Who Looks Down', one of the most popular Bodhisattvas; also known as Padmanpāni.

avatāra Incarnation of a god, especially Vishnu.

Balarāma Brother of Krishna.

Bhagavad Gītā 'Song Celestial'; section of the *Mahābhārata* in which Krishna reveals himself as god incarnate.

Bhāgavata Purāna A principal text on the life of Krishna.

Bhairava Fearsome aspect of Shiva expiating his crime of having cut off the fifth head of Brahmā.

bhājan Communal singing celebrating Krishna and Rādhā.

bhakta Devotee.

bhakti Intense devotion to a personal god.

Bharata Brother of Rāma.

Bhūdevi The earth goddess rescued by Vishnu.

bīja Seed; sacred syllable used mostly in meditation.

Bodhisattva Saintly and compassionate being destined to become a Buddha.

Brahmā Maker of the universe; sometimes considered part of a trio of deities including Vishnu as the preserver and Shiva as the destroyer.

brahman Soul or universal spirit, identified with the real self (*ātman*).

brāhman Member of the highest Hindu class, divinity in human form; professional priests are invariably *brāhmans*.

Brāhmanas Texts on Vedic sacrificial ritual.

buddhi Intellect; hence the *bodhi* or wisdom tree, and the Buddha – 'The Enlightened'.

chakra Disc or wheel, concentration of psychic force; sun symbol, weapon of Vishnu.

Chāmundā Goddess created by Durgā to destroy evil.

Chandra Moon god.

darshana Auspicious viewing of a deity within the temple, or outside at a public festival.

deva God.

devapūjā Worship of the gods, usually in a temple.

Devī The Goddess, incorporating both benign and fearsome aspects.

dharma Righteousness or sacred law, one of the four goals of life; individual's class duty.

dikpālas Guardians of the eight directions of space.

Durgā 'Difficult to penetrate', goddess, destroyer of the buffalo demon.

dvārapāla Door guardian, usually armed.

gana Impish dwarf attendant of Shiva.

gandharva Celestial being, often a flying musician.

Ganesha Elephant-headed god, the remover of obstacles; sometimes considered the son of Shiva and Pārvatī. Also known as Ganapati.

Gangā Goddess, personification of the Ganges river.

garbha-griha 'Womb-chamber', temple sanctum.

Garuda Eagle mount of Vishnu, symbol of the sun.

Gaurī Goddess, a name of the consort of Shiva (also Pārvatī etc.)

Gīta Govinda Devotional text describing the life of Krishna, particularly his dalliance with the beautiful Rādhā.

gopīs Cowherdesses, much loved by Krishna.

Hanumān Monkey god, friend and ally of Rāma as described in the *Rāmāyana*.

hamsa Goose, the vehicle of the god Brahmā.

Harihara Shiva and Vishnu joined together in a single figure.

Hiranya-garbha The Golden Egg, or Womb.

Indra War god and rain god of the *Vedas*.

Jātakas Stories of the former lives of the Buddha.

Jatāyu Vulture that attempts to rescue Sītā in the *Rāmāyana*.

jnāna Knowledge.

Jyeshthā Goddess of sloth and bad luck; closely related to Sītalā; sometimes connected with Alakshmī.

Kālī 'The Black', fearsome goddess of death and destruction; also known as Chāmundā.

Kāliya Serpent demon subdued by Krishna.

kāma Desire, physical love, pleasure of all kinds; one of the four goals of life.

kāma-dhenu Wish-fulfilling cow.

Kāmasūtra Treatise on eroticism.

karma Effect of former deeds, performed in this life and in previous ones, on one's present and future condition.

Kārttikeya Warrior god, considered to be the son of Shiva, also known as Skanda, Kumāra or Subrahmanya.

Ketu Planetary deity; god of the comet.

Krishna Pastoral hero and amorous lover of Rādhā; as the supreme lord is an incarnation of Vishnu and preacher of the *Bhagavad Gītā*.

kshatriya Ruling warrior aristocracy in Hindu society.

kshetra-devatā *Naga* guardian of the fields.

Kubera Guardian of the treasures of the earth; regent of the northern quarter.

Kumāra See Kārttikeya.

Kūrma Turtle; second incarnation of Vishnu involved in the myth of the churning of the cosmic ocean.

Lakshmana Brother of Rāma.

Lakshmī Goddess of the lotus, good luck and prosperity; also known as Shrī; also the consort of Vishnu.

linga Phallic emblem of Shiva, symbol of the god's cosmic energy; sometimes combined with one or more faces of the god.

Mahābhārata Epic poem telling of the great civil war in the kingdom of the Kurus.

Maitreya One of the Bodhisattvas, destined to be the next Buddha.

makara Aquatic monster associated with Ganga.

Manasā Protective goddess of snakes.

mandala Geometric design of cosmic order. Used in conjunction with *bījas* in meditation.

Manikkavāchakar Saintly Tamil poet.

mansabdār Military rank at the Mughal court.

mantra Magical verbal formula used in worship and meditation.

Mātrikā Mother goddess; sometimes standardized into groups of seven (Saptamātrikās).

Matsya Fish, first incarnation of Vishnu.

māyā Illusion, dream or mirage; interpretation of the whole phenomenal universe including the gods themselves.

mithuna Embracing couple found in temple art.

moksha Enlightenment or 'release', the aim of all Hindu philosophy; one of the four goals of life.

Muchilinda Multi-headed serpent protecting the Buddha at the moment of enlightenment.

mudrā Hand gesture indicating a specific mood or action – protection, compassion, meditation, teaching etc.

Mughals Muslim dynasty that ruled large parts of north-western India from the early 16th–mid-18th century.

nāga Protective snake or snake spirit, often taking a hybrid human-animal form.

nāgī/nāginī Female *nāga*.

Nandin Bull, mount of Shiva.

Narasimha Man-lion; fierce fourth incarnation of Vishnu.

Natarāja 'Lord of the Dance', a form of Shiva.

navagraha Nine planetary deities including the sun and the moon.

Nāyanār Devotee of Shiva.

nāyaka Hero.

nawab Local ruler.

nīlgai Blue bull.

nirvāna In Buddhism, the complete 'extinction' of all ties to the conditioned world of *māyā*.

padma Lotus.

Padmapāni 'The Lotus Bearer'. (=Avalokiteshvara), one of the principal Bodhisattvas.

padmāsana Lotus position adopted for meditation.

pān Betel-nut, chewed rather as tobacco is.

parinirvāna Death of the Buddha, ie., his total 'extinction'.

Pārvatī 'Daughter of the Mountains', consort of Shiva, embodiment of peace and beauty.

pati Lord, husband.

pradakshinā The clockwise direction of auspicious circumambulation around a *stūpa*, temple or sacred image.

prajnā Knowledge; tantric Buddhist equivalent of Hindu *shakti*.

prakriti Primeval matter identified with the female principle – energy, vitality and diversity; counterpart of *purusha*.

pralaya Undifferentiated cosmic matter.

prāna Breath, the control of which is the aim of yogic practices.

prithvī Earth.

pūjā Worship of gods usually in the form of icons; essentially an act of ritual homage, address and entertainment.

Purāna Collection of Hindu myths and legends.

pūrnaghata Motif of pot overflowing with leaves and blossoms.

Pūrneshvarī Buddhist mother goddess.

purusha Primeval man; male creative principle, counterpart of *prakriti*.

Rādhā Consort of Krishna, his favourite *gopī*.

rāga Musical mode (masculine).

Rāgamālā Series of paintings based on musical modes, identified with the different times of the day, seasons of the year, etc.

rāginī Musical mode (feminine).

Rāhu Planetary deity; god of the eclipse.

Rāja (raja) Ruler.

Rājput Hindu rulers of Rajasthan and the Punjab hills.

Rāma Hero of the *Rāmāyana*; one of the incarnations of Vishnu.

Rāmāyana Epic story of Rāma and Lakshmana, the abduction of Sītā by the demon-king Rāvana, and her rescue with the help of Hanumān.

rasa Essence or emotion.

rāsamandala Circular dance of Krishna and the *gopīs*.

Rāvana Multi-headed demon from Lanka who abducted Sītā in the *Rāmāyana*.

Rig Veda Early collection of hymns used at sacrifices embodying the religious beliefs of the Indo-Āryans.

rishi Sage, seer.

Sadāshiva Form of Shiva with five heads.

sannyāsin Hindu ascetic, often devoted to Shiva.

Sarasvatī River goddess identified with knowledge, music and the arts; identified with the Vedic goddess Vāch; sometimes daughter and consort of Brahmā.

satī Good wife.

Shaivite Pertaining to Shiva; worshipper of Shiva.

shākta Worshipper of The Goddess.

shakti Active energetic aspect of a god, sometimes personified as his wife.

shālabhanjikā Motif of girl beneath *shāla* tree which she both clutches and kicks with her foot.

shālagrāma Fossil ammonite believed to be a self-willed manifestation of a deity, especially Vishnu.

shārdūla Mythic tiger-like beast.

Shāstra Expert treatise or manual on any subject.

Shesha Serpent supporting Vishnu on the cosmic ocean.

shikhara Mountain-like temple tower.

shilpin Stone mason, sculptor.

Shiva Hindu god characterized by his cosmic energy manifested in many creative and destructive forms.

Shrī Goddess (=Lakshmī), consort of Vishnu.

Shrī Nāthjī An image of Vishnu worshipped at Nathadwara in Rajasthan.

shrīvasta Auspicious diamond shaped symbol.

Shūrpanakhā Ogress disfigured by Lakshmana in the *Rāmāyana*.

Siddhārtha Name of the Buddha.

Sītā Virtuous wife of Rāma.

Sītalā Goddess of smallpox.

Skanda Son of Shiva and Pārvatī (see Kārttikeya).

stūpa Hemispherical mound associated with Buddhism and Jainism; originally intended to enshrine relics of the great teachers, the *stūpa* symbolized the form of the universe itself.

sūfi(sm) Muslim mystic; in India often closely linked with non-Muslim ascetic traditions.

suparna Winged celestial being.

Sūrya Sun god.

Svayambhū 'Self Existent'; primeval man.

svayambhū-linga Naturally-occurring stone identified with the cosmic egg of creation, and with the *linga*.

Tantras Tantric scriptures.

tantric Cults and sects worshipping goddesses with magical ceremonies.

Tārā Buddhist goddess, consort of a Bodhisattva.

thikana Small fiefdom or state.

Tīrthankaras 'Ford Makers', the twenty-four saints of Jainism.

tribhanga Pose with three bends common in sculpture.

trimūrti Divinity expressed by the three gods Brahmā, Vishnu and Shiva together.

Trivikrama Aspect of Vishnu pacing out the three cosmic steps.

tulsī Household tree (basil), sacred to Vishnu/Krishna, tended by women.

Upanishads Philosophical and mystical texts.

Vāch Goddess of speech.

vāhana Animal mount or 'vehicle' of a deity.

Vaikuntha Form of Vishnu combining the boar and man-lion incarnations.

Vaishnavite Pertaining to Vishnu; worshipper of Vishnu.

Vāmana Dwarf incarnation of Vishnu.

Varāha Boar; third incarnation of Vishnu.

varnas The four classes of Hindu society – *brāhmana, kshatriya, vaishya* and *shūdra*.

Varuna Vedic god of the waters.

Vāyu Vedic god of air.

Vedas Ancient religious texts of the Indo-Āryans; see *Rig Veda*.

Vedic Pertaining to the pre-Hindu, Indo-Āryan culture whose members compiled the *Vedas*.

vīnā Stringed musical instrument.

Vishnu Hindu god associated with creation and preservation myths; his various incarnations restore the balance of cosmic forces which sustain the universe.

Vishvarūpa Omniform; especially the cosmic manifestation of Vishnu.

vyāla Imaginary lion-like beast, personification of rampant natural forces.

yaksha Male nature spirit.

yakshī Female nature spirit, associated with trees; images often located at entrances to sacred places.

Yama Ruler of the dead.

Yamunā Goddess, personification of the Jumna river.

yantra Geometric diagram used to focus concentration during meditation.

yoga Both a school of philosophy and a psycho-physical discipline emphasizing physical control.

yogī (*yoginī*) A practitioner of *yoga*.

yoni Female organs of generation; also a pedestal symbolically encircling the *linga*.

yuga One of four vast measures of time, which in aggregate form a time-cycle (*mahā-yuga*), at the end of which the world is purified through the total destruction, after which a new time-cycle commences.

zenana Women's quarters in a palace.

SELECT BIBLIOGRAPHY

General Books

Bahsam, A. L., *The Wonder that was India: A Survey of the Culture of the Sub-Continent before the coming of the Mughals*, London, 1954.

Brown, Percy, *Indian Architecture (2 vols): Buddhist and Hindu Periods, Islamic Period*, Bombay, 1942

Commaraswamy, Ananda, K., *The Dance of Shiva: Fourteen Indian Essays*, New York, 1962

Daniélou, Alain, *Hindu Polytheism*, London, 1964

Fischer, Eberhard and Jain, Jyotindra, *Art and Rituals: 2500 Years of Jainism in India*, New Delhi, 1977

Gascoigne, B., *The Great Moghuls*, New York, 1971

Ions, Veronica, *Indian Mythology*, London, 1967

Jahangir, *The Tuzuk-i-Jahangiri; or Memoirs of Jahangir*, trans. by A. Rogers and S. Beveridge, London, 1909–14

Lannoy, Richard, *The Speaking Tree: A Study of Indian Culture and Society*, London/New York, 1971

Michell, George, *The Hindu Temple: An Introduction to its Meaning and Form*, London/New York, 1977

Mujeeb, M., *The Indian Muslims*, London, 1967

Shastri, H. P., *The Ramayana of Valmiki*, London, 1957

Smith, V. A., *Akbar the Great Mogul*, Oxford, 1917

Spear, Percival, *History of India*, vol. 2, Harmondsworth, Middlesex, 1970

Spink, W., *Krishnamandala*, Ann Arbor, Michigan, 1971

Stutley, Margaret and James, *A Dictionary of Hinduism*, London, 1977

Stevenson, Mrs S., *The Rites of the Twice-Born*, London, 1920

Books on sculpture and painting

Archer, M. and W. G., *Indian Painting for the British*, London, 1955

Archer, W. G., *Indian Paintings from the Punjab Hills* (2 vols), London, 1973

Banerjea, J. N., *The Development of Hindu Iconography*, Calcutta, 1956

Barrett, D. and Gray, B., *Indian Painting*, Geneva, 1963

Beach, M., *The Grand Mogul*, Williamstown, Mass., 1978

Beach, M., *Rajput Painting at Bundi and Kota*, Ascona, Switzerland, 1974

Bhattacharya, B. C., *The Jain Iconography*, Varanasi, 1974

Binney, E., *Indian Miniature Painting from the Collection of Edwin Binney, III: The Mughal and Deccani Schools*, Portland, Oregon, 1973

Brown, P., *Indian Painting under the Mughals*, Oxford, 1924

Desai, Devangana, *Erotic Sculpture of India: A Socio-Cultural Study*, New Delhi, 1975

Ebeling, K., *Ragamala Painting*, Basel, 1973

Goetz, Hermann, *India: Five Thousand Years of Indian Art*, London, 1959

Grey, Basil (ed.), *The Arts of India*, London, 1981

Harle, James, *Gupta Sculpture*, Oxford, 1974

Kramrisch, Stella, *The Art of India*, London, 1954

de Lippe, Aschwin, *Mediaeval Indian Sculpture*, New York, 1978

Rawson, Philip, *Indian Sculpture*, London, 1966

Rowland, Benjamin, *The Art and Architecture of India: Buddhist, Hindu, Jain*, London/Baltimore, 1953

Sivaramamurti, Calambur, *The Art of India*, New York, 1977

Snellgrove, David (ed.), *The Image of the Buddha*, New Delhi, 1978

Taddei, Maurizio, *Monuments of Civilization: India*, London, 1977

Welch, S. C., *A Flower from Every Meadow*, New York, 1973

Welch, S. C., *Indian Drawings and Painted Sketches*, New York, 1976

Welch, S. C., *Room for Wonder*, New York, 1978

GUIDE TO DEITIES

APPEARING IN THE CATALOGUE

This is a brief, simplified guide. It is not definitive and should be used in conjunction with the Glossary of terms and deities, and the text of the catalogue. It does not include the references to Islam; Muslims worship one god, ´Allāh.

HINDU PANTHEON

Basically three principal deities are worshipped: **Vishnu, Shiva** and **The Goddess**; each commands a following which reveres one above the others and hence their devotees are known as **Vaishnavites, Shaivites** or **Shāktas** respectively.

VAISHNAVITE PANTHEON

VISHNU 'The Pervasive'

His vehicle: the eagle **Garuda**
His consort: **Lakshmī** (also known as **Shrī**)
Identifying features: he usually carries a mace, a disc, a conch shell and a lotus (which are sometimes personified as attendant figures); he sometimes lies or sits on the serpent **Ananta** (also known as **Shesha**).
Principal incarnations (*avatāras*) (*The sequence is that used in this catalogue; it is not invariable.*):
　First **Matsya** (the fish)
　Second **Kūrma** (the turtle)
　Third **Varāha** (the boar)
　Fourth **Narasimha** (man-lion)
　Fifth **Vāmana** (the dwarf, who also grows into the giant **Trivikrama**, *see below*)
　Sixth **Parashurāma** (Rama with the axe)
　Seventh **Rāma** (the hero of the *Rāmāyana*)
　Eighth **Balarāma** (Krishna's brother)
　Ninth **The Buddha** (as a false prophet)
　Tenth **Kalki** (an equestrian warrior-priest who may also appear in horse-headed form)
Vishnu also appears as:
　Vishvarupa 'The Omniform', the embodiment of the universe, multi-headed and surrounded by small figures
　Viakuntha 'The Penetrating', combining human, lion, boar and usually demonic heads
　Trivikrama, the giant who takes the Three Steps which spatially define the universe
Principal myths:
　As Varāha he rescues the earth goddess, Bhūdevī, from dissolution in the cosmic ocean.
　As Kūrma he appears in the churning of the ocean as the fundament upon which the mountain, used for churning, rotates.
　As Narasimha he destroys the heretical king Hiranyakashipu and saves one of his devotees.
　On Garuda he overcomes a serpent-demon and rescues the elephant king Gajendra.
　As Rāma he destroys the demon king Rāvana who has abducted his wife Sītā.

KRISHNA, integrated into the theology as an incarnation of Vishnu, is frequently confused with the god Vishnu himself. (Originally Vishnu was a Vedic god; Krishna very probably an apotheosized human war-leader; the two were combined to make up the god generally known as Vishnu, but even early mediaeval Sanskrit texts still confuse the two names or use them interchangeably, notably in the *Bhāgavata Purāna*. The god was and still is sometimes called Vishnu-Krishna, but technically Krishna is listed as an *avatāra* of Vishnu.)

SHAIVITE PANTHEON

SHIVA 'The Auspicious'

His vehicle: the bull **Nandin**
His consort: **Pārvati** (also known as **Gauri** or **Devi**, The Goddess)
His sons: **Karttikeya** (also known as **Skanda, Kumāra** or **Subrahmanya**)
    : **Ganesha** (the elephant-headed god of auspicious beginnings)
Identifying features: he usually carries the trident and snake, or axe and deer; he
    has long matted hair with a crescent moon in it (instead of a crown); he often has
    a third eye, vertically placed in the forehead.
Cult emblem: the *linga*, in which form he is usually worshipped; the *linga* may be
    combined with one or four faces of the god

Shiva also appears as:
    Kālāntaka 'Death Destroyer', from within the *linga*
    Bhairava 'The Terrible', a wandering, naked ascetic, wearing skulls
    Ardhanārishvara, the androgynous 'Lord Who Is Half Woman'
    Natarāja 'Lord of the Dance'
    Sadāshiva 'Eternal Shiva', the multi-headed form of the god
    Tripurāntaka 'Destroyer of the Three Fortresses'

Principal myths:
    He spears the demon Andhaka.
    As Tripurāntaka he destroys the triple fortress (or three fortresses) of the demons.
    Shiva is often accompanied by dwarfish imps, the *ganas* (whose lord is **Ganesha**).

SHAKTI CULT PANTHEON

THE GODDESS (considered the female energy of the gods)
    Also known as **Pārvati**, 'Daughter of the Mountains', **Gauri** and **Devi**

The Goddess also appears as:
    Durgā 'Difficult to Penetrate'
    Chāmundā (also known as **Kāli**), the terrifying goddess as destroyer of evil
    Matrikās 'The Mothers' (These are listed as a group of seven or eight and include
    Indrāni, Brahamāni Maheshvari, Kaumari, Vārāhi, Vaishnavi and Chāmundā)

Principal myths:
    As Durgā she slays the buffalo demon.

JAIN PANTHEON

Jainism was established by **Vardhamāna**, known both as **Mahāvira** 'Great Hero'
and **Jina** 'The Conqueror'

There are 24 Jain saints, termed **Tirthankaras** 'Ford Makers', of whom
Mahāvira himself became the 24th. Others include:
    Pārshvanātha (the 23rd, who is protected by the multi-headed serpent)
    Neminātha (the 22nd)

Associated goddesses:
    Lakshmi, goddess of plenty (who is also thought of as Vishnu's consort in
    the Vaishnavite pantheon)
    Ambikā, a mother goddess depicted with symbols of fertility (children, mango
    leaves and fruit)

BUDDHIST PANTHEON

Buddhism was founded by **Gautama (Siddhārtha)** who became the **Buddha**
'The Enlightened', who is sometimes protected by the multi-headed serpent
Muchilinda

Buddhist saintly beings, termed **Bodhisattvas**, include:
    Avalokiteshvara 'The Lord Who Looks Down' (also known as **Padmapāni**)
    Maitreya, the future Buddha
    Manjushri (also known as **Siddhaikavira**) whose consort is **Bhrikuti**

Associated goddesses:
    Pūrneshvari, goddess of abundance
    Māyā, the mother of the Buddha

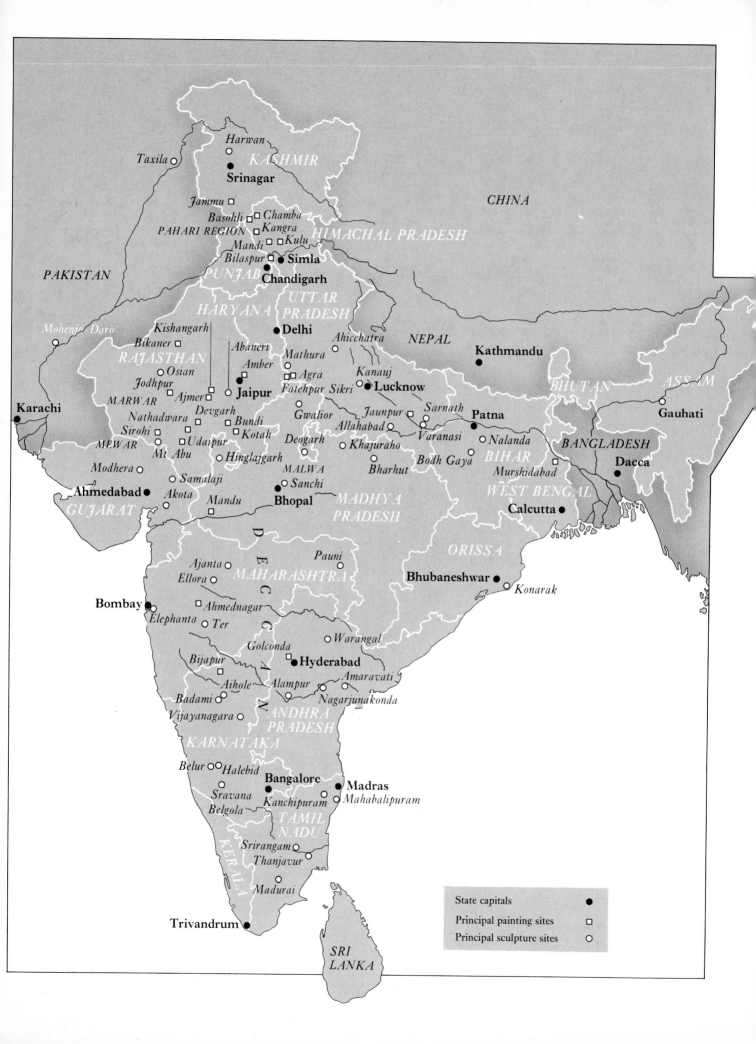

Taxila ○
Harwan ○
KASHMIR
Srinagar ●
CHINA

Jammu □
Basohli □ □ Chamba
PAHARI REGION □ Kangra
Mandi □ □ Kulu
Bilaspur □ ● Simla
HIMACHAL PRADESH
Chandigarh ●
PUNJAB
PAKISTAN
HARYANA
UTTAR PRADESH

Mohenjo-Daro ○
Kishangarh
Bikaner □
RAJASTHAN
Osian ○
Jodhpur ○
MARWAR
Ajmer □
Abaneri
Amber
Jaipur ●
Delhi ●
Ahicchatra ○
Mathura ○
Agra □ □
Fatehpur Sikri
Kanauj ○
Lucknow ●
NEPAL
Kathmandu ●
BHUTAN
ASSAM
Gauhati ●

Karachi ●
Nathadwara ○
Sirohi □
MEWAR
Devgarh □
Udaipur □
Mt Abu ○
Modhera ○
Samalaji ○
AHMEDABAD ●
Akota ○
GUJARAT
Bundi □
Kotah
Hinglajgarh ○
Gwalior ○
Jaunpur
Allahabad
Deogarh ○
Khajuraho ○
MALWA
Sanchi
Bharhut
MADHYA PRADESH
Bhopal ●
Mandu □
Sarnath ○
Varanasi ○
Patna ●
Bodh Gaya
BIHAR
Nalanda ○
Murshidabad □
WEST BENGAL
BANGLADESH
Dacca ●
Calcutta ●

Pauni
Ajanta ○
Ellora ○
DECCAN
MAHARASHTRA
Ahmednagar □
ORISSA
Bhubaneshwar ●
Konarak ○

Bombay ●
Elephanta ○
Ter ○
Bijapur □
Golconda □
Warangal ○
Hyderabad ●
Amaravati ○
Aihole ○
Alampur ○
Nagarjunakonda ○
Badami ○
Vijayanagara ○
ANDHRA PRADESH
KARNATAKA

Belur ○ ○ Halebid
Bangalore ●
Sravana Belgola ○
Kanchipuram ○
Madras ●
Mahabalipuram ○
TAMIL NADU

KERALA
Srirangam ○
Thanjavur ○
Madurai ○

Trivandrum ●

SRI LANKA

State capitals ●
Principal painting sites □
Principal sculpture sites ○